BEHIND CLOSED DOORS

National Library of New Zealand Cataloguing-in-Publication Data
Thomas, Ngaire, 1943–
Behind closed doors : a startling story of Exclusive Brethren life / Ngaire Thomas.
Originally published: Palmerston North, N.Z. : N. Thomas, 2004.
ISBN 1-86941-730-5
1. Thomas, Ngaire, 1943– 2. Plymouth Brethren – New Zealand.
289.90993-dc 22

A RANDOM HOUSE BOOK
published by
Random House New Zealand
18 Poland Road, Glenfield, Auckland, New Zealand
www.randomhouse.co.nz

This edition first published 2005. Reprinted 2005 (four times)

© 2004 Ngaire Thomas

The moral rights of the author have been asserted

ISBN 1 86941 730 5

Text and cover design: Katy Yiakmis
Printed in Australia by Griffin Press

BEHIND CLOSED DOORS

A startling story of
Exclusive Brethren life

Second Edition

NGAIRE THOMAS

RANDOM HOUSE
NEW ZEALAND

Dedicated to

Denis

You gave me a precious gift.
I let you go,
But you set me free,
To be whatever
I wanted to be.

Contents

Introduction   7

1 Public perceptions   9
2 Heritage, culture and values   15
3 Born Brethren   20
4 Dare to be different   28
5 Meetings, meetings, and more meetings   33
6 No nervous breakdowns allowed!   39
7 When he comes like a thief in the night   45
8 The age of responsibility   53
9 Trash in a paper cover   59
10 An end to innocence   67
11 Tried, convicted and excommunicated   75
12 Creative teenage rule breaker   82
13 Born to be Brethren   90
14 For better or for worse   100
15 No compromise   106
16 Let parenthood begin   113
17 Double-dipped for good measure   118
18 The Aberdeen ambush   123
19 Vatican roulette versus the pill   129
20 Shut up, then shipped out   139

21	Judge, jury, and executioners	150
22	Life on the outside	158
23	Learning a new culture	166
24	You've got to take your medicine	178
25	The next generation	187
26	An upside-down world	191
27	Other people's stories	200
28	If you love her let her go	206
29	Peace reigned at last	214
30	Goodbye, my friend	218

Epilogue   229
Appendix 1: Exclusive Brethren history   236
Appendix 2: Is the Exclusive Brethren Church a cult?   240
Appendix 3: An ongoing nightmare   245

Introduction

The plea 'Tell me a story' has been echoed down through the ages from children and adults alike because storytelling is a useful way of conveying an image of a bygone era. Some of my early memories are from stories passed down from parents and grandparents, while others come from actual happenings and are etched forever on my mind. No two people's memories are quite the same, even between those who have been exposed to the same events that caused the memories. I don't expect others to have exactly the same recollections of growing up Exclusive Brethren as I remember it, but many of their experiences will be similar.

Although some of this book is told in a storytelling genre, it is not dramatised or exaggerated. At times I have used a fictional dialogue style of writing to help convey the type of language used in this particular cultural environment. It is written in the past tense because I left the Exclusive Brethren in 1974 and some of their rules may have changed.

I wrote this book for many different reasons: to record the history and evolution of a fascinating and microcosmic part of society; because I like writing and everyone has the right to record, publish and sell their personal memoirs for the interest of future generations without fear of being intimidated and censured by wealthy groups or individuals; and to satisfy the curiosity of all those people out there who have ever asked, 'What was it like being an Exclusive Brethren?'

I would like to sincerely thank family and friends who have

helped and supported me. Thank you to those who designed the cover, gave me permission to write their stories, and helped by proofreading the many drafts for accuracy. For fear of implication you shall all remain nameless but appreciated.

Where appropriate, or requested, real names have been used, but all other names have been changed to protect privacy.

You can contact me by e-mail by visiting my website: www.behind-closed-doors.org

1

Public perceptions

Some things come as a shock. They wake you up; make you sit bolt upright and take notice. One Sunday evening, near the end of 1997, I was listening to talkback radio and heard a young lady make an unusual request.

'I want to join the Exclusive Brethren,' she said. 'Is there anyone out there who can tell me something about them?'

Perhaps I hadn't heard right. This couldn't be happening. I waited for the talkback host's comment.

'Thank you, Jane. Jane would like to join the Exclusive Brethren. If there are any listeners out there tonight who can tell Jane something about them, please give us a call.'

Just like that. No surprised tone of voice for this cool, laid-back radio host, who had been fielding a range of theological dilemmas for the past twenty years. This was just a simple plea for information. I couldn't believe my ears! Here was a young lady who actually wanted to join the Exclusive Brethren, a religious sect I'd been born into in 1943 and stayed with until 1974 when I left with my husband and children. I expected the lines to run hot with ex-members ringing to advise Jane to think very carefully before she made a decision that would significantly affect the rest of her life. Exclusive Brethren don't listen to the radio, so I knew that no current member would have heard her request, and maybe I was the only ex-member listening that night. I waited for half an hour then dialled the radio station and was put on hold for a moment.

Before I had a chance to hang up in a panic, I heard myself replying to the talkback host, 'If the young lady who was inquiring about the Exclusive Brethren would like to ring me, I would be happy to talk to her.'

'Are you an Exclusive Brethren member?' he asked.

'No, I'm an ex-member.' I was hoping he wouldn't ask me any more questions; I didn't want to discuss this on air.

'I can't imagine why anyone would want to join the Exclusive Brethren,' he said with a laugh. 'Jane, if you are still listening, give Ngaire a call, she'll tell you what you want to know.'

For the next few hours I was inundated with calls from people who wanted to know something about this little-understood group of fundamentalist Christians. Some callers used it as an opportunity to vent their anger and frustration.

'Those people have a lot to answer for,' the first caller hotly exclaimed. 'They ruined my friend's life; she can't even see her parents. They could be dead for all she knows, and she could be dead for all they care!' I ended the call as soon as I could. What had I let myself in for? I consider myself a caring, mild mannered, friendly person; I hadn't expected a barrage of expletives! The next caller was less volatile.

'My husband and I are pastors of a small church down south,' she began. 'Why don't the Exclusive Brethren mix with other churches? Why do they refuse to join in with other Christian activities? They say they are Christians, but don't even allow the children to attend religious instruction at school. We have so many questions,' she added. I tried to answer her as best I could. I understood the questions and I knew the answers, but trying to explain over the phone was a daunting task.

'The family next door has eight children and another on the way,' said the next caller. 'The mother always looks so tired. I wish I could do something to help her. Do you have any suggestions?' This caller could not understand why her offers of help were often turned down.

One caller worked at a liquor store, and was openly derisive. 'Drink like fish they do, all top-shelf stuff, too. One way to cope with their stressful lifestyle, I suppose.'

'They don't have the right to call themselves Christians,' said one man. 'They split families, ruin good marriages, severely restrict their children's social activities and deny them a comprehensive education. They're barbaric, still in the Dark Ages, they should be lined up and shot. If they call themselves Christian, then I'm glad I'm an atheist.' He was getting wound up.

'They're not Christians, they're not "Christ like", just sanctimonious hypocrites. They give us Christians a bad name,' said another.

There was one caller who spoke in favour of them. 'I would like to know more about them, too,' he said. 'We need more hard working, honest people like them in our communities. They keep to themselves and don't cause any trouble, they are good business people, and their children are mostly well behaved and polite.'

Some people were curious; most were ill informed, knowing only what had been reported in the media. Others, knowing ex-Exclusive Brethren who had been badly treated, were angry. The calls continued one after the other, until I finally left the receiver off the hook at about two o'clock in the morning.

The next evening I heard from the young lady herself. Her request for information was genuine. I gave her what I hoped was a balanced overview of the lifestyle she would be expected to follow should she decide to join the Exclusives. I first pointed out the many positive aspects of joining such a close-knit and caring group of fundamentalist Christians, a group who rigorously endeavour to follow their leaders' interpretation and understanding of the Bible's teachings. I explained that passages from the teachings of the apostle Paul, particularly regarding the subjugation of women, were of particular importance to them.

It soon became clear to me that it was not their belief system that was attracting her, but rather an affair of the heart. She had fallen in love with a workmate, an Exclusive Brethren boy. She found it hard to understand why so many restrictions had been put on their relationship. No hanky panky in the back room she could understand, but no kissing? No holding hands? No dates? No un-chaperoned outings? She couldn't even get to know the guy until after the wedding! In fact, there wouldn't even be a wedding until she became a member. I told her of some of my own experiences, both positive and negative.

I told her that, for me, being an Exclusive Brethren woman hadn't been much fun. I didn't enjoy being subservient, and dictated to by an all-male hierarchy who expected strict and absolute obedience to an ever-increasing number of fanatical rules. Their rules didn't make any sense to me even after being a member for over thirty years. I pointed out that if she decided to join the Exclusive Brethren, that would be, in effect, the last personal choice she would make for as long as she remained with them. All decisions regarding beliefs, lifestyle and behaviour are dictated by the church as set down and modified by each successive 'Man of God'. (The 'Man of God' — a term I have abbreviated to the 'MOG' — and the 'Elect Vessel' are terms the Exclusives use for their world leader.)

I've had no further contact with Jane, although I did hear that she was eventually received into the Exclusive Brethren fellowship.

There are times in our lives when, in hindsight, we can say, 'That was a red letter day.' Deciding to respond to Jane's call changed the direction of my life — not immediately, mind you, but eventually. Six months later I had almost forgotten about Jane and the interest her call had caused.

'Phone for you, Mum,' called Vicky from the kitchen one Friday evening in April.

'Hello, you are speaking to Ngaire.'

'Hello Ngaire, my name is Daphne,' said the voice of a woman on the other end of the line. 'Does the name Exclusive Brethren mean anything to you?'

'Sure does,' I replied. 'Why?'

'I'm so glad I've tracked you down. You've been hard to find,' she said. 'I recorded your name and phone number when you called a talkback radio host last year.'

'Yes, I remember the call. How can I help you?'

Daphne and I talked about a number of things that evening. She told me about Esther, a young Exclusive Brethren girl she had befriended in the 1970s. Esther, her husband and their ten children had recently been 'shut up' and, Daphne had paid them a visit.

Being 'shut up' is a form of isolation in which no social contact is allowed with members (or outsiders) other than approved 'priests' who observe and assist towards a state of contrition. This period of isolation is followed either by being accepted back into the flock, or by being 'withdrawn from'. 'Withdrawn from' is the Exclusive Brethren expression for excommunication, the ultimate and final step in their disciplinary process.

Daphne knew very little about Exclusive Brethren history and was glad of a few explanations. I told her how I eventually wanted to write a book about my life. 'Just as soon as I've finished my university degree,' I explained.

'I know someone who would love to talk to you,' she said. 'Hang up the phone; you can expect a call from him very soon.'

Within a few minutes I was talking to Robert, an ex-Exclusive who had meticulously recorded events surrounding his own excommunication from the church some years before. He invited me to visit his family, which I did, and I made plans to return in the second semester of 1998 as an exchange student at Edith Cowan University in Western Australia.

Hearing about my plans for writing a book, an Australian friend sent me a packet of newspaper clippings about recent confrontations between the Exclusives and some ex-members. The headlines looked interesting.

Families divided — Christian sect splits families — Strict rules dictate way of life for sect families — Brethren deny strict rules — Sect ties prove hard to break — Not easy to leave — Victim recalls ordeal — Strict rules tore family apart forty years ago— Leave them alone, they're not doing any harm — Excommunicated member's world in tatters — Threat to family unit exposed — Lifetime of faith ends in torment — I fear for my son, says angry father — Father says pleas for son's return ignored . . . Father's request for visiting rights refused —'There ought to be a law against it!'

Are embittered ex-members and the media painting the wrong picture? What is the real story? What goes on behind the closed doors of those mysterious windowless buildings? How do people learn about this interesting sect and its background when there are no books or written records available? With strong financial backing, the Exclusives have a reputation for suing people who defy them, ensuring that books such as this are not easily published. However, my faith that they would want to be seen as reasonable people who will recognise truth is stronger than my fear of being sued by them.

2

Heritage, culture and values

Although I would prefer to launch straight into telling my own story, I think it is important to first give a brief overview of the group of people commonly known as the Exclusive Brethren but sometimes referred to as: the 'Jims', 'Taylorites', 'Peebs', 'Plyms', 'Scarfies' or 'Hanky Heads'.

The Brethren movement began in the 1820s in Ireland and spread throughout the world to about 30 countries. The first Exclusive Brethren group in New Zealand was formed in 1860. You will find a more detailed history in Appendix 1.

I have often been asked to tell of my experiences as an Exclusive, and one of the questions most often asked is 'Why did you join?' I didn't join them by personal choice or by being recruited, as is often the case when joining a cult, nor was I 'evangelised' as an outsider. Like all but a small percentage of their members, I was born into the sect. Membership of the Exclusive Brethren is thought to be between 30,000 and 45,000 worldwide. Practically all of these people are heritage members, there initially through no choice of their own. Like me, they were born into Brethren families, automatically becoming members after 'partaking of the emblems' at a young age. The 'emblems' is a Brethren term for the bread and wine used for the breaking of bread or communion service. Apart from 'street corner preaching', public evangelism has never been particularly strong, and the teaching of separatism further discourages 'outsiders' from joining.

I was twelve when I first broke bread. This was the age when one was expected to make a commitment. During the 1960s the age became progressively younger, and by the early 1970s babies of a few months old were automatically received into fellowship when they reached out for the bread and wine as it was being passed around during the Sunday morning meeting.

I started thinking about writing a book back in 1975, soon after we left the Brethren fellowship. However, even though I assured him it was a 'love story', my husband asked me not to publish it in his lifetime. I agreed to wait, perhaps never to write it at all, but now I have his blessing to tell people what it was like growing up Exclusive Brethren, and how difficult it is to adjust to life on the outside after being withdrawn from. Their uniquely curious term 'withdrawn from' is a consequence both revered and dreaded by their members. It derives from the Exclusive Brethren 'Charter' found in JN Darby's translation of 2 Timothy 2:19–21, in particular the end of verse 19: 'let every one who names the name of the Lord withdraw from iniquity.'

Most people are withdrawn from for no other reason than that they are not 'good Assembly material'. Others commit so-called 'unforgivable' misdemeanors and are suddenly stunned to find themselves on the outside, ostracised by family and friends and afraid to seek help from strangers. Some leave of their own accord, as individuals, families or groups. For whatever reason members are withdrawn from, all are regarded as outcasts by the Exclusives and treated with equal severity. Being classified as a wicked person, an unbeliever, a reprobate, and being denied access to family and friends, is always heart-wrenchingly traumatic. It is intended to be so. That, according to the Exclusives, is the only path that will lead to true repentance and acceptance back into the fold.

Once you are on the outside you can't immediately get on with your new life and forget all about the past; it's not that easy, and it takes time. You feel very vulnerable, fragile and at times angry. Fortunately today there is a network of ex-members ready and willing to help make the transition easier, but back in the 1970s we were on our own. Members are threatened with the likelihood of all manner of divinely evoked disasters should they dare to leave. In the first three years after we left I can remember waiting for something dreadful to happen to us like losing one of the family, becoming terminally ill, having financial difficulties and not being able to make friends on the outside. Then, of course, there was the ultimate fear of being unsaved for eternity, the fear of the 'Lake of Fire'. There was also the prospect that the Exclusive Brethren might try to persuade my children to return to the fellowship. We were very fortunate to leave with our whole family intact. I was very protective of my family; I didn't want to be separated from them and didn't want anything untoward to happen to them.

Collectively, the Exclusive Brethren are very powerful people, and very persuasive. It can take years to stop feeling intimidated by them. Their leaders have been convincingly plausible yet excruciatingly cruel in their efforts to ensure a 'pure' Assembly. If you want to be sure of keeping your place in the fellowship you are duty bound to toe the party line or you might get dispensed with. If you leave, you face the overwhelming consequences of causing deep distress to family and friends and losing home and employment if these are connected with Brethren. People with close extended families don't usually want to leave because no contact is permitted between the 'Ins' and the 'Outs'. If you are deemed to be unfit for fellowship, then no matter how badly you want to stay in the fellowship, you can't. There is a category of sins for which excommunication is the inevitable consequence. Repentance is not even looked for until the shock of being cast out is experienced. Being withdrawn from is moral, physical and legal. When one partner in a marriage is withdrawn from, legal separation papers are quickly drawn up between husband and wife, ensuring that the Exclusive Brethren retain control of the remaining partner and usually a substantial portion of their finances. Once stripped of all they have, the despairing victim is told that this is the only way to a full and complete recovery, and often waits in vain for years, while the family gradually grows further and further apart. It is understandable why some people call the Exclusives a cult.

I don't want to be unfair to them. As individuals most of them are good, obedient but simple-minded people who genuinely believe they are doing God's will. The Exclusive Brethren have always been 'God-fearing' people. They are usually well respected as devout, if extreme, fundamentalist Christians. In the main, these people are very zealous individuals, sincere but, to my way of thinking, deluded into accepting the strangest of practices, without any right to question. The Exclusives' behaviour, especially toward ex-members, is becoming more bizarre and cult-like. Their cultural heritage is strongly biblical and they still retain some positive and wholesome behaviour patterns. In spite of public opinion and media reports, it would be fair comment that, generally, they live a type of high-quality Christian life, loving and caring for one another, and doing little harm to the wider society. Maintaining this high standard is what makes their behaviour toward ex-members so cruel. They ensure full employment with each other, are seldom involved in crime and have a clean lifestyle. These good points have a flip side that includes mind control based on three main tactics: fear, finance and family. Their practice since the 1960s of extreme separatism, particularly from ex-members, results in guilt, financial ruin and severely divided families. I believe Exclusive Brethren demonstrate both the strengths and weaknesses of being bound together in commitment to the 'common good' of their group.

I value my past. I was an Exclusive Brethren member for over thirty years. It's my culture, my heritage. In the end, although I learned their values, I didn't always appreciate or practise those values because I found it so difficult to be separate from the world. I also learned to be crafty and deceitful, not telling lies but turning things around to my own advantage so I could get away with them. This was a survival mechanism frequently adopted by Exclusives but not readily acknowledged. I eventually found it too hard to live like that. I would rather be open and honest, but it was too difficult to keep up with the changes to the rules. There were so many changes, so many rules. Each time a new MOG came into power, he brought with him new, stricter and more extreme directives, which were often traumatic and confusing. Today, John Nelson Darby's teachings are scarcely recognizable. In fact, it has been noted that the Exclusive Brethren are now characterised by the very things that their earlier leaders denounced. Among other things, Darby condemned the idea of a clergy or official leaders, saying that the clergy in effect placed themselves between the 'believer' and God. Although the church may strenuously deny it, an Exclusive would find it impossible to express anything like a personal link with God, other than something received through the Man of God, who is regarded as wholly pure and irreproachable, and whose teachings are seldom questioned. As the Brethren movement evolved, strong universal leadership became the pivotal point of its continued survival.

I'm pleased to observe that in recent years Exclusive Brethren attitudes have changed slightly. In an effort to woo ex-members back into the fold, communications between family members within the fellowship and those who have been withdrawn from are improving.

I was born and grew up Exclusive Brethren in the 1940s and 1950s, during the reign of JT Snr. This is my story, told the way I remember it and as accurately as memory allows.

3

Born Brethren

It was 1943 and the world was at war. My own war was only just beginning. Any moment now I would be thrust into this world, free. Free from the confines that had cradled and protected me these past months, but yet not free. My family carefully bundled me up against the cool June day, took me home, loved me and nurtured me in the way good families do. When I was a few months old, they fully immersed me in the waters of baptism, as is the Exclusive Brethren custom. They called me Ngaire and they brought me up Brethren. That was their choice, not mine. But it wasn't quite their choice either because, as Exclusive Brethren, they had no choice but to do what was expected of them.

I know that none of us has a choice about the family, culture or circumstances we are born into. That's the exciting thing about life — we always start off by belonging to someone else.

First there was Mum. She was the most beautiful person in my world. She was like a delicate little porcelain bird, a small, fine-featured lady, with blue-grey eyes, light brown hair and fair skin. She always looked up to Dad, and was the most loyal, submissive and subject wife in the world. Dad was dark. His skin was light, but everything else was dark, especially his eyebrows. He had a stern yet kindly face, and nobody dared argue with him because Father was always right. Dad was an outgoing and friendly man who could always be relied on to help someone out if they had a problem.

I had an older sister, too. Her name was Pearl. Pearl was dark like Dad, and very pretty with her mop of black curls and her big brown eyes. Everyone loved Pearl. Then there was Grandma Ruth. Grandma Ruth was the most special person in my life. She was the matriarch of a large family of aunts, uncles and cousins. There wasn't a Grandpa. He had died when Dad was seventeen. There were some older people, too: two great-grandmothers, a great-grandfather, some great-aunts, and even some great-great-aunts. I'll tell you more about them later.

I even belonged, a little bit, to Grandfather and Grandmother. They were Mum's parents, but they weren't Exclusive Brethren like us, and never had been. There was always an air of mystery about these relatives, as if they were different somehow. Later on I would realise it was we who were different — very different.

Dad went to work to pay the bills, while Mum stayed home to make the beds, wash and mend the clothes, clean the house, cook the dinner and wash the dishes. Dad was the breadwinner. Mum was the homemaker. They each had their carefully defined roles. This is how it was in most of society in those days, and still is in Exclusive Brethren families because, according to them, that's the way it's supposed to be. Grandma Ruth made our clothes and gave us hugs and kisses. Big sister Pearl played with me and made sure I didn't eat the snails in the garden or walk too close to the swing.

My feelings of belonging extended far beyond the immediate family. We belonged, body, mind and soul, to the Exclusive Brethren. They were like a big, happy, close-knit family, and I was part of it. We went to lots of meetings, and not just on Sundays. With all those loving and caring people around me, I was one very lucky little girl.

When Dad was away at the war, we all lived together with Grandma Ruth and numerous aunts and uncles. In the evenings, one of them would read to us. Sometimes Grandma Ruth told us stories. I liked the one about how Mum and Dad met.

Mum wasn't brought up (as an) [in the] Exclusive Brethren. She worked as a nanny and housemaid for an Exclusive Brethren family. One day Dad was at their house, fixing Mr Olsen's car. Mum was asked to take Dad a cup of tea. She couldn't find him. She looked all around the car. He wasn't there. She looked in the garage. He wasn't there either. She went back to the car, and then she saw his feet poking out from underneath. She got down on her hands and knees to peer under the car. Their noses almost touched.

'Cup of tea?' she asked.

Dad sat up so fast that he banged his head! He came out from under the car and took a long hard look at the young lady who by now was smiling at him.

'How do you do? I'm Lawrence, what's your name?'

'I'm Victoria, and you've got a big black smudge on your nose,' she laughed.

Dad wasn't laughing. He had just seen the girl he wanted to spend the rest of his life with. He quickly rubbed the end of his nose, making it worse, before reaching out for the teacup.

Dad was in a quandary. He had fallen in love. He was sure that Victoria felt the same, but he couldn't ask her to marry him. Victoria was Church of England, all her family was, had been for generations. Victoria couldn't see why there was a problem.

'You could be an Anglican, too,' she suggested.

'Mm, I suppose I could,' said Dad doubtfully. Dad knew he couldn't marry an Anglican, definitely not in an Anglican Church; the Exclusive Brethren would withdraw from him for that.

'Or, you could (become an) [join the] Exclusive Brethren,' he offered hopefully. And so she did.

When Mum asked to 'break bread' the Brethren said yes. By 'breaking bread' she was accepted into Christian fellowship with the Exclusive Brethren, giving her the privilege of partaking of the 'emblems' (bread and wine) at the Lord's Supper each Sunday morning. She was baptised in the bathtub. Dad and Mum got married, but not in the Anglican Church. Mum's family didn't like it much. I think they could see the writing on the wall. Little did Mum know at the time that in a few short years she would be completely alienated from her family, cut off from them by the Exclusive Brethren's practice of separatism.

During the war we lived with Grandma Ruth because Dad was a soldier, and was away for months at a time. Dad wasn't in the armed forces. As an Exclusive Brethren [Brother] he wasn't allowed to use a gun. He was a conscientious objector who worked in the non-combatant Medical Corps. Dad enjoyed working in the hospital. He had always wanted to be a doctor, but he came from a very poor family. He was the oldest of eight children in a family who had always struggled to find enough money for food and shelter. His father had been an editor and roving reporter for the *Wanderlust* magazine, and the family had shifted from place to place. Dad had lost count of the number of different schools he had gone to when he was a boy.

Grandma Ruth had a big old house on the Great South Road in Auckland. To one side of the house was a sprawling orchard with many trees badly in need of pruning. There were always plenty of peaches, nectarines, pears and apples, and the little cape gooseberries we called 'apples in paper bags'. There were chickens and bantams pecking around the yard and a cat or two to keep down the mice. Grandma Ruth had a goat called Bunty, which she tethered to a post; just far enough from the clothes line to keep the washing safe. I liked Bunty, even when she butted me and sent me sprawling on the grass. Grandma Ruth milked the goat and gave the milk to us children to drink.

The war was almost over, but there were still the occasional army parades with the rumble of trucks and the sounds of foot soldiers marching down the Great South Road, past our house, around the corner by the primary school, and into the town. I wasn't afraid of the soldiers on foot, and would sit on the letterbox and wave to them as they marched down the road, but I was scared of the big army trucks. As soon as I heard them coming I'd run down the drive, dive behind the shed and hide in the hydrangea bush growing by the shed door. Some nights we could hear the wail of the sirens. We would quickly run to the window, pull up the blackout blind just a teensy wee bit and watch the searchlights sweep across the night sky. Our uncles told us scary stories about the war. They thought it was fun, but Dad didn't talk about the war. He said it was best forgotten.

During the 1947 polio epidemic, when I was four, I spent six weeks in hospital. I had woken one morning complaining of a headache, a sore throat and pains in my legs.

'I'm afraid she will need to go to the hospital,' the doctor said after he had listened to my chest, and read the thermometer. 'There's an epidemic of polio going around and we need to do some tests.' Our family had no car, so the ambulance came and took Mum and me all the way into Auckland city, to the big hospital by Grafton Bridge.

It was a long way to the hospital. They lifted me out of the ambulance on a stretcher and wheeled me away, into the lift and up to the sixth floor. They put me on a big bed with high pillows and a white counterpane. Then they poked me and prodded me, and listened to my chest again.

'She doesn't have polio,' said the doctor. 'She has diphtheria. We will need to keep her here for a while.'

They put me in a room all by myself and sent Mum home. Two weeks later I developed whooping cough, then pneumonia. I didn't have any visitors for a long time because by then I was in an isolation ward with only one other patient. Visitors were not encouraged unless they were close relatives. I suppose my family came to see me sometimes, but I have no recollection of it. Maybe they didn't visit because I was infectious, or maybe it was too far to travel.

I remember the boy in the bed opposite because his mother visited every week, and would always include me in some way. Tony was older than me, and the nurses came in every afternoon to read to us, and help Tony with his schoolwork. One day they carried a big wooden box into the ward and put it beside Tony's bed. They told Tony he could listen to school on the air, broadcasting from the correspondence school in Wellington.

'Want to come over and listen?' asked Tony, pointing to the box.

'What is it?' I asked.

Sensing my hesitation, he said, 'It's a radio, silly'. 'Come and listen, it won't bite you.'

I'd never seen a radio like that before. Exclusive Brethren families didn't have radios, and for some reason I had never noticed one on the few occasions I visited Mother's relations. I was absolutely fascinated. There was someone talking inside the box. One of the aunts had a gramophone that played music when you wound the handle at the side, but this box didn't have a handle, just a few knobs on the front. After that, I joined Tony every day and listened to the teacher talking. Sometimes children rang up and asked questions, or talked about the books they liked, or about their pets.

'There are a lot of children doing correspondence lessons,' explained the nurse. 'Most of the schools are closed because of the polio epidemic.'

I was a bright child, a very sociable and friendly little girl, always looking on the sunny side of any situation. I didn't understand then about Exclusive Brethren being separate from the world. I was only four, and this was my first taste of the outside world. I was behaving just like any other outgoing, happy, carefree four year old. After six weeks in hospital, I returned home, thin, scrawny and hardly able to walk.

I was gradually becoming aware of a world outside of the family; as yet, a world that had had no tangible impact on me. Ours was an elite and exclusive lifestyle, a strong, safe and dependable environment that dominated everything the family did from the time we opened our eyes in the morning till we went to sleep at night. The Exclusive Brethren meeting room was a place we went to on Sundays and other days, dressed in our best clothes. I can still remember the people there: old Mr Holmes who wore a wig, and Mrs Rowe who sat behind us. She would poke me in the bottom with her umbrella if I wriggled too much. Mr Haines started all the hymns as there was no organ accompaniment. Mrs Haines was nice; she kept peppermints in her pocket. Everyone had their own favorite seat in the meeting room. The older men sat at the front, and others sat with their wives to help look after the children. I didn't understand what they were talking about, so Grandma Ruth would take a little celluloid kewpie doll out of her handbag and wrap it in her handkerchief for me to play with. After the meeting the children played together outside while the big people chatted in groups around the doorway. So there was I, a kid growing up in an environment of strict separatist fundamentalism, and not even realizing I was any different from any other kid in the world.

I lived in this delightfully warm fuzzy haze until I was old enough to go to school. It was there that I learned about a world outside the Brethren — a world so different from mine that I began to feel like a misfit, alone, isolated, and longing to make friends with the other children but not knowing how.

Now I knew I was different, as different as a five-year-old kid can feel, wanting to belong but always being outside the circle. We were taught that we were different, kind of special, chosen to be God's earthly people. Besides, I looked different. My hair was long and so were my dresses. Other girls wore long hair and dresses too, but we had to, and that's what made the difference. The Exclusive Brethren weren't worried about fashion. When the other girls wore their dresses above their knees, ours modestly covered our knees. If the fashion had been for really long dresses, then ours would be shorter. We had long hair because the Bible, and the Brethren, said so. We had no choice.

Thank goodness we didn't have to wear scarves to school in those days like they do now. We wore hats to the meetings but not to school. There was no rule about it then, but later on there was.

Half the time I didn't know what the other children were talking about, our home life was so different from theirs. My parents usually just said 'bother' if something went wrong, but at school I heard a whole range of foreign slang and swear words. These of course could not be repeated at home or I would have my mouth washed out with soap.

Everything in our lives was centered on the Bible and being separate from the world, so there were a lot of 'Thou Shalt Nots'. I could have coped with the Ten Commandments, but we had so many rules or directives. Rules may not be the best word, certainly not one the

Exclusives use. It was more like disapproved conduct that you couldn't expect to openly get away with. There was never a list that we could refer to or memorise, but for simplicity I will refer to them as rules. Although they were unwritten and kept changing we always knew what they were; we were too scared not to. It would have been easier to list the things we were allowed to do! It got a lot worse of course; that was just the beginning. The other children were curious. They wanted to know why I couldn't go to the pictures, why I didn't know about children's programmes on the radio and why I didn't read comics. I had always just accepted the rules as a way of life. Now these kids were asking why. Never before in my life had I thought to question such things. I had no sensible or appropriate answers, and the very fact of being asked by my school friends made me feel awkward and self-conscious. This was the beginning of a process of shutting down that would continue for the next two decades.

4

Dare to be different

There were some things in our house that never changed, like having Bible reading every morning.

Before every meal we thanked our Heavenly Father for the food, but breakfast time was different; it took longer, much longer.

When we were all quietly seated around the large family table, Dad reached for the stack of old well-worn Bibles from the mantelpiece above the fireplace. Dad sat at the head of the table, Mum sat at the other end, and we children sat like little statues on each side. (There were four children by now; my brother Daniel and my sister Christine were both younger than me.) Mum always cooked the porridge and dished it up so that it would cool down during 'morning reading'. I loved the smell of hot porridge and looked forward to the brown sugar and clotted cream — from our own house cow — which Mum spooned liberally on the top. We didn't eat our porridge straight away. We had to wait. Dad handed out the Bibles. He and Mum, and the older children who could read, had one each. Dad selected the chapter for the day and everyone took their turn to read a few verses, around the table.

'We have finished the Old Testament and now we're reading from the book of Matthew,' said Dad. 'Chapter one, verse one.' He waited while we found our places. In those days, before the exclusive use of JN Darby's Bible, mine was a King James Version. It had a cut-out and labelled index making it easy to find the various books of the Old and New Testaments and a ribbon for marking the page. 'Are we all ready? Quietly now, children.' Dad began to read.

'Book of the generation of Jesus Christ, Son of David, Son of Abraham.' He stopped after the fifth verse. 'Your turn, Ngaire.'

'And Boaz begat Obed of Ruth; and Obed begat Jesse, and Jesse begat David the king. What does "begat" mean, Dad?' I asked.

'Shush, it's Pearl's turn to read.'

Even the younger children were encouraged to repeat a few verses. Morning reading and prayer could take up to half an hour. To a child, it was a long time. When everyone had had a turn reading, Dad read the rest of the chapter. After he had finished, he would tell us what it all meant. He was a very learned and intelligent man, but he didn't know how to explain what we were reading in language that I could understand. We couldn't ask Mum; she didn't understand either. We were not encouraged to discuss what we had read, or to ask questions, so I found this daily ritual very boring. Asking questions was being argumentative. We were told to sit up straight, be quiet and not fidget. Looking back on it now I wonder why Dad made morning reading such an event, other than to condition us for going to meetings.

After the reading, the Bibles were stacked tidily on the mantelpiece. Dad always finished off the family devotions with a prayer. We would all kneel down on the cold, hard floor and keep very still and quiet while Dad prayed. During prayers, Mum covered her head with her apron and we girls placed a handkerchief or a serviette on our heads — according to the Brethren custom of women having their heads covered while praying. Usually the porridge was cold and we were all very hungry by the time Dad finished his prayer with 'Our God and our Father, we thank you for this food, in the name of the Lord Jesus Christ, Amen.' We always knew exactly what he was going to say. He used the same words, every day, every year, for the rest of his life. Morning reading took longer on Saturday and Sunday mornings because there was no rush to get to school.

After breakfast, Mum brushed the knots from my long straight brown hair which, according to the Brethren rules, must never be cut. All the Exclusive Brethren women and girls had long hair, but it was sometimes hard to tell how long it was because the women wore their hair 'up'. How long was long? If you kept the scissors away you would find out!

'Ngaire, will you please stand still,' pleaded Mum, 'I don't know how you get your hair so knotty.' It was very straight, parted in the middle, plaited into two long braids, and tied at the ends with ribbons. Sometimes Mum burned the ends of my hair with a candle to get rid of the split ends. For some reason, burning our hair was acceptable but cutting it was not! On Saturday nights, after my hair had been washed, Mum wrapped it in rags so that I could have curls for Sunday. The curling rags were strips torn from old sheets. I would hold one end on top of my head, out of the way. When all the hair was wound around the rag, Mum wound the rag around my hair from the bottom up, and tied it together at the top. I went to bed looking like a rag doll.

Exclusive Brethren men quote St Paul's words in 1 Corinthians verse 11 that a woman's hair is her crowning glory, that her beauty is in her long hair. The men liked the ladies, especially the young teenagers, to have beautiful long hair. We all wanted to look beautiful and attractive to the men. Like everything else they wanted to enforce, the Exclusives quoted a Bible verse to support this custom. We took the Bible very literally. For us, the Bible had to be followed in whatever way the MOG said it should. As God's 'chosen' people, looking different from the world was supposed to be a privilege, but it was rather irksome for us kids.

Although the Exclusives believed in the Bible, we weren't allowed to go to Bible in Schools. Parents, in particular mothers, were responsible for teaching the children at home.

At our school there was Bible in Schools once a week for children between the ages of about seven and eleven. For these weekly lessons the Exclusive children were expected to leave the classroom. They sat together in the library or in the corridor outside the classroom. The Exclusives wouldn't like just any old 'worldly' teaching them about the Bible, even if they were very good Christians. They considered that Christians from other churches had 'departed from the truth'.

I think by now I was about seven or eight, and this was one time I felt the sting of being different from other children. I badly wanted to be like them so I did go to Bible in Schools, but at first it happened quite by accident. During a wet lunch recess, I stayed in the classroom reading. I was so absorbed in my book that I didn't notice the other children coming in. I looked up and saw the lady who was teaching the class. She smiled and invited me to stay. I was too embarrassed to get up and walk out. I enjoyed the lesson. After joining in once, it wasn't hard to convince myself that there was nothing wrong with going again, so long as I didn't get caught! It was there that I learned about the famous stories of the Old Testament, about Daniel in the lion's den, about the three men in the fiery furnace, Shadrach, Meshach and Abednego, and the story of David and Goliath. I memorised 'The Lord is my shepherd' from the 23rd Psalm, and the Lord's Prayer. I learned about Christmas and Easter, festivals seldom spoken about in the Exclusive Brethren meetings.

I continued going to Bible in Schools for some time, but my parents eventually found out. I got the leather razor strop around my legs. I knew I was being naughty and disobedient. I just couldn't help myself!

We didn't celebrate Christmas. We had been taught that Christmas was a pagan festival, and the birth of Jesus Christ was not so important as His death and resurrection. The Exclusive Brethren don't celebrate Easter either, but they do remember Christ's death at the Breaking of Bread every week, and not just once a year or once a month as we were told other churches were in a habit of doing. The Exclusives have no children's church or Sunday school, and we were expected to sit quietly and listen to meetings designed for adults and far beyond a child's understanding. To me, as a child, they seemed dull, tiresome and boring.

I was afraid of being caught doing wrong things and at times I felt guilty. Dad said that having a guilty conscience was a good thing because it reminded us that we were sinners. My conscience had to work overtime! I didn't like being reminded that I was a sinner. Well, I suppose if you are a sinner, you can be saved. The most important thing was to be saved. First you say you're sorry, and you stop doing whatever it was that you were doing wrong. It was a vicious circle really. You had to sin so that you could be saved. If you thought you weren't a sinner, then you were a sinner for sure, just for thinking you weren't!

To me the meetings made very little sense. They were just a bunch of old men trying to outdo each other, each one thinking more about what they wanted to say next than what the previous person had said. Boring!

Everything in my young life centered on the Exclusive Brethren and their meetings. Because we spent so much time there, the meeting room was a very important part of our daily life, and as familiar to me as my home.

Back in the 1950s the meeting rooms didn't look the same as they do now — warehouses with no windows and high fences around the outside. That trend has developed in the past twenty or so years. When I was a child it was quite different. The buildings didn't look like churches, but they did have windows!

5

Meetings, meetings and more meetings

I will try to give you an idea of the type of meetings we attended regularly each week. There have been changes over the years to time, frequency and content but the basic format remains the same.

Sunday was called the Lord's day because when Jesus rose from the dead, after he was crucified, he appeared to his disciples on the first day of the week to break bread with them. The Exclusive Brethren celebrate a re-enactment of this event every Sunday morning at the 'Lord's Supper'. During the thirty or so years I was with the Exclusives the general format of the Sunday morning meeting stayed much the same, although the time changed from eleven o'clock to ten o'clock, nine o'clock and then later to six o'clock in the morning.

Everyone sat on seats or forms set out in a rectangle or a circle, with a small table in the centre. The table, covered with a white linen cloth, held a round loaf of bread on a plate, a large glass or crystal goblet of real red wine or port, and a basket for the collection money.

At eleven o'clock the meeting would begin. As usual, our whole family walked to the meeting room and I sat between Grandma Ruth and the aunties. We usually knew what was going to happen, and the old regulars were almost predictable in their habits. The meetings had a safe sameness about them in those days. As I remember it, the routine went something like this. The door handle slowly turned. They were late again. Miss Graham came in first, her stick tapping on the bare wooden floorboards of the meeting room. Naomi Graham was a big woman, slightly stooped, and her tread was heavy as she stumbled, trying unsuccessfully to slip unobtrusively into her seat on the outside of the third row. Not that there were any designated seats mind you, but it was understood by all that that particular seat belonged to Miss Graham, maybe because she was more often late than not. Next came Mrs Holmes, who sat down in the seat next to Grandma Ruth. Mr Holmes, a small, bird-like man, followed her and headed straight for the front row. He sat down in front of his wife to a chorus of twitters and giggles from the young and the not so young in the congregation. Mr Holmes's toupee was crooked again. It sat on a rakish angle, slightly over one ear, showing a glimpse of his shiny baldpate and a wisp or two of fine grey hair. 'Willie,' hissed his wife, 'straighten up.' She tweaked his hairpiece back into place. There were more giggles from the other side of the room.

Almost as if on cue, the meeting began. The weekly notices were read, the first hymn was given out, and we all sat quietly with heads bowed. After a loud clearing of the throat and a shuffling of feet, Mr Kent rose to his feet. 'Let us give thanks,' he intoned.

As far as I know the rituals have remained almost unchanged. The Brother giving thanks offers an impromptu thanksgiving prayer to God, then breaks the loaf of bread open before passing it to the person next to him, who takes a small piece and passes it on. When the loaf has finished its circuit, it is returned to the table. He then gives thanks for the cup (the wine), which is passed around for everyone to touch to their lips — some more eagerly than others! The expression 'let us give thanks for the cup' (or the bread) didn't literally mean the cup or the wine it held, or the bread itself, but the 'blood of Christ' or 'the body of Christ' which they represented. Then (without a prayer) the offering basket is passed around to gather in the collection money. The meeting then proceeds through a sequence of spontaneously chosen hymns, and contributions of praise and worship offered by the Brothers, all in an understood sequence. The hymns, sung unaccompanied, were always chosen by the men — until about 1970 when the MOG decreed that the women should choose the hymns. This meeting, sometimes called 'The Essential Occasion', was for worship and thanksgiving, rather than instruction, not prearranged but apparently spontaneous. However, it has a prescribed form and a strong sense of what is or is not appropriate, expressed in language full of often-repeated clichés and recycled phrases similar to a liturgy.

Grandma Ruth usually invited us to her house for lunch on Sundays before we went back to the meeting room again for the afternoon meeting. In some country areas the Brethren stayed at the meeting room for lunch. However, the practice of meeting together for a meal at the meeting room — including Fellowship Meetings — was stopped in the late 1950s because the Bible asks, 'Have you not houses for eating and drinking?'

The next meeting — at about two o'clock in the afternoon — was a 'reading meeting', so called because it originally took the form of reading a passage of the Bible followed by a discussion. This meeting was a less formal affair, and again the women and children sat quietly, while the Brothers were expected to participate. After a hymn and a prayer, a Brother would suggest a paragraph or two from the Bible (or they might work their way through a complete book of the Bible, a chapter at a time, spread over several meetings). The Brothers discussed the verses read and related them to the Brethren teachings.

If children didn't sit quietly, mothers had their own ways of surreptitiously controlling distracting behaviour! A short sharp pinch on the leg or arm usually did the trick. Many years later I think I might have been guilty of doing the same to my children, too. You couldn't be seen to punish the children in front of everyone, but strict control was expected.

The gospel was preached at the third meeting, on Sunday at seven o'clock in the evening. Prior to the 1960s, there would be only one preacher, but later that was changed to a group of three preachers speaking consecutively. The Brethren had a scarcity of good preachers who could hold your attention for half an hour or more, so it was a relief to have the variety of three speakers. Speaking was a mixed blessing for the younger Brothers, many of whom shivered in their shoes for fear that they would be asked to participate. Fortunately there was a scriptural basis in 2 Corinthians 1:19 for having three preachers: 'Jesus Christ, he who has been preached by us among you (by me and Silvanus and Timotheus).' Grandma Ruth said that the Exclusive Brethren could find a scripture for almost anything, even if they had to work backwards by searching the scriptures to find if it was not so.

As far back as I can remember, the men preached on street corners on Sunday evening before the gospel. Open air preaching was a good training ground for the young men. A long time ago they used to be genuinely evangelical, but now I often wonder what they would do if someone actually stopped and listened to them, or asked them questions. With their 'closed door' policy, I can't imagine why they still preach on the street corners. There are still a lot of things I don't understand.

There was a time, prior to the 1950s, when all the Exclusive Brethren meeting rooms had notice boards outside. Although separation from the world had always been part of their creed, the Exclusive Brethren used to invite people to hear the gospel preached on Sunday nights. On the notice board was an open invitation:

> The Gospel of our Lord Jesus Christ
> Will be preached here
> Each Lord's Day (God willing)
> At 7 pm
> ALL WELCOME

The gospel preaching was the one I liked best. Some of the preachers talked so that outsiders (Worldlies) and children could understand. They told us stories about the prodigal son, or about Jesus healing blind people and lepers. I liked listening to Mr Watson, from the South Island. He was what they called an evangelist. He would make people cry by telling them about Jesus, the Lamb of God who died on the cross, shedding His blood for their sins. If people cried at the gospel because they had 'come under conviction', then they might ask to 'break bread' and so be accepted into fellowship with the Exclusive Brethren.

On Monday nights there was a Prayer Meeting where the men and older boys were expected to stand and audibly pray in turn. Tuesday evening was the Ministry Meeting where two or three Brothers would voluntarily stand and deliver a short message, usually about some matter of local concern. (A good time to have a dig at someone when they couldn't answer back!) The meetings on Wednesday, Thursday and, in later years, Friday evenings were Reading meetings, similar to those on a Sunday afternoon. All meetings started and ended with a hymn and a prayer. A similar format was used for Saturday Fellowship Meetings, and Three-day Meetings.

In the 1950s the Care Meeting was held once a month on a Saturday night, and would sometimes go on until after midnight. At first this meeting had only been for the Brothers. Later, all who were members were expected to attend. This meeting was where they took care of the administrative and business side of things. They decided whether or not someone who had asked to break bread was 'ready', and who would be asked to take the lead in the next Fellowship Meetings. In the distribution of the collection money (tithes), first call would be for 'those in need', but there were rarely any cases of need. Next call was for 'matters of righteousness', which meant payment of bills, rental etc. Then the balance, usually substantial, would be distributed to 'those serving the Lord' — meaning those such as the MOG and men who were asked to lead in special meetings. If the Brethren needed money to pay for a new meeting room they had a 'special collection', and everyone would dig deep into their bank accounts till the building was paid for. At times the Care Meeting was like a court. Your 'matter' or case was discussed and you were 'dealt with', if you had come to the notice of the elders or priests for some misdemeanor. This was very shameful. If you had done something so bad that they couldn't forgive you, they convened an Assembly meeting where you would be withdrawn from, and then you couldn't go to any more meetings until you had 'got right'. It seemed to me that 'getting right' was very difficult for some people. No matter how hard they tried to remember and confess all the wicked things they had ever done, it seemed as though there was no forgiveness for them. The Exclusive Brethren were very wary of words of repentance that did not have a ring of sincerity. Others seemed to have their sins forgiven without much trouble. I think it all depended on who you were. It didn't seem to me to be very fair.

6

No nervous breakdowns allowed!

We weren't allowed to make friends with worldly children at school and our sport was limited because we couldn't play in a team out of school hours. Ours was just basic schooling with no extra-curricular involvement. Apart from family outings like visits to the beach or a day in the city looking in shop windows, going to meetings was our social life. Fellowship Meetings were about the closest we got to social outings. I'll explain more about that later.

The Brethren fellowship had no events dedicated to children or youth — no Sunday school or youth groups whatsoever. All formal activities included all members of the fellowship; they weren't arranged according to subgroups of age, gender or secular interests. Women's meetings? Certainly not! The only recognised groupings were the family unit and the 'local meeting'. These local or satellite meetings consisted of small groups of families and any single brothers and sisters who lived within a zoned area.

We relied a lot on the extended family for fun and entertainment. I have many happy childhood memories of short camping holidays (always close enough to a meeting room so as not to miss a meeting), and numerous picnic outings with our cousins. Dad came from a large family, and most of his siblings had large families of their own. I had always thought that Father's family members were all Brethren born, but now I know different. It's quite an amusing story because my great-grandmother Henrietta was a Catholic, and the Exclusive Brethren didn't seem to like the Catholics!

Because most members of our extended family were Exclusive Brethren I thought the way we lived was the same way most people lived. Only as I grew older did I learn that not all people lived like we did. In fact, not all of our relatives did either.

My whole world centered on Grandma Ruth, and would remain that way for the rest of her life. Maybe that was because we had lived with her for so long. She was the centre of our extended family and everyone loved her. Grandma Ruth would take the grandchildren on the bus and the tram, then across the harbour in the ferryboat to see her mother, Great-grandmother Henrietta, who had chickens and goats in the backyard. Sometimes the chickens went inside the house. She shooed them out, flapping a tea towel at them. Great-grandfather Edmond didn't live with her; they had separated. She was Catholic and he was Exclusive Brethren. Two, or maybe three, great-aunts, Grandma Ruth's sisters, lived with Great-grandfather Edmond in a big house on the slopes of Mount Eden, in Auckland.

Grandma Ruth told us the story about when she was young. A long time ago, back in about 1899, Great-grandfather Edmond, Grandma Ruth's father, met a man called John at the Newmarket railway workshops, where he worked as a carpenter. Great-grandfather Edmond was an Anglican and John was an Exclusive Brethren. They had many interesting conversations as they travelled to work together on the train each day. Eventually John persuaded Great-grandfather Edmond to join the Exclusive Brethren. Great-grandmother Henrietta, being Catholic, was not at all pleased. She heard that the children were to be baptised into the Exclusive Brethren church, so she hurriedly and secretly had them sprinkled with Holy Water at the Catholic Church! Now that the children were Catholics, it was harder for them to become Exclusives until they were old enough to renounce their Catholicism.

However, because Great-grandmother Henrietta didn't go to church very often, the children were all taken along to the Exclusive Brethren church with their father. Fourteen years and another three children later, Edmond and Henrietta parted company. All the girls, including the youngest who was only four, stayed with Edmond. Their only son went with Henrietta to look after her. The three younger girls grew up as Exclusive Brethren and eventually became members. The older girls, one of them Grandma Ruth, joined at a later date.

There was another great-grandmother, too. She was Dad's Grandmother Ellen. Her long thick white hair was neatly coiled into a large bun on the back of her head. Great-grandmother Ellen was a Baptist. She often had high-spirited arguments with Dad about the difference between the Baptists and the Exclusives. She thought it was a pity that Mr Darby had changed the words of the 23rd Psalm in the Exclusive Brethren Bible.

'Jehovah is my shepherd' doesn't sound anywhere near as good as 'The Lord is my shepherd' like it reads in the King James Bible, she would say.

I wasn't sure what the difference was, but I liked Great-grandma Ellen, who went to the Baptist Church every Sunday with Aunt Edith and Uncle Jim in their Model T Ford car.

The Exclusive Brethren didn't celebrate Christmas, Easter or birthdays. These weren't forbidden, just discouraged. We knew when it was Christmas, and Easter, and we knew that we had a birthday every year, but there were no celebrations. We didn't have birthday parties, cakes and candles like other children. Sometimes we were asked to our school friends' birthday parties but Dad always said we couldn't go.

But Grandma Ruth believed in Christmas — she called it 'Children's Day', and would work late into the night making little gifts for all her grandchildren. She would take a bus ride into the city and look for bargains like little dolls and pieces of fabric to dress them in. While Grandma Ruth and the aunts made 'girl' things, the uncles would make 'boy' presents. Sometimes I was allowed to help. I learned to sew dolls' clothes and make little dolls and beads out of bread dough, which were placed around the fire to dry. By the time I was four, Grandma Ruth had taught me how to make chocolate fudge biscuit cake and home-made sweets. They were good for giving away as presents. The aunts kept pieces of pretty wrapping paper and coloured cellophane to wrap the presents in. We saved all the beautiful foil wrappings from chocolates and Easter eggs (when we were young, Mother's family gave us Easter eggs, until Dad told them to stop!). Aunty May showed us how to draw outline pictures on glass with black paint and a fine brush, and how to stick the coloured foil onto the back of the glass.

We knew that Mother's family was different — a nice, almost exciting kind of different. Mother's family were not Exclusive Brethren. They had proper Christmas, with parties, paper hats, balloons and presents. They even had chocolate eggs and hot cross buns at Easter. They had a radio, but I think it was turned off while we visited. Dad said that visits with people who were not Exclusive Brethren were to be kept to a minimum. Visiting Grandfather and Grandmother was always exciting because it didn't happen very often. Grandmother made delicious puffy white scones. While Mum and Dad ate afternoon tea, she let us girls play with her old china doll in the wicker basket. Grandfather loved rugby. He came from a large family of boys, a rugby team on their own. One day they shifted from their farm in Hunua to a little white cottage by the Papakura railway station, near the big rugby field where Grandfather mowed the grass on Fridays.

There were uncles, aunts, and cousins on this side of my family, too. Sometimes, when we were very young, we went to stay with them at Christmas time, in a little beach house that belonged to Grandfather. We always looked a little enviously at all their lovely Christmas presents. Of course, they gave us some too, but they knew Dad didn't approve. As I got older, we saw less and less of Mother's family, until finally Dad told us that because of the 'eating matter' we had to be totally separate from the world. The 'eating matter' is the expression used to describe the edict of not eating or drinking or having any type of fellowship or friendship with persons who were not breaking bread with the Exclusive Brethren. This meant that we could no longer fraternise with worldly relatives. This made Mum very sad. I think that's why she got sick.

I knew something was wrong with Mum. She was crying a lot and the house was messy. Dad said she was depressed.

Dad was already doing more than was reasonably expected of Brethren men, like helping with dishes and putting out the trash. Mum couldn't cope with all the housework, the cooking and getting the family ready to go to meetings. Mum was at breaking point. Even I knew that. The doctor suggested a long holiday without the children.

When Mum came home after their holiday she wasn't much better. She would always find it hard to cope. I think she missed her family. I don't think Exclusive Brethren people were allowed to have nervous breakdowns, especially not about something as unimportant to them as separation from worldly relatives! Nervous breakdowns were thought of as an unacceptable display of weakness, like pandering to 'the flesh'. 'The flesh' is one of those strange Exclusive terms encompassing *any* personal weakness, the 'natural' order of things, and was to be denied, rejected and avoided at all cost. Although I felt very sorry for Mum, I was left with the feeling that she was inadequate in some way because she couldn't cope very well.

We were, first and foremost, Exclusive Brethren. That was the core of our being, the main influence that superseded everything else. Our values and standards came from the top down; God, the MOG, the leading Brothers (later to be called 'Levites and Priests') and the rest of the Exclusive Brethren. Then there was father, mother, son and daughter, in that order. As they got older, sons were even higher up the pecking order than their mothers, especially if the mother was the quiet submissive type that Exclusive Brethrenism required. Anything taught at home was necessarily an extension and enforcement of the Exclusive teaching. I know that there would have been a slight variety of lifestyle between families, but we all had the same basic rules.

In theory, the Bible was the authority for all our conduct and beliefs but, in practice, the teachings of our leaders were what we obeyed. The

Bible requires that we 'obey [our] leaders, and be submissive' (Hebrews 13:17). Meetings led by the MOG were recorded (shorthand in those days, taped in later times) and then transcribed and printed in books known as 'Ministry Books'. These books became the references for our conduct, with recent books having preference over earlier ones.

In spite of all this, my childhood was probably no more unusual than or different from that of any other child growing up in a middle-class, European, strict fundamentalist Christian family in the 1940s.

My whole concept of Jesus, of good and evil, right and wrong, heaven and hell, God and Satan, and their relevance to my personal spirituality has now changed. Going back to what I was taught at the beginning is an interesting experience showing me just how much my thinking has evolved, developed and matured over the past fifty years.

7

When he comes like a thief in the night

I seldom went to other children's homes to play, and on the odd occasion when I did I would be reprimanded because I hadn't asked Mum first. Mostly I didn't ask because I already knew the answer. Mum always said no. In fact, Mum had to say no to almost anything, just in case. At this stage I was permitted to bring my friends home, but they seldom came a second time because Mum would preach to them. She would tell them about the 'end times' from Revelation, the last book in the Bible. The Exclusive Brethren believed that we were in the 'last days'; Christ was soon going to return.

Our world was disciplined, ordered and predictable as we lived our lives according to a set pattern. We were God's chosen people and, as such, we should be showing the world that we were happy with our 'position' (an almost indefinable Brethrenism meaning that we knew our place in the broader scheme of things). Children have a habit of being happy anyhow, and I was no exception. However, I was beginning to understand that Exclusive Brethren children didn't have quite as much freedom as other children. Other children seemed familiar with things that I seldom heard of, like radios, make up, picture theatres and comics — especially comics. How I envied them, and how thrilled I was to be lent one occasionally, but never to be taken home, of course! At first, this dawning of awareness went almost unnoticed because my life was very busy, and there were plenty of other Exclusive Brethren children to play with.

I can remember getting very worried about being a sinner. I think being a sinner, and needing a savior, was the most salient part about being in the Exclusive Brethren. It was enough to scare the living daylights out of a kid. For example, one day a neighbour gave me some letters and money to buy her some health stamps (which would apparently contain a small contribution to a Health Camp and cost more than ordinary postage stamps), asking me to stick them to the envelopes and post them in the big red letter box outside the post office. I purchased the required number of stamps and was given some change. After posting the letters, I realised that there shouldn't have been any change. Instead of telling my neighbour that I had forgotten to ask for 'health stamps', I spent the money! I figured that if I confessed to making a mistake, I would be in trouble, so I sinned a second time so that nobody would know about it. As I walked home very slowly, my conscience was working overtime. I was bad, wicked, and dishonest. God would find some way of punishing me. I worried about it for weeks, wondering and waiting for God to make the next move.

What if Jesus came one day while I was at school and took the family up to heaven and left me behind? I knew he could come at any time, unexpected and unannounced, to take all the saved people away. I might be abandoned, left alone with the bad, unbelieving people who weren't Brethren, to face the Day of Judgement before going to hell. Belief in Jesus saved people from their sins. I had always believed that the Exclusive Brethren, who had asked Jesus into their hearts, were in fact the only 'saved' people. However, even though I was afraid of God, I didn't believe enough to want to be 'saved' myself. I was taught that Christians in other churches were only nominal Christians and not really 'saved' at all. Because they didn't have the 'Light of the Assembly', as the Exclusive Brethren claimed to have. According to Mum, it was very doubtful that they would go to heaven.

'Jesus will come secretly, like a thief in the night, to take all his loved ones home, and nobody will know they have gone,' she said. Mum was always telling us about the 'Rapture, the Second Coming', the 'Book of Life' and the 'End Times' when God would judge the people. Rapture is the term used by fundamentalist Christians for the moment when, at God's command, Christ comes to meet believers, who will then be taken away from this wicked world to be with Him in heaven forever.

'Mum, what's in the book of life?' I asked her one day.

'That's where God records our names if we are "saved". If we belong to the Lord Jesus, we will go to be with Him in heaven.'

'How are we going to go to heaven?'

'We will be caught up to meet Jesus in the air when He comes to collect us. Before Jesus can take us to heaven, we will have to stand before God at the judgement seat while he reads through the Book of Life to see if our names are recorded in it,' Mum explained. 'God records all our sins and deeds in books. If your name is recorded in the Book of Life it is because you have put your faith in Jesus, your sins are washed away and you will be saved for eternity.' *[margin note: not accurate]*

Sometimes Mum would say, 'Now you behave yourself Ngaire, or I'll tell your Father when he gets home and he will give you a grandfather of a hiding, and God will punish you too!'

I was sure that Mum and Dad and the Exclusive Brethren knew exactly which of my sins God had recorded in his books. They were very worried about sin. Some sins were so bad that the Brethren couldn't forgive them, and that is why some people were withdrawn from, even when they had said they were sorry. If we had somehow evoked the wrath of God, and not repented, then the Exclusive Brethren (our mediators!) would withdraw from us. God might sometime grant repentance but, if not, he would eventually punish us by throwing us in the Lake of Hell Fire, where we would burn forever but never die!

Sometimes I would run home from school and, if no one were home, I'd pound on the door, begging God to forgive me, and crying with relief when Mum arrived home. She hadn't gone to heaven after all, she'd only gone shopping! That's scary stuff for a kid. I think the terror of the 'thief' who would secretly and silently whisk the good people away and leave the bad ones behind was every Exclusive Brethren child's nightmare. It would haunt them till they became 'saved' or until they defied the whole concept and eventually left the fellowship.

I don't really believe that Jesus is coming back secretly and silently for some special people and that other ordinary folks like me will be left behind not knowing about it.

We didn't have to think about what was right and what was wrong. We just knew. It was ingrained. We knew what the rules were and instinctively obeyed them. There was no way we were allowed to break them. If you were to ask the Exclusive Brethren for a list of their rules, you would be told the Brethren don't have any rules, we just follow 'Divine principles'. This, of course, left those of us who were rebels with very little leverage for an argument in self-defence. It was easier and safer to do what you knew was expected of you than to make your own judgements.

The safest thing for me was to do what Dad said. Dad was the head of our house. His word was law. I knew I should never disobey Dad; it was as bad as disobeying God. I had become a very confused child! Was my father God? No, I was told often enough that God was like a father. But I already had a father I was afraid of; I didn't need another one. God made the rules, and my father enforced them. Were the Exclusive Brethren leaders God? No, but God was out there somewhere watching me. I couldn't see him but he could see right through me! God knew everything I did and everything I thought. God was big, God was powerful, and there were those books, mentioned in Revelation. How I hoped my name was recorded in 'the Book of Life', although sometimes I was sure it wasn't.

I didn't know a loving and compassionate God. I knew all about him, but I didn't love him. I had only been taught to *fear* him. I don't think this was supposed to be an *afraid* kind of fear, but a type of reverence, reserved only for God. How do you teach a kid how to love God when God was portrayed as a sadistic ogre? I knew more about fear than about love. My parents probably loved me in the best way they knew how but I don't remember feeling loved. Perhaps I was a difficult child to love, or maybe I just didn't fit the Exclusive Brethren mould and that made me unlovable.

For whatever reason, I always felt like the black sheep, the odd one out, and the one that attracted trouble like iron filings to a magnet. Everything was my fault. I just didn't belong. If the other children had these fears I was unaware of it. It wasn't talked about. I felt terribly alone. Maybe I was adopted. No, I knew I wasn't. The Exclusive Brethren didn't adopt babies; they had plenty of their own!

Dad could be very stern sometimes. I used to think he was too hard and legal minded, but Dad always thought he was right, and was doing all the right things according to the Brethren rules. Being first to comply with any new rule was Father's way of being personally committed to rising up the ranks of Brethren leadership, and he would allow nothing to get in his way. I found it best to keep out of trouble and just to do what I was told, but I often wanted to do the opposite. Sometimes Dad would say, 'Ngaire, wait for me in the bathroom.'

When he said this, I knew I was in trouble, that I had been disobedient again and Dad was going to strap me with his razor strop. The razor strop was a piece of leather about eighteen inches long and three inches wide. The strop hung behind the bathroom door and Dad used it to sharpen his razor every morning. Sometimes I got the strap for hitting out at Pearl when she whispered 'Fatso' in my ear. Other times it was for staying at a friend's house after school and getting home late. I even got the strap for reading, but that was because I was reading when I should have been working, or because I was reading a forbidden book, a novel or a paperback (rare in those days) under the bedclothes with the torch on. Sometimes it was because I was caught telling lies, making up stories, exaggerating and letting my imagination run away with me. Dad would tell me I was rebellious, insolent, impudent and independent. Any one of those things was evil enough to be punished for. Thwack, thwack went the razor strop on my legs and bottom. Mum didn't often hit us, she just said, 'Wait till your father gets home, he'll deal with you.' Then I had to wait all day and think about my impending punishment. I would rather Mum had done the punishing.

Mum was very loyal to Dad and would never listen to anything said against him. We were not allowed to criticise him or complain about him in any way. Mum was a very good (Exclusive) Brethren lady. She was 'subject' to her husband, which means she always honored him and did exactly what she was told, often before she was told. Because she had only joined the Exclusive Brethren so she could marry Dad, she had conditioned herself to renounce her own way of thinking. I have heard that converts to a group often become even more committed than people who are born into it. Mum was like that. I felt sorry for her; she never got to do or say what she really wanted, she just said, 'If your father says so.' Sometimes I think she would have liked a life of her own instead of being pushed around like a pawn on a chessboard, but she seldom complained. I think she really believed that all that happened was God's will for her.

I never heard my parents argue. If they ever disagreed with one another, it was not in front of the children. I sometimes thought Dad was so clever that he could read Mum's mind, that he loved her so much that he always knew what was best for her. I am sure they loved each other, but there was no outward show of affection, no hugs or kisses, just devoted and unquestioned obedience from her, and powerful domination from him. This is the way that I, too, would be expected to behave when I grew up.

I was a well-developed child, old for my age, prematurely mature, and given a lot of responsibility. By the time I was nine, I had developed an independent spirit, something that would become the bane of my life, and the cause of despair for my family. A 'spirit of independence' usually meant that a person had begun to think for themselves rather than obeying the MOG — an undesirable trait that needed to be dealt with.

I was not much more than ten years old when I knew that I no longer needed my mother. I could already do some things better than she could. I had outgrown her. My mother was the most beautiful person I knew, small, delicate, fragile, but apathetic and unable to cope with the pressures of everyday life. Mum needed me to take care of her. I looked after my younger sister, too.

It was I who took my sister Chris to school to enrol her when she turned five. I knocked on the headmaster's door.

'Come in,' he answered.

'This is my sister Chris, she is starting school today and I am going to look after her,' I proudly announced.

I loved Chris more than anyone else in the world. I wasn't going to let anything happen to her, ever. I protectively watched over her like a clucky mother hen.

A few years after the war, Grandma Ruth and Dad had started a manufacturing business in the back shed, sewing black school gym frocks and drill rompers. Drill rompers were made of black Italian cloth and looked like a short pleated skirt, gathered in with elastic around the legs, with a buttoned band around the waist. They were part of our school uniform for physical education and sports. Of course, drill rompers, even though Dad made and sold them, were not to be worn by Brethren girls because shorts and trousers were considered to be men's clothing, and were, perhaps, too revealing. For some reason, the Exclusive Brethren thought that wearing drill rompers was worse than a girl showing her panties when she turned flips and did handstands! Sometimes I would sneak a pair of rompers out of the factory and into my bedroom. I'd shut the door and pull the dressing table over so the door couldn't be opened, then I would try them on and twirl in front of the mirror. I wouldn't dare 'borrow' a pair and take them to school. A kid might get withdrawn from for something like that! I am sure it would have deserved at least a belting with the razor strop! I shudder at the thought, having spent so much of my young life avoiding the strap.

Children don't understand 'fear' as it relates to reverence, but they do, usually through an unpleasant experience, understand 'fear' as it relates to being afraid. I was brought up on a diet of fear, fear of God, fear of men and fear of being an outsider. I knew that if I didn't ask to become a member soon, I would be treated like an outsider.

At that stage I had to make a decision. I could ask to break bread with the Exclusive Brethren and become a committed member, or I could refrain and eventually become an outcast, estranged from church and family. What a choice! On the one hand I could be sure of salvation for eternity by staying with the Exclusive Brethren, or I could look forward to hell and damnation and certain destruction sometime in the future, after my vain pursuit of the 'temporary pleasures' of sin! At the age of twelve, the choice was easy, and predictable. At least I had a choice. Nowadays, the children don't have a choice; they become accepted as members of the church at a few months old, as soon as they are old enough to reach out and grab a handful of bread at the communion service. Their happy parents nod and smile at one another and say how blessed they are and how wonderful it is that their precious child has voluntarily partaken of the emblems. But these babies have no choice, only a primal instinct to reach out for food. Maybe it's easier that way, but the Exclusive Brethren have taken away the rights of the children to make responsible choices for themselves when they are older. When teenagers are eventually faced with a decision either to stay in the fellowship or to quit, the consequences of their actions are almost too much for them to comprehend. Misguided choices can then lead to the very disasters that the Exclusive Brethren predict for them. You might even say it's a form of emotional child abuse.

8

The age of responsibility

When I was about twelve I was expected to commit my life to Jesus and become a member of the Exclusive Brethren church. Dad became concerned about the fact that I had not yet asked to 'break bread' (or take communion as it is known in some churches).

'Ngaire, I want to speak to you in the lounge, please.' When Dad spoke to me in that particular way, I knew it was serious. I went into the lounge and sat on the edge of the chair, waiting for Dad to tell me what I had done wrong this time.

'Ngaire, you are nearly twelve and you haven't asked to break bread yet,' he said. 'Your younger brother Daniel has been breaking bread for nearly two years. What is wrong with you?' Dad asked in his stern voice.

The breaking of bread is a very important and essential ritual to the Exclusive Brethren, and they celebrate this event every Sunday morning no matter what. To participate in this ritual, you had to be a member and I, alas, was not.

'The Brethren have taught us that twelve years old is the age of responsibility and all children of twelve should already be breaking bread,' said Dad.

'But I don't want to be in the Exclusive Brethren,' I answered. 'I'm not going to ask to break bread. I'm not ready yet and I don't know the answers to all the questions,' I added lamely.

'I will arrange for you to be visited by Mr Johns,' said Dad, and that was that. Mr Johns and his wife, a nice old couple, asked me to their house for dinner one night.

'Do you have something to ask me, dear?' prompted the kindly Mr Johns, beaming at me from behind his half glasses.

'No,' I replied nonchalantly. I sat, slowly chewing the tough piece of meat Mrs Johns had put on my plate. That night at home, Dad asked me to come into the lounge.

'Ngaire, I am disappointed in you. You know what this means, don't you.' This was not a question. I knew very well what it meant. I nodded my head but kept my eyes on his shoes. 'Ngaire,' Dad said more gently, 'children who are not breaking bread by the time they are twelve are to be treated like outsiders.' Dad was using his most persuasive tone of voice to explain.

What child of twelve wants to be treated like an outsider? I knew what this meant. I would be able to go to the meetings but I would have to sit in the back row as if I was a stranger, someone who didn't belong but who was permitted to attend the meetings. What a disgrace to a family to have a child 'sit back', and I was becoming a disgrace to our family. Any Exclusive Brethren man who had ambitions of being a leading Brother could ill afford a child who didn't toe the line. It says of aspiring leaders in 1 Timothy 3:4–5, 'Overseers [Deacons] conducting his own house well, having his own children in subjection with all gravity.' I imagined that even at home I might be treated like an outcast, like someone 'out of fellowship'. I didn't want to be an 'outsider'; I didn't want to be different from my family. The fact that I didn't really believe — in the Brethren way — in Jesus as the Son of God who died for my sins didn't seem to matter, so long as I said I did and conformed to my parents' expectations.

'OK, I'll ask to break bread,' I promised Dad one night after a gospel preaching. Although I had not 'come under conviction' (I had not cried with remorse about my 'sins'), I knew that it was time I did something about it. 'I will go and see Mr Robinson on the way home from school tomorrow.'

The next day I went to see Mr Robinson.

'I want to break bread,' I blurted out when he came to the door.

'You had better come in,' said Mr Robinson. 'We will sit in the kitchen.' He gave me some biscuits and a glass of milk. I was glad that we didn't have to sit in the lounge. The Robinsons' house was very posh and expensive looking; they were quite 'upper class' compared to us.

'Why do you want to break bread Ngaire?' asked Mr Robinson.

'Because I know it's the right thing to do,' I replied, hoping that was the right answer. We talked about it for a while and then I left for home.

'I don't think Ngaire is ready to break bread yet,' said Mr Robinson to Dad. 'She doesn't have the Holy Spirit.'

'But she is nearly twelve,' Dad said disappointedly. 'How long do you think it will take?'

'I think we should make her wait for at least another six months,' replied Mr Robinson.

I did have to wait six months. I certainly was a problem, a young lady with a strong mind of my own. Wilful and independent, Dad called it. He didn't want any of his children to be independent, disobedient or rebellious. That would be a reflection on him. He was the father, the head of the house. The expectation was for a father to make sure that all the people in his house were committed, obedient and compliant Exclusives.

Because there was no Sunday school, and the church services were at an adult level of understanding, the Christian teaching of the children was the responsibility of the parents, mostly the mothers. Since my mother had not been brought up Exclusive Brethren she found it hard to teach us a belief system that she often didn't understand herself. She sometimes read us stories directly from the Bible, but not very often. There are no books written by the Exclusive Brethren for the children, but we did have a few other Christian books like *The Beacon Light*, *Uncle Arthur's Bedtime Stories* and the *Gospel Stories for the Young*. We would wait eagerly for Dad to bring home his monthly ministry books and there, tucked in between the big books (transcripts of recorded meetings with the MOG), would be the *Gospel Stories for the Young*, a small monthly publication for children by the publishers Stowe Hill Bible and Tract Depot, in England. In this little book there were stories, poems and questions about Bible verses. We were called 'gleaners', and if we sent in the right answers to the questions our names would be published as prizewinners. Unfortunately, the Exclusive Brethren children are no longer permitted to read Christian books like *Uncle Arthur's Bedtime Stories*, written by 'outsiders', and the *Gospel Stories for the Young* are no longer printed.

There were so many good things about Brethren life. We knew everyone in our local meeting and even further away. The Brethren are very hospitable, and we often went out for lunch or dinner on a Sunday or had visitors at our house. Dad loved entertaining guests and, as soon as we were old enough, we would help prepare for Sunday by cooking and cleaning all day Saturday, unless of course we were going to Fellowship Meetings somewhere.

Fellowship Meetings were a great opportunity to meet other girls our own age and make friends. When we got older, we made friends with the boys too! Let me explain a little more about Fellowship Meetings as I remember them in the 1950s.

They were held on a Saturday afternoon, every two or three months, in each main locality where there was a group of Brethren. It was not unusual to go to a Fellowship Meeting somewhere quite frequently, especially if your father was (or aspired to be) a respected, leading Brother. Brethren from other nearby meetings would be invited, sometimes travelling several hundred miles to attend. There was a meeting at about four o'clock and another at seven o'clock, with a sandwich tea in between. We referred to Fellowship Meetings as 'Tea Meetings' because of the light meal served between the two services. Tea usually consisted of sandwiches and cakes followed by tea and cordial.

On the morning of Fellowship Meetings in the Auckland area, Pearl and I would walk about a mile to the nearest bus stop and ride the bus twenty miles into the main city meeting room. We got off the bus at

Karangahape Road, and walked several blocks, past the hotel with its horrid beery smells, past the big city stores, which in those days were shut for the weekend, and into the old brick building in East Street. It was a large two-storey building, which the Brethren had purchased and used for many years. The gallery, used only for Fellowship Meetings or when there were large crowds, had a sloping floor and seating around three sides. At the back of the gallery was a large long room, used by parents with very young children, and frequented by me whenever I could find a baby to look after. The lower floor, on street level, was the main meeting room and the stage sloped up so that the top row of seats was level with the lower row in the gallery. Underneath the stage was a long narrow kitchen, and this is where we were headed to help make the sandwiches.

On the long tables were loaves of sliced bread, bowls of softened butter and larger bowls with sandwich fillings such as mashed hard-boiled eggs, and smoked fish in white sauce. There would usually be about twenty teenagers there to make the sandwiches, supervised by a few older ones. We looked to see if our name was on the roster to serve at teatime. If it was, we were given a block of several rows of seats to look after, handing the sandwich trays and the cakes (usually shop-bought ones) around three times each. The tea boys carried the big teapots, topping up the cups that were passed to the end of the rows.

Fellowship Meetings were a very important part of our social life as young teenagers, and were very much enjoyed by all, and not just for their spiritual content. This is where we met people from outside our own little circle of local Brethren, and this is where we might eventually meet our prospective partners. And this is where the great things of God were propounded!

We sometimes went to the Three-day Meetings, which the Exclusive Brethren regularly organised in different parts of the country. Three-day Meetings were similar to Fellowship Meetings only on a much grander scale. They lasted all day for three days. Originally they were held on Saturday, Sunday and Monday, often in large public halls or hired picture theatres, and were open to any Brethren who wanted to go. Later they were changed to Friday, Saturday and Sunday and were by invitation only. These meetings were often very social occasions and jokingly called the 'heifer sales', where the young men looked around for their future wives. I can remember, when I was about thirteen, staying with a family during some Three-day Meetings. I was in the backyard peeling a huge bucket full of potatoes ready for all the dinner guests. I looked up and saw a young man approaching on a motorbike. He was collecting an older girl to take her out for the evening. How I wished I could go for a ride on the back of that motorbike. The rider was so good looking. I found out later that his name was Denis. He was considered a 'good catch' and was never short of a willing pillion passenger, but he didn't even give me a second glance back then.

9

Trash in a paper cover

When I walked through the school gates, I put aside all thought of home and church and tried to blend in as if I were normal. Normal? What is normal for a young teenager? I wanted to be the same as my classmates, even if I had to pretend. I took note of those around me and tried to behave like them. I even learned a few swear words but, of course, I was very careful not to use them at home or Dad might wash my mouth out with soap. I was always the one who got caught by the teacher if I swore at school, and eventually I was summoned to the headmaster's office.

'If you continue to use bad language I will send a note home to your parents,' threatened Mr Robbie.

'Yes sir. I'm sorry, sir.'

'That's not the only thing. You started off well this year but your grades are slipping,' he added. 'What have you got to say about that?'

'Nothing, sir.'

'I've had the stick in the pickle for you all year,' he said. 'I've got a good mind to hold you back a year.'

'I will try to do better next year, sir,' I replied. It was the end of 1956 and the following year I would be a foundation pupil at a brand new high school being built not far from our home.

This was a new school and a fresh start. I was going to change. There were several times during my life when I had tried to turn over a new leaf, and this was one of the more successful of them! I worked hard to improve my grades to show everyone what a girl could do if she set her mind to it. I had learned to read; now I read to learn. I spent all my spare time in the school library, a library full of brand new books. I needed a talisman. Exclusives didn't believe in luck, but I needed a good luck charm — something small, something I could keep with me while I studied. I found a small brass sewing pin and pretended it was gold. I slipped it into the seam on the lapel of my school blazer. Now I had something to bring me good luck, to remind me of my promise to myself to do better. I only half believed in it. I knew it would take more than a gold pin to improve my grades, so I did my bit by putting in some extra effort. By the end of that first year I was top in my class, and I continued to stay at the top until I left school.

Although education is seen to be important, the Brethren discourage schooling beyond high school level, or past the age of about sixteen or seventeen. All Exclusive Brethren children are expected to do well at their lessons. A high standard is expected in every area of life.

Coping with the so-called 'evil influences' of the outside world has always been a problem for Exclusive children who attend worldly schools. When I was going to school, I played with the other children in the playground, but by the time my own children went to school, they had to come home for lunch every day. Separation from the world became very important, especially the part about not eating with 'Worldlies'.

I have heard that nowadays they have the choice of going to a public school until they are about ten or eleven, or being home-schooled. After that they are taught at home by correspondence or, as in Australia, through the long-distance education system. I think before long they will turn completely away from public schooling. In areas where there are enough children of school age, they sometimes set up a separate classroom within an existing school and hire a teacher to work with the children at several different levels. Even more recently they have opened their own regional high schools, employing state-trained teachers and bussing children in from outlying areas. They try to find a balance between being separate and being a visible testimony to the world. The children learn all the basics like English, maths, economics and business studies but no fun things. They can't watch a video, even if it's educational, and there's no drama or play-acting, although hopefully this will all change under the influence of 'worldly' teachers. Their reading material is restricted, too. Nothing is taught about sex or contact between sexes, and there are no gender studies, although lessons involving violence and retribution are fine. Then, of course, there are supposed to be no computers at work, home or in the classroom.

Although most of the Exclusives' children are highly intelligent, their education appears to be restricted and inadequate. From the time they are born they are read to from the Bible and, even before they start school, some would already have started reading at the family morning reading session. When they leave school, they learn the skills to work in the various businesses they operate, and have enough general knowledge to have a limited understanding of the world around them. The girls don't need a high level of education because they are not permitted to be in paid employment after they marry. Many of the Exclusive Brethren own their own businesses, so their young people work for Brethren, and need only learn the subjects necessary to work in those areas. Education is for literacy and for skills needed to earn a living.

As an Exclusive kid, life for me was very dull and uninteresting. The more I learned about the pleasures and challenges of the outside world, the more discontented I became. School was like an oasis in the desert, an escape from the reality of my home life. It gave me an excited feeling of anticipated daring and adventure; it was a place where I could eventually be the 'real self' of my imagination, even though I was different from the other children.

I loved school. Not the social side; I was a bit of a nerd in the playground, but I had a natural love of learning. I liked the home economics classes best. Mum would let me try out the recipes at home and, because I was used to helping her in the kitchen, I found that I already knew a lot about cooking. The same thing happened in the sewing class. Dad had a sewing manufacturing business and had taught me how to use all the different sewing machines, so I would get my own sewing done quickly and then help the other girls. When I was going to intermediate school, I was making my own dresses. At high school I remember making a bright yellow corduroy velvet dress with black trim on the pockets. My sewing teacher said she couldn't fault it, but she didn't give me full marks because that would leave no room for improvement. I proudly wore the dress to some Fellowship Meetings and was reprimanded for being too conspicuous. The next time I wore it, the dress had been dyed a dull muddy brown. I loved special fabrics like silk, satin and velvet and the embroidered fabrics that were popular at the time. One day I bought a length of beautiful cherry red velvet with some matching satin lining to make a coat. I just couldn't resist it. I didn't show it to anyone until it was finished. I knew it wouldn't meet with parental approval. Mum tut-tutted when she saw it. She was a very conservative lady and the sight of my beautiful red coat was almost too much for her. I put it away in the cupboard until the right occasion came along. Of course, when I did venture out in it, I was told never to wear it again! I still didn't learn because many years later I cut it up for outfits for my little boys and was told, 'Don't dress your children in red, it's a worldly colour!'

[Margin note: "God hates red, GC"]

Like most Exclusive Brethren children, once I had set my mind to it, I did very well academically. My ability to read well, the strict discipline at home and nothing outside of home and church to distract me from study combined to assure me of a place among the top students. I entered all the writing competitions and accumulated an impressive collection of books given as prizes for stories and poems and for coming first in the class exams. I was often given a choice of books for prizes but had to be very careful not to choose fiction or anything to do with religion. Several years later, most of those books, along with my dolls and other valued possessions, were destroyed by my father in accordance with some new rule.

Paperback books were always suspect. Dad seemed to think they were all trash. I borrowed a copy of *The Diary of Anne Frank* from the school library. I was born on Anne Frank's thirteenth birthday, and although our lives were vastly different, I too felt as if I was hiding from the authorities. I had been reading it at school and took it home to finish. I was reading it one night, curled up in front of the fire in the lounge, knowing that Dad was at a meeting. I didn't notice him come in.

'Ngaire, what's that you are reading?' he asked suspiciously.

'Just a book,' I mumbled, trying to stuff it under a cushion, out of sight.

'What's it called?' he barked at me.

'*The Diary of Anne Frank*,' I replied, trying to look as innocent as possible.

'Give it to me,' he said in a cold, quiet voice, holding out his hand for it. After I had reluctantly given it to him, he turned it over in his hands and read the blurb on the back cover.

'Where did you get it?'

'From the school library,' I replied. 'It's required reading,' I lied, hoping he would give it back.

'You know you have to show all your books to me or your mother before you read them,' Dad reminded me. 'We can't trust you, you read too much rubbish.'

'It's all right Dad, this one's about a young Jewish girl who hid from the Germans during the Second World War.' He'd been a hospital orderly in the war. I thought he would understand.

'I've told you not to read paperbacks,' he said, looking up over the top of his glasses.

'But Dad, it's a true story,' I pleaded. 'I thought we were allowed to read true stories.'

'That's enough of your impudence,' he replied as he shredded the book, and fed each page deliberately into the fire. 'Some true stories are worse than fiction, and this is trash in a paper cover,' he added unreasonably. Not only had he destroyed a wonderful book, but now I would need to find some way of replacing it. I was beginning to realise that there were many things in life that just weren't fair. In later years I would read books like *Peyton Place* and *The Life of Suzie Wong* and know how to get away with it.

Dad would not have needed to be so strict had I been more obedient. My life was very structured. As an adult, I'm aware that it's hard to differentiate between what were family rules and what were church rules. I'm also aware that other Exclusive Brethren families had slightly different rules from those of my own family. There were very strict guidelines for every facet of living and, if my father was stricter than most, then he assumed that gave him more credence in the eyes of the church. I knew exactly what I was and was not allowed to do. The greatest fun in my life at that stage was constructing creative ways of disobeying those rules. And break them I did, I can assure you. However, there were numerous occasions when I didn't win. The fact that I could, and often did, get caught just added adrenaline to the bloodstream and made me even more daring and rebellious!

At high school, I had other Brethren friends. There were four of us, and we went to three different Brethren Fellowships. One friend was an Open Brethren; another girl went to an Exclusive Brethren breakaway group called the Plymouth United Brethren. We were not really allowed to associate with them because the Exclusive Brethren taught us that breakaway groups of Brethren were the worst kind of Christians because they had 'turned their backs on the light'. Two of us were Exclusives, and our friends called us Peebs or Plyms. We didn't join in any social things at school, except once when I agreed to help with the school concert. The school students were organizing the concert to raise money for a new school gymnasium and I had been asked to be an usher at the door and to sell tickets. Of course, Dad said no. I don't know why I asked; the answer was always going to be no. I went anyway, and I dressed up and borrowed some lipstick from a friend! Dad was waiting up for me when I got home and sternly said he would deal with me in the morning. The next day was Sunday and, as a punishment, I had to stay home from the meetings and read a ministry book called The Way Everlasting, a collection of writings and poems by Exclusive Brethren. I didn't understand what I was reading, and didn't want to, but managed to answer most of the questions Dad asked me, enough to convince him that I had read it.

I was fifteen when I knew that one day I wanted to be a schoolteacher. Dad said this would be out of the question. My school friends were going on to university, but I knew that, for us Exclusives, higher education was now forbidden. Many of the Brethren rules had recently been changed. No longer were members permitted to study at university or teachers training college. They could not study to become doctors, nurses, teachers, lawyers, accountants or any other profession that required an education beyond high school. Any members who already had a university degree were expected to disown it because a degree gave them status and meant they were associated with people in the world. Like many Brethren terms, 'the world' meant whatever they said it did, and, in practice, 'the world' boiled down to whatever was outside the Exclusive Brethren fellowship. I was taught that people in the world were on their way to hell — but they seemed to be having so much fun getting there! My life wasn't any fun at all, at least not compared to theirs. A Brethren's life is full of 'Thou Shalt Nots' and 'Don't do this, I'll tell on you if you do that!' They thought they were on their way to heaven, and the only way to get there was along the narrow path of complete separation from the world and all its evil influences. I knew why Exclusive was their middle name. It was because they thought they were better than everyone else.

I dreamed of a future as a schoolteacher. But it was only a dream. By the year 1959, the Exclusives had already decided that higher education was a doorway to corruption, apostasy and evil influences.

'But Dad, I want to go to university, I want to be a teacher,' I wailed when he told me of the new edict.

'Universities are dens of iniquity and the Man of God has seen fit to prohibit our young people from entering them. You will be leaving school at the end of the week,' was his answer.

School was the best thing in my life, and I didn't care what the MOG said, I wasn't about to give it up that easily. Stamping my foot, I turned on Dad.

'Dad, I am not going to leave school. I don't care about the Exclusive Brethren and their stupid rules, I'm staying at school until I pass all my certificates and then I'm going to university.'

'Ngaire, your insolent behaviour makes your mother and me very sad,' he said, turning on his hang dog look. 'I want you to go to your room and think about it. I have arranged an interview for you at the Commercial Bank next Monday. There is no more to be said about it,' he added.

Well, I did think about it. The more I thought, the more I wanted to run away and live my own life. But running away was not really an option. If I did that, I would be an outcast. I would never see my family again. I would be treated as if I were dead. Besides, if I worked at the bank for a while, I could save some money, and then I would be better able to start a new life.

All hopes I had of becoming a teacher were dashed. My teachers felt sorry for me and appealed to my parents to make an exception. It was no use; in fact it made things worse.

Within a few days I had been removed from school and I started working at the bank. Those were the days when women worked in the background on accounting machines while the men were up front as tellers. I replaced a woman who was leaving to get married because in the 1950s the banks didn't employ married women.

The Exclusives were just entering a new phase in their already strict fundamentalist system. Separation from the world became the cornerstone of their beliefs, and separation meant complete isolation from anyone and everyone who was not in the fellowship. Eating in the presence of other people had always been discouraged. Now it was forbidden to the point that if you were caught having a cup of tea or eating with someone who was outside the fellowship, you could be put under investigation and eventually withdrawn from. People outside of the church found it very hard to understand this rule, and I can remember that Mother's parents were very hurt because we had to stop seeing them. The 'eating matter' and the directive of complete separation from the world became a test of fellowship, which for many members was the last straw.

But wait, I'm getting too far ahead here. I want to go back a year or two.

10

An end to innocence

Most Exclusives are very uncomfortable discussing sex, and in many homes sex education was considered unnecessary. In our day sex education in schools had not yet been introduced, and when it became part of the school curriculum, Brethren children were not permitted to attend those lessons. The Exclusive Brethren believed that all we needed to know about sex was in the Bible. To my way of thinking there are many interesting things that children can learn from reading the Bible, but some things need to be explained simply and clearly in language that children can understand.

The Exclusives see themselves as a very puritanical group. Talking about sex publicly was taboo, and as a result most Brethren children, me included, were innocently ignorant of the facts of life until we were much older than would be expected of children these days. If sex was ever talked about among the Brethren it was in the context of sin, and this would usually take place at a Care Meeting where the sins and misdemeanours of Brethren members were discussed and members dealt with, often by being withdrawn from. The positive references to sex in the Bible were always given a safe, sanitised, spiritual meaning. The Exclusive Brethren, by reputation, had very high moral standards, and immorality was not to be tolerated among them.

New leadership brought changes, and by the late 1950s, dealing with sexual impropriety in the meetings had become a more common practice. Any outward expression of sexuality might have been curbed by severe repression, but in reality, Brethren members had no special immunity when it came to lustful thoughts and actions. It now appeared that sexual immorality among the Brethren was rife, as was attested to by the regular and numerous public confessions and private whisperings. (I only became aware of all this when I was old enough to go to a Care Meeting.) I had the unfortunate experience of being brought before the members of the Brethren to be 'dealt with' at a Care Meeting, when I was only about fifteen. It was certainly a terrifying and horrific experience.

I'm not saying that I never did anything wrong; I enjoyed a bit of fun as much as anyone else, but I will never forget the embarrassment, shame and humiliation of being publicly censured for something I didn't do.

The story goes like this. A leading Brother from another town visited my father. After the leading Brother had been talking to Dad in the lounge for a while, Dad called me in.

'Ngaire, I wish to speak to you in the lounge, please,' he said sternly. My father was really upset about something, and I was soon to find out what. When we were seated in the lounge with the door closed, the questions began. I sat very still on the edge of the sofa, looking at the ground with my hands clasped firmly in my lap. Being 'visited' by a leading Brother from another town was serious stuff and usually meant trouble of some kind for someone. With a certain amount of trepidation I sat waiting for the inquisition to begin, and with many things going over in my mind I wondered if there were any rules I might have broken recently. The questions began with the visitor starting off by asking me about my friendships with some of the Brethren boys who were near my age.

'Have you ever been on your own with a boy?' I was asked.

I thought they were probably expecting a confession of some sort so I told them about the time I missed a meeting, going out with a friend to try out his new car and having a quick hug. My father was looking very uncomfortable by now.

'What about your cousin Trevor?' the visitor asked.

My cousin was about a year older than me. We had always been good friends but lately we had started getting more interested in each other. I didn't see him very often because he lived in a different city, but I sometimes went to stay with his family during the holidays. We talked and joked about sex as young teenagers do, but mostly we were just too busy having fun and enjoying each other's company along with his sister and mine. However, we did experiment with kissing on the odd occasion that we were alone together, so I confessed about the times my cousin had kissed me down in the garden among the bushes.

'So, are you admitting that you have committed fornication with a young man?' Dad asked.

'Well, yes, I suppose I must have,' I answered, nodding my head, not knowing what he meant by 'committing fornication'. I only vaguely understood their biblical terminology as having something to do with the opposite sex.

'I told you so, and she's not even ashamed of it,' said the visiting Brother in a smug, self-satisfied voice. 'This is a matter that should be dealt with by the Assembly in Auckland. I will contact the Brethren about it.'

With that Dad let his visitor out the front door, and then walked slowly back into the lounge.

'Your matter will probably come up before the Assembly meeting next Tuesday night,' said Dad, as he dismissed me without asking any more questions or even explaining to me the seriousness of what I had unwittingly confessed to. We didn't discuss sexual things in our house and I honestly didn't have a clue about the accusation being made against me. I had learned about the birds and the bees from playground discussions and innuendos, and I had looked at the pictures in the big medical book on the top shelf of the bookcase, but I still didn't know about words like 'fornication' and 'adultery'. These are adult terms and don't mean much to a child unless they are explained in context. I do not doubt that some Exclusive parents may have explained these biblical words to their children and young teenagers, but mine didn't, and I had not yet discovered the exciting, but illicit, thrill of going through the Bible with the express purpose of finding all the juicy bits.

If Dad had sat down there and then and talked about it with me I'm sure what followed would not have needed to happen. I expected him to explain to me what I had let myself in for, but he didn't. He seemed so cold and distant, so sullen and embarrassed, as if I had let the family down. I believe he thought I knew what the Brother was talking about. I was in trouble, and the family was disgraced. As my matter was now under Assembly investigation, no one wanted to talk to me, not even my mother, and everyone in the family knew I had been unspeakably wicked. For quite some time I stayed in my room feeling sorry for myself, and I was worried enough to pray a foxhole prayer. I pleaded with what was to me an unsympathetic God, asking Him to forgive me for whatever it was that I had done wrong. I knew that what I was supposed to have done was a serious matter because they were going to talk about me at the Assembly meeting. I was in dire trouble, in a tight spot, and I wasn't sure, in fact I had not the slightest idea, how I was going to get myself out of this terrible situation.

As the day of my humiliation drew near, an elderly gentleman from our local meeting came to see me and to talk over my matters with me before the meeting on Tuesday night.

'Do you know how serious this is?' he asked in a quiet, kindly voice. 'Do you know what the act of fornication is?'

'I'm not sure that I do, but I think it's something to do with holding hands and kissing' I replied.

He soon realised that I didn't really have a clue what the word meant. After he explained it to me I went all red and burst into tears. I understood then what all the fuss was about and felt quite relieved that I hadn't been guilty after all. I was young enough and sufficiently naïve to believe that if I hadn't done what they were accusing me of, then I was innocent and that would be the end of the matter. My fears were again heightened when I began to understand that this was not going to be the end of the matter, but that trouble was still in store for me. I wanted the priest who had come to visit me to make this whole ugly scenario go away, but that was only wishful thinking on my part. I hoped that he could arrange it so I wouldn't have to have 'my case brought to the Assembly', but it was too late, the wheels of judgement had begun to turn and the fact that I was innocent was of no consequence.

I had plenty of time alone to think, and I did a lot of thinking. I knew that it was wrong to kiss and cuddle the boys, and what I had done was never any more than that, and it hadn't happened very often, so I thought I should be able to get off the hook. I concluded that what had been going on for quite some time in my own bedroom was far worse than that. I waited for Dad to come and talk to me about it all, but he didn't.

Tuesday night came and we all went into that dreaded city meeting. The time came for my 'matters' to be heard, and someone outlined the facts according to what they had been told. Then Mr Kent stood up on my behalf and explained that he had visited me. He explained that he had talked to me about the matters that were now before the Brethren and he believed I was still a virgin, that I had not committed fornication, and in fact I was somewhat ignorant of the meaning of the word. This development caused much discussion to and fro, but I have no clear recollection of what was said until they addressed me when they had come to a conclusion. Some Brothers were sure that I must be guilty of something, so they went ahead and read Deuteronomy 22:24, a verse in the Old Testament about 'not crying out'. They seemed to be able to find a Bible verse for every situation! (They appeared to have little or no concern as to whether the verse of scripture they applied was relevant to the situation or not.) I think they meant that I should have cried out and said 'No' when my cousin had wanted to kiss me. I was given the microphone and told to say I was sorry for not crying out. I stood up in front of about five or six hundred people with the microphone in my hand. The sea of stern and solemn faces was just a blur in front of me as I apologised for something I didn't do. After I had said I was sorry and had been graciously forgiven by the Brethren, I sat down in my seat and cried with humiliation and shame.

It was uncharacteristic for Exclusive Brethren priests to back down, apologise, or say they were sorry, even when they were proven wrong. (However, in 2002, my younger brother came and told me that he was very sorry for what had happened to me.) As it turned out, what had happened was that someone had made a careless mistake about the details of my friendship with my cousin Trevor, and I was left to wear the shame and ignominy of someone else's assumption. Someone had heard wrongly and passed it on as fact, resulting in something similar to a game of Chinese whispers. These situations were aggravated by a lust for sexual gossip, and a readiness to believe the worst, even of their own members. Knowing the way the Exclusives operate, I can well understand how such a mistake came about.

In hindsight I believe this whole horrible scenario was really just the playing out of a hideous and disgusting adult game. It seemed to me that publicly exposing sensuous, lustful behaviour in other people made the rest of the Brethren feel that they were more holy. I think this was really just one of their ways of internalising and excusing their own secrets and inhibitions. For the Exclusive Brethren, dealing with sin was supposed to be all about maintaining holiness and purity, but it didn't seem to matter about the traumatic effect such exposure had on young and relatively innocent people. I have never seen and certainly never experienced any concern for the victims of their bizarre procedures. There was no focus on healing the affected party, nor was there any type of counselling available. Any counselling outside the confines of the fellowship of the Brethren was considered evil and unnecessary. I now wonder if maybe this was to discourage members from exposing Exclusive Brethren practices to people on the outside. Many years latter, I still feel angry and violated. I am angry that adults could be so ignorant and callous as to publicly inflict on a teenager such an unnecessary and damaging experience. I now regard this type of violation as part of their extreme subjugation of their members, and of women in particular.

Although it was a very traumatic experience, something good came out of it. At fifteen, although still rather ignorant of some things, I was old enough to know that if it was wrong for my cousin to hug and kiss me, then what my father was doing to me was very, very wrong indeed. Being of a determined character, and by now out for revenge, I took the opportunity to retaliate. I threatened my father that I would 'cry out' and cause a public scandal, much worse than the experience I had endured, if he did not stop his inappropriate behaviour. I knew I now held the key to his continued church membership. The abuse ended there and then; he was careful never to touch me again.

As a result of my unfortunate experience with the Exclusives, and with my father, I built a hard protective shell around myself and made out that I was tough. On the inside I was hurting, and I tried to compensate by overeating. Sometimes I got to the point where I would hate myself. In my distress I assumed that it must be all my fault, that God was punishing me for some reason, and that I just had to put up with it. Nothing more was said about my case after that Tuesday night. At least I had been forgiven and wasn't put out of fellowship, and that was something to be thankful for, or at least I thought so at the time.

Unfortunately, my kissing cousin didn't come off so well. Trevor was a year older than me. He was withdrawn from in 1959. There had recently been a change of leadership. It was a difficult time for many Exclusive Brethren members as they could not accept the teachings of the new MOG (Man of God) and, after a season of 'purging' confessions, some of them left the fellowship or were withdrawn from. Trevor just got caught up in it somehow. Trevor's story is similar to those of many other young people who eventually found themselves out of fellowship and completely estranged from parents, siblings and friends. It's not easy to get over an experience like this, especially after living a life that is seemingly sheltered and protected from the sins and evils of the world. It is very hard to come to terms with being thrown out into the wicked world by the very same people who had proclaimed its wickedness.

Most people who have been put out of the fellowship of the Exclusive Brethren carry scars of trauma for the rest of their lives. This problem is particularly evident when death separates them from loved ones before any reconciliation takes place. Trevor belonged to my extended family, and I contacted him after not having seen him for forty years. He told me his story with a hint of rebellious bravado, a bravado that only thinly obscured the deep hurts he has carried with him for so long.

11

Tried, convicted and excommunicated

I remember Trevor as a good friend who was a fun person to be with; full of bright ideas and taking outrageous risks by disobeying the rules of the Exclusive Brethren. As a result of this behaviour, he came in for a fair share of parental discipline. Not all punishments meted out to him were for anti-church behaviour. Most were for normal, high-spirited boyish pranks. His father had a short fuse and would let fly at him with a broom, a stick or his fists. Sometimes the dreaded razor strop would be brought down hard on his legs and buttocks making red welts and bruises. Added to that was the occasional kick in the shins and a cuff around the ear. The Exclusive Brethren believed in strict discipline — 'Spare the rod, spoil the child' sort of stuff — but in most homes, physical punishment was not extreme or excessive. Trevor regarded home as an extension of the church. He felt resentful about heavy-handed punishments but thought the rough treatment was normal. Sometimes it's easier to fight a group like the church than to go against your parents, so Trevor blamed the Brethren.

There were times when the restricted Exclusive Brethren life got too much for Trevor and, being a bright boy, he had learned to think things out and come up with ways to beat the Exclusive system. Beating the system, in some way or another, was the survival tactic of many

Exclusive Brethren kids. There were a lot of young people at the meeting room where Trevor and his family went, and it was not unusual to find Trevor and his friends down the back of the car park, hatching up some mischievous plan.

Trevor knew one very important fact of life: possession of money assured power and independence. He was the oldest in the family and had always been encouraged to work for his pocket money. He mowed lawns, weeded the garden, took out the trash and helped his mother with the younger children, as well as delivering groceries for the local store. Trevor always kept the lawns neat and tidy, and, before long, other people wanted their lawns mown too. He knew what he wanted to do with the money he earned. Like his father, Trevor was very keen on inventing things. He needed all manner of bits and pieces for his experiments, so he carefully calculated how much he could spend, giving him enough left over to put in the bank for when he needed something big. His aim was to have enough money at fifteen to buy a car.

Trevor used his knowledge of tinkering and technology to build himself a radio. Trevor knew very well that the Exclusive Brethren had forbidden radios, but he knew how to make a crystal set from bits and pieces. Trevor worked out a way to turn his bed into a radio. Using the crystal set as a receiver, he connected it to the wire-wove base of his bed, and with the help of some earphones he could lie in bed and listen to the radio.

Because he liked tinkering with technology, Trevor often sat at the back of the meeting room, helping with the sound amplifying system. Among other things, it was fun to fiddle with the tapes, recording loud windy noises in the most inappropriate places! Trevor and his friends were never short of bright ideas to relieve the boredom of having to go to so many meetings. Although some of the Brothers suspected Trevor and his friends of these pranks, I am sure they saw the funny side of it, and made no serious attempt to nail down the culprits. Trevor was a boy with an irresistible sense of humor.

And he liked the girls — all girls, any girls, he just liked girls. He had two sisters and several girl cousins and, wow, there was no shortage of lovely young ladies at the meeting room. At fifteen, there was only one thing Trevor liked better than girls, and that was his little red soft-top car, which he called Noddy. Of course, Noddy was usually full of girls, and so Trevor was often to be seen with a smile from ear to ear. On Saturdays, Trevor and Noddy would take off to Fellowship Meetings in neighbouring towns. These tea-meetings were the hub of the Exclusive Brethren social life in those times, and Trevor was a very sociable lad. At Fellowship Meetings there was many a girl who was enticed into Noddy's passenger seat for a spin around the block during the break between meetings. Sometimes these little jaunts would take a little longer and the last meeting would be finished before their return.

During the summer holidays, Trevor drove Noddy up north to stay with relatives. Most Exclusive Brethren were related to others in some way and everyone knew everyone else all over New Zealand. Trevor enjoyed staying on his cousin's farm. He liked the animals. The oldest girl in the family wasn't too bad either! It was a busy time of the year, and Trevor was only too happy to throw in his weight with the rest. When work was done for the day he would sit and talk with his friends, or take Noddy for a spin around the countryside. Returning home, he stopped in Auckland to stay the night with his uncle and aunt. He knew there was always a welcome at their place for him.

But this time something was wrong. Uncle was very stern and asked Trevor to come into the lounge, he had something to say to him. Uncle had had a phone call from a Brother up north. Trevor was being accused of immorality, of 'unclean' behaviour with girls, of sleeping around and goodness knows what else. Although vehemently declaring that it wasn't as bad as they made out, he was not believed. Trevor knew he wasn't perfect, but how else can a boy have fun if not with the girls? Uncle said he was in disgrace, he could not speak to his cousins, and although he could stay overnight in the shed, he would have to pack his bags and leave early in the morning. Trevor made his way home after a sleepless night. This was all a misunderstanding; his mum and dad would know what to do, they would believe him. Trevor says his father often belted him cruelly for his misdemeanors, but this was serious stuff. Trevor knew that he had sailed pretty close to the wind with some of his girlfriends, but this was a bit over the top. Not that he hadn't daydreamed a little! If thoughts were deeds, then Trevor was guilty of having gone the whole way.

His welcome home could hardly be called warm. His mum had been crying and his father was angry. His brothers and sisters were told to keep away from him. Thus started the nightmare, and visits from the church elders that would go on for months. After the first Care Meeting, where the Brethren were told all the details of his apparently sinful behaviour, the news spread quickly throughout the country, and letters started arriving from other areas accusing Trevor of sinful behaviour with girls up and down the North Island. It must be remembered that this was one of those times in the history of the Exclusive Brethren when many of them were making confessions about their past sins, both real and imagined, and often these would be embroidered. At the end of the 1950s many of the Brethren were purging themselves in accordance with strong new directives from the current MOG. Trevor just happened to be on the receiving end. It was Dump-on-Trevor time, and he was sure made an example of. Trevor was, without doubt, a daring and experimental trendsetter. His name had acquired a special significance among the teenage girls. To the ruling patriarchy Trevor was seen as a vector for a plague of leprosy.

After three or four Care Meetings (very similar to a court hearing) where his case was discussed, and in spite of him protesting his innocence to all but the pettiest of the accusations, Trevor was declared guilty. An Assembly meeting was arranged after the Ministry meeting one Tuesday night. The three Brothers (elders/priests) dealing with his case outlined the details and called upon the Brethren to make their judgement. After reading a few passages of scripture from the Bible, one Brother rose and said that, in the light of the facts brought before them, and without tears of remorse or other evidence of repentance, they could no longer walk with (break bread with) Trevor. He rose and slowly left the room, leaving behind him the only friends he had ever been allowed to know. Trevor, only seventeen, was an outcast. The Exclusive Brethren had withdrawn from him, the worst punishment they could mete out.

He drove home and walked through the house. His young brothers and sisters were in bed. His aunt, who was looking after them, looked straight through him as if he wasn't there. She knew what the meeting had been about and she had already guessed the outcome. Trevor sat on his bed in the front room, which would become his prison for the next three months, and he cried. His whole life was tied up with the Exclusive Brethren. He didn't know anyone on the outside, and even his job was at stake because his boss was a Brethren. The only thing he could think of was how to get back into fellowship. By the time his parents had returned from the meeting, he had resolved to 'get right'. However, getting right is not easy when no one believes you. He thought back over his life. He feared God. Trevor's father was given to bouts of violent punishments and if God was 'Father' then God's eternal punishment was something to be feared. God knew everything and abhorred sin. Some sins could be forgiven but Trevor had not been forgiven that night. He wondered if he could ever be forgiven. What if he had done something really bad? Trevor's feeling of guilt for the things that he *had* done overshadowed his understanding of the more serious unsubstantiated charges the Exclusive Brethren were bringing against him.

Trevor remained confined to his room for three months. He wasn't allowed to have his meals with the family. His mum put his meals on a tray outside the door. He still went to work but he couldn't eat or drink with his boss. He went to a few of the Brethren meetings during those three months but he couldn't break bread or talk to the other young people. He sat at the back of the meeting room by himself. So long as he was trying to get back into the Exclusive Brethren fellowship, Trevor was tolerated, at home, at work and at the meeting room. He felt like he was being dangled on a rope, out of reach of terra firma, and swaying this way and that. No matter how he pleaded, grovelled and begged, the Brethren were not ready to take him back. In Trevor's opinion he was made a scapegoat by accusers who were too anxious to comply with higher orders to make certain that the charges against him were merited. Those responsible for enforcing discipline could lose face if they were too lenient or too quick with their forgiveness.

One day Trevor met a young man who turned out to be a distant cousin. This cousin invited him to a youth meeting at the local Open Brethren Gospel Hall. What a contrast! The Exclusive Brethren had no youth group activities except for the occasional sing-along at someone's house, after the gospel on Sunday nights. The Open Brethren young people had so much fun! One of the girls invited him to their Breaking of Bread meeting the next morning, and he went. When he arrived home at the end of the day, his parents already knew where he had been. Exclusive Brethren members are prohibited from attending any other church service. Although Trevor was no longer breaking bread with them, he was bound by their rules because he was trying to 'get right'. Now that he had broken the rules by attending another church, and because he had been seen with a 'worldly' girl, he could no longer live at home. He put all his possessions in the back of Noddy and drove to the park, where he slept for the night. Next morning, after a wash in the men's changing rooms by the beach, he arrived at work to find his tool bag packed. He was ordered off the site. He had no job, no contact with his family, nowhere to live and no friends apart from the ones he had met at the Open Brethren meeting the day before.

He lived in the park for a week, washing in the men's changing room and sleeping in the car. One day a lady saw him and recognised him as he walked along the beach. She and her husband had left the Exclusive Brethren fellowship a year before. She gave him their address and invited him to dinner that night. With an overwhelming feeling of gratitude he then set off for a stroll on the beach. He returned to his car a while later to find that his possessions had gone. The car was empty. All he owned had been in the car. If only he hadn't left the soft top down and the car unlocked. He turned up to dinner that night and poured out his problems to his new-found friends. They took him downstairs, and there in the basement room were all his things. She had taken them home, washed his clothes and set everything up for Trevor to live with them until he could get himself sorted out.

It may be hard to believe these things can happen, but it doesn't take much imagination to see how someone can blow the whole thing out of proportion and then judge accordingly. Once the Brethren have got it in for you, there is very little opportunity for self-defence, or forgiveness. You can repent until you're blue in the face but it doesn't mean that you're going to be forgiven.

Trevor visited his mother before she died. She was still with the Exclusive Brethren but living part-time in a rest home. A photo of them together is proudly displayed in Trevor's family album. The natural love between mother and son had remained intact.

12

Creative teenage rule breaker

I think I was a normal enough teenager, but as I grew older my basic personality began to show more clearly. I just happened to be questioning and rebellious, rather than compliant and submissive. To an Exclusive Brethren parent these are the worst characteristics they would ever want to see in a daughter. After being publicly humiliated I sensed I was morally ugly – add to this being called 'fatso' and 'uglymug' by my siblings and you have the potential for one very screwed-up teenager. I wanted to rebel, to get even but not get caught. The more things I was not allowed to do, the more I tried to do them anyway.

All the women and girls wore hats when we went out and when we went to meetings. We had to wear a scarf to work. I hated wearing a scarf as much as wearing a hat, so I would take it off when I left the house and stuff it in the hedge and retrieve it on my way home — if I remembered. I got caught several times and was given extra chores to do as a punishment. Brethren women and girls don't cut their hair, so it grew very long. While we were young enough to go to school we could wear our hair in a ponytail or in plaits, but when we left school, we were expected to put our hair 'up', which was a sign of being almost grown up. There were several ways we could do it. We could twist it into a bun, wear a plait around the head, roll it up or under into a pageboy style or, if it wasn't very long and thick, we could make a French roll. The older ladies rolled it up or made a bun, but young girls usually chose a pageboy style or the more fashionable French roll. I preferred a pageboy style. I had two pieces of cotton-covered wire about twelve inches long, secured together at the ends with rubber bands. Tied tightly to the rubber bands were narrow ribbons, which were usually black, brown, or navy blue. I would put my hair between the two wires and pull the wires to the ends of my hair and roll it under. Because my hair was long and thick, I had to roll it very tightly then bring the ends around and tie the ribbons together at the top of my head. This little bow on the top then became a 'token'. A token, worn twenty-four hours a day, was a small piece of ribbon tied into the hair or worn on a hair clip. The token showed the angels that we women were in subjection to men and it was thought that we would be more likely to be protected by the angels if they thought we ... Oh dear! This is too complicated to explain and I do believe now that it was more superstition than spiritual belief!

All the women and girls wore a token in their hair. The symbolic token is derived from St Paul's writings in 1 Corinthians, and who was I to argue with St Paul?

I had a creative personality, and so I directed it towards creative disobedience of the rules. I became friends with the other staff of the bank where I worked, who took great delight in helping me escape the net with prohibited visits to the cinema, the occasional staff drinking party and the inevitable subtle changes to my appearance. The day I put a purple plum rinse in my hair was a red-letter day indeed. You would have thought I had committed the most heinous of sins. I was 'visited' by a concerned Brother whose wife had assured him that my hair was no longer the natural colour that God had made it. I thought it looked rather nice. Mum and Dad said nothing. I don't think they even noticed. When we got home from the meeting on Sunday afternoon the phone was ringing. Dad answered it. It was Mr Wilson.

Dad looked very solemn and he kept looking at me.

'What on earth has Ngaire done to her hair?' asked Mr Wilson, already knowing the answer. 'Mrs Wilson says it is very obvious that she has coloured it.'

'I will speak to her about it,' replied Dad. 'Ngaire, I want to see you in the lounge please, at once.'

Oh dear! More trouble. A long time later, Dad and I emerged from the lounge and my eyes were as red as my hair. Dad said I had to wash all the dye out before the next Sunday. Easier said than done! Of course I knew that dyeing my hair was against the rules, along with using make-up, perming hair and having a fringe, but if ever anyone needed to enhance their looks, it was me. Now that I'm free to do it, I don't know how to!

Some of the Brethren must have wondered about all the ever-tightening rules that were actually excluding people from joining the fellowship and alienating many who already belonged. I am sure that many had their own private doubts; some may even have dared to question the rules. But almost as though they were anticipating these questions, the leaders would say that 'the refining process is getting more intensive, the mesh is getting finer, and only the truly faithful will make it to the glorious end. The less faithful will be "ashamed at His coming".' Those who upheld the standards were the honoured faithful who carried authority in the fellowship. People like me were confused stragglers, trying to appear as though we measured up to the almost unattainable standards.

And still I stayed. Sometimes I wanted to scream, 'Set me free, kick me out, and withdraw from me.' I don't actually remember seriously contemplating leaving the Brethren at that stage, but my stroppy behaviour was causing concern.

One day we were at Fellowship Meetings in the city.

'If anyone asks you where I am, please, please could you say I have a headache and I'm sitting in the car or I've gone for a walk?' I pleaded to my sister.

'Ngaire, what are you going to do?' she asked, 'Please don't do anything you shouldn't.'

'I'm going out with Lenny, we are going up the hill to look at the lights,' I replied. 'Remember, if anyone asks, I've got a headache.'

'Bother,' I thought as I slipped out through the side door of the meeting room. Mrs Bluett was standing in the shadows rocking the pram gently to get her youngster off to sleep while keeping half an eye on another child sitting just inside the door. But one eye I am sure was on me and then on Lenny as he slipped out a few moments later and followed me down the street. The next day I was summonsed to the lounge.

'Ngaire,' Dad said angrily, 'I want to speak to you in the lounge, now, do you hear?'

'Yes, Dad.' I knew Dad had been speaking to Mr Bluett and I knew what Dad was going to say.

'Ngaire, who was the young man you were with last evening?' he asked.

'What young man?'

'You were seen leaving the meeting with young Lenny Roberts, is that correct?'

'Whoever told you that is just trying to make trouble,' I replied.

'Mr Bluett is coming to visit you on Monday night after the Prayer Meeting. You had better tell him the truth because his wife saw you.'

I knew I was in trouble but I had had enough. What I did was none of their business. I was skating on very thin ice, but I was not about to admit that I had not only missed a meeting to go out with a boy, but I had lied about it. Worse still, I had let him kiss me!

'Please own up and tell them you did it,' pleaded my sister. 'I hate it when you get into trouble, and this time they might put you out of fellowship.'

I didn't own up, and after several visits from Mr Bluett, spurred on no doubt by Mrs Bluett, I was visited by old Mr Bates who had, in his younger days, been a school headmaster and knew all about difficult teenagers.

'Ngaire dear, you know, and I know, and God knows that you and Lenny missed the last meeting on Saturday, so why don't I tell the others that you have admitted it? I think that would be for the best. Don't you, dear?'

'Yes, Mr Bates,' I replied.

'Before I go, I want to tell you about a few verses in Exodus. When I have gone I want you to look them up and read them for yourself,' he said. 'It says there that God has mercy over thousands, forgiving sins, but by no means clearing the guilty,' he went on. 'If you do something wrong, you will have to pay the consequences for your wrong actions. Your parents and the Brethren have only your good at heart and are seeking the salvation of your soul through confession of your sins and the forsaking of evil. Goodnight, Ngaire,' he said as he left the room. I have never forgotten his kind words of wisdom and often wished that other Brothers had the same gentle and effective ways of explaining things. I did try harder after that.

At sixteen I was old enough by law to leave home, but as an Exclusive Brethren I was forbidden to leave until I married. This was another new rule. Some of our older friends had left home to work in other towns or on farms, some had even gone overseas for their big 'Overseas Experience', but this was no longer allowed. This would have been the best time for me to break free from this restricted life, before I found a mate, because he too would be tied to his family. But being free was always in the future, being free meant never again seeing my family or friends, and being free meant something terrible could happen to me: an accident an incurable disease, or I could die and spend eternity in hell!

It was time for me to turn that leaf over once again. I made a vow. I had an aggressive and volatile personality, and I had flown off the handle just once too often, punching a hole in the lounge door! I had become very angry because the Exclusive Brethren had forbidden me to see a young man I had become friendly with. They said he was 'morally married' to another young woman because he had been intimate with her. He had already told me about this incident, which happened when he was fifteen, and now the Exclusive Brethren were insisting that he marry her to 'fulfill righteousness'. After my parents had calmed me down, I felt ashamed of my violent outburst. I vowed never again to let anyone experience my bad temper and aggressiveness. I would build an impenetrable wall of protection around myself.

Did anyone notice the change? I doubt it. It's a sad fact of life that, when we do something good, something positive, it often goes unnoticed, but when we do something negative, we get pounced on. I'm not aware that anyone noticed the change at the time, but I kept that vow, and before long it had become part of my personality and it was hard to believe that I had ever had a bad temper.

It is very hard to permanently change an attitude or type of behaviour or to keep a volatile temper bottled up indefinitely. I think it was my way of changing my outer world. If I couldn't change what was going on around me, then I wanted to be a better person for me. It was almost as if I had more control over my life because I had control of my 'inner environment'.

In short, I had decided that I would not allow the Exclusive Brethren, or anyone else, to hurt or humiliate me ever again. I worked hard at being calm, compliant, obedient, submissive, and everything the Exclusive Brethren expected me to be, but what went on inside my head belonged to me. On the outside I had learned to hide my true feelings by maintaining respectability while in my imagination I lived in a different world. I knew it was considered to be wicked to have an imagination. 'It was all lies' they told me, just a world of make believe that came from reading too many novels. I had learned to be independent, deceitful, to lie to keep out of trouble, and never, ever to trust anyone, a trait that remained with me until I left the fellowship.

The list of 'Thou Shalt Nots' kept growing. I seldom spoke to anyone about my discontent, and when I did, I was told that the best thing was to get married. Being married and having children would keep me occupied and give me more purpose in life. Exclusive Brethren girls were encouraged to get married while they were very young, and sixteen to eighteen was considered the best age. But I didn't really want to get married. I didn't like men because you had to obey them and be subject to them, even if it went against your conscience. But most scary of all, a man might expect me to do things that I didn't want to do.

If I didn't marry before I turned eighteen, I would need to apply for exemption from joining a trade union. At the end of the 1930s, the Exclusive Brethren had taken the stand that belonging to a union was wrong. In those days trade union membership was compulsory in New Zealand. The Exclusives appealed to the government of the day against becoming union members on the grounds that they were conscientious objectors. I would be drilled on the correct answers to give to the inevitable questions posed by the Tribunal committee. What church do you go to? Are they a sect? Are you appealing because of your own conscience or because you belong to the Exclusive Brethren? I had been drilled in the correct answers. 'No, I do not belong to a sect; I am a believer in the Lord Jesus Christ, and in the absolute authority of God's inspired Word, the Holy Bible.' I would quote 2 Corinthians 6:15 about being unequally yoked with unbelievers. I would point out that submission to trade union influence accepts interference in the employer (master) and employee (servant) relationship, which is divinely ordained.

I didn't like these answers that I was expected to learn off pat. I looked up the dictionary meaning of the word 'sect': Confined or devoted to a religious denomination, adherents of a principle or school of thought. How could I truthfully declare that the Exclusive Brethren were not a sect? I sidestepped the issue by just not turning up for my union appeal. I had a year to wait before the next appeal, maybe I could think up an excuse, or maybe I would be married by then, and would no longer be allowed to go out to work.

It was part of the Exclusive Brethren strategy that our lives should be so entwined with the fellowship that it would be very difficult to separate from it. This was seen to be part of God's way of salvation. We were told it was His 'provision' for us. I felt like I was being swept along in a strong current, unable to stand alone but in reality seeing nothing stable to grab hold of to avoid being swamped or drowned. Then I met Denis at some Fellowship Meetings, one Saturday near the end of 1961.

I have pieced together Denis's story from the many things he has told me, and from his diaries, which he kept from the time he was about nine years old. I would have loved to discuss this next chapter with his sisters, but because they are still in the Exclusive Brethren fellowship I can have no contact with them. Denis's story is an almost lyrical account of Brethrenism at its best. I have included it here as a contrast to my own and Trevor's stories and to show that not all Exclusive Brethren families are the same.

13

Born to be Brethren

The farmhouse stood back from the road a little, on a hill, overlooking the lush farmland on the outskirts of the town. Along the roadside marched a row of trees, originally planted as a hedge but now so tall they seemed to go up forever.

It wasn't too far to walk to the small general store, and Agnes had put Denis and Carol in the big pushchair and, with Jenny running alongside, they set off toward the shops. Jenny was tall for six, and already her dark hair was long, almost to her waist. Denis was nearly four, dark like his sister, but with beautiful hazel eyes framed by the longest, darkest lashes ever seen on a boy. As Agnes pushed the pram along the country road, Carol fell asleep, lying curled up behind Denis, who was sitting at the front, very still so as not to overbalance. Carol was eighteen months old, as fair as the others were dark, a halo of soft, gold curls framing her face. Agnes was proud of her three children. Sometimes women stopped to admire the baby with her blonde hair and fair complexion contrasting with the older ones with their dark hair and skin tanned from running around the farm.

The walk home seemed to take forever. The children were tired and Agnes glanced anxiously at her watch. Henry would be home for dinner soon. The cows were walking in single file down the race and would soon be munching the grass in the home paddock. The winter sun was already low in the sky by the time they tripped wearily up the back steps. The evening was going to be cool, so Agnes started the fire already set in the grate and settled the children in front of it, each with a mug of warm cocoa. As soon as he had finished his drink, Denis was off to meet his dad. He would slip his small hand into his father's big one and walk with him toward the house, neither of them needing to say a word.

Henry was a big man of very few words, well respected in the Exclusive Brethren church to which he took his family every Sunday and several evenings during the week. Today was Monday, and tonight he was going to the Prayer Meeting where all the Brothers would pray and the Sisters could say a quiet amen to show that, if they had been permitted to pray themselves, they would have said the same thing. Good, the fire was lit. It would have been so much easier to stay home by the fire, telling his children stories from the Bible, but Henry was a good man and he knew that, no matter what, he would be at that Prayer Meeting.

Agnes had cooked his favorite meal: sausages in gravy, mashed potatoes, peas and yellow butter beans preserved from their own garden. Although some food items were rationed because of the war, there was always plenty of meat and vegetables, and Agnes made bread several times a week to feed her family. It was 1943 and there was a war raging somewhere on the other side of the world. Henry, being a farmer, had been exempted from signing up. He was needed at home to run the farm.

Henry and Agnes had both been born Exclusive Brethren, as had their parents and grandparents before them. Their forebears had been Brethren in England, Ireland and Wales, probably as far back as the beginning of the Brethren movement in the mid-1800s. They both came from large families and expected to have several more children of their own. They were good parents, teaching their children well. The strict moral and isolated lifestyle of the Exclusive Brethren was not irksome for them. They had known no other. That was the way it was, and hopefully that was the way it would stay. Some time ago, Agnes had made a text to hang on the wall: 'This is our God for ever and ever, He will be our guide until death.' Another hung beside it: 'But as for me and my house, we will serve the Lord.' Henry told the children that the 'But' was very important. It meant 'no matter what happens' we will serve the Lord. These Bible texts, along with other Brethren beliefs, would govern all decisions made in this household.

Denis was a quiet child, not shy but reserved. He didn't have much to say to anyone, but for most of his life he kept a diary, starting in 1948 when he was nine years old. He mostly wrote about home and meetings, but sometimes he would just write one word, 'school'. He would write that same word five times followed by, Saturday, 'went to Fellowship Meetings in Cambridge', and Sunday, 'went to meeting, Uncle George preached'. Denis liked listening to Uncle George; he always made the lessons sound interesting. After one of his preachings, Denis told Uncle George that he would like to ask Jesus into his heart, and in his nine-year-old way, he made a commitment to love the Lord for the rest of his life.

Sunday was a busy day. All the children had their baths on Saturday night and on Sunday morning they had to stay indoors so they wouldn't get dirty. Sometimes Martin would sneak outside and play in the sandpit. That made his mother very cross; didn't she have enough to do with the new baby and the lunch to pack and the breakfast dishes to do? Jenny was almost grown up, and after she had brushed and combed and braided her own hair she would do Carol's. Carol wore hers in long ringlets, tied each side with ribbons to match her dress. Denis was wearing his first pair of long pants, a white shirt and a tie just like father's. At last they were all ready. Today was very special; Denis would break bread at the Lord's Supper for the first time.

They were late again. The milking had taken longer than usual and so the drive into town was a little over the speed limit, and not for the first time either! They slipped into the meeting room just as the first hymn was being given out. Father led Denis to the seats in the front row with the other Brothers, and Mother and the children sat at the back so that Jenny could take the baby out for a walk if he got restless. Denis liked to sing. He had a very good singing voice and was soon joining in as they sang the second verse. They all sat quietly for a few minutes, then a Brother got up and stood by the table in the centre of the room. On the table were a small loaf of bread on a plate, and a large goblet of dark red port wine covered with a crocheted cloth weighted down on the corners with glass beads. Beside the bread and the wine was a small basket without a handle. Around the top of the basket was a piece of fabric, stitched to the top edge and gathered into a circle leaving a small hole in the middle, big enough to poke in a coin or a pound note but not big enough for the money to fall out if it got too full while it was being passed around for the collection.

'Let us pray', said the Brother, and they all bowed their heads. He thanked the Lord Jesus for dying on the cross for their sins and then he broke the bread, which represented Christ's body. He nestled the pieces of bread carefully on the plate, so they wouldn't fall off, and passed it to another Brother on the front row. When it came to Denis's turn, he carefully pulled off a small piece — must leave plenty for everyone else — and popped it into his mouth. It tasted good, and it had been a long time since breakfast. What a pity he couldn't have some more. Never mind, after the meeting he would ask if he could have some of the leftovers.

'Let us give thanks for the wine', said the Brother. After lifting the cover off the goblet, he gave thanks for the wine and handed it to the same Brother on the front row. Denis had never tasted wine before, and it was so sharp in his throat that he began to cough. Like most of the Exclusive Brethren back then, his parents didn't drink alcohol, but the Brethren always used wine for the Breaking of Bread. Now it was time for the collection to be taken up. Denis did a giggle to himself. When he was younger, he used to think that they had something to eat and something to drink and then they had to pay for it. Now he knew that the money would be used to help other Brethren who needed it, and some would be sent to the Very Important Brethren People from all over the world who took Fellowship Meetings and Three-day Meetings.

They sang some more hymns with prayers of thanksgiving in between, then the meeting was over and they all went outside to talk.

The children were free to run and play while the Sisters admired the babies, the little girls' dresses, and the latest style in hats for the women. Because they lived in an area where many of the Brethren managed dairy farms, most had lunch at the hall so that the next meeting could follow on quickly so as to allow plenty of time for the afternoon milking. Sunday lunch was a great social occasion, and soon they were all sitting down in the back room, the tables laden with the goodies that each family had prepared that morning. Denis hoped that Lester's mother would ask him to sit at their part of the table; they always had a nice lunch.

It was hard to keep awake during the next meeting, especially in the summertime. Sometimes Denis would jerk awake just as his head was about to flop onto his chest. This meeting was called a reading meeting, and after one of the Brothers had stood to read the passage aloud from the Bible, the Brothers would talk about it. They used the Bible that was translated by John Nelson Darby, the founder of the Exclusive Brethren movement. There wasn't any Sunday school for the children, but Denis didn't miss it because he had never heard of such a thing. All the children stayed in the meeting with their parents, and woe betides any who talked, or made a noise, or kicked the seat in front. He was too big now to play with his hanky, folding it up like a fan or a hat, so Father gave him a pencil and a piece of paper from his pocket and Denis drew pictures of tractors, trucks and bulldozers.

Hopefully, after the meeting someone might ask him home for dinner. He liked going out for dinner. He could stay all afternoon and play. There were lots of other children at their meeting, and they took it in turns going to each other's houses. Denis's father had to go home to milk the cows, so they usually had one or even two families home to share the Sunday evening meal. Before every meal they thanked their heavenly Father, in the name of the Lord Jesus, for the food. On Sunday nights after the meal, they all kneeled on the floor in front of their chairs to pray for the evening gospel preaching. The women and girls put a hanky or a table napkin on their heads as a covering, while the Brothers, even the small boys, prayed. If there were a lot of people home for dinner, the prayers would take a long time and they would all be late for the gospel. It was always a privilege to entertain the preacher's family for dinner on Sunday evening, especially if he was a visitor from another meeting. The same preacher would preach for three weeks in a row, and this was the meeting that Denis liked best because he could understand some of it. The worst part of Sunday was that it was followed by Monday, and school.

Sometimes he wrote 'horrible old school again' in his diary. Denis didn't like school. He loved the farm. He was old enough to help Father in the milking shed, and he loved the swish, swish of the milk as it hit the bottom of the empty bucket. The cows were all milked by hand. He watched the foam and froth while the milk gradually rose to the top. He carried the bucket very carefully up the hill to the house for Mother, who poured it into large jars to settle. When the cream came to the top, she skimmed it off into another jar, and they would have delicious cream on their morning porridge, topped with a generous helping of brown sugar. She always saved enough cream to make butter. Denis loved to turn the handle of the butter churn and watch the thick yellow curds separate from the whey. There was nothing quite like fresh bread, spread with home-made butter and wild blackberry jam.

One day he wrote in his diary, 'tomorrow I get my pigeons'. He had been working hard, cutting wire and sawing bits of timber to make a pigeon house. He had a new friend at the meeting. Rob had recently arrived in New Zealand from Ireland. Rob had some racing pigeons and he sold a pair to Denis.

Uncle George wanted to sell his bike, and Denis saved hard so he could buy it. He and Jenny sometimes rode tandem on their horse, but usually they walked the mile or so to school. Denis longed for a bicycle like some of his friends, and he was saving the money that Father gave him for helping with the haymaking and the shearing. Denis had other jobs to do, too. He helped in the vegetable garden, hoeing and raking and weeding between the small carrots that grew so thick they needed to be thinned out so they could develop properly. He grew beans and peas and potatoes, but best of all, he grew beetroot. Mother bottled the beans and the beetroot for the family to eat over the winter.

Denis was a good boy, mostly. But no boy can be good all the time. One day he wrote in his diary, 'Today John dared me to jump out of the schoolroom window while the teacher was writing on the blackboard. I did it. I got the strap, but it was worth the five shillings!' During his high school years he recorded thirty-two times when he got the strap, or the cuts, as he sometimes called it, for a variety of misdemeanors like setting off crackers in the science room, pulling girls' hair and, most of all, for not paying attention in class. He couldn't wait to leave school and work on the farm. His schooling finished the day he turned fifteen, the minimum leaving age.

Besides working on the farm, Denis helped his father in his small logging business. They cut and carted logs to be loaded on boats at the nearest port. He learned all about the different trees and the types of wood grown in the area that could be used for building houses and farm fence posts and trees to be turned into wood chips for paper making. His love of wood stayed with him for the rest of his life.

Although he loved the farm life and working in the logging forests with his father, his first love was the meetings. He liked being an Exclusive Brethren boy. He may have strayed a little during his teenage years but he always came back to the beliefs of the Brethren. When he was growing up in the 1940s, the Exclusive Brethren were much the same as many other fundamentalist Christian groups, dedicated to the teachings of Jesus Christ found in the Christian Bible. Their doctrine was sound and their lifestyle was strict, but they were good people, well respected in the community. They kept to themselves as much as possible, but their meeting rooms were open for the preaching of the gospel and all were welcome. It was a good life for a boy. The men were in charge and the women and girls knew their place. What more could a boy want?

What this boy wanted was to see more of the country, so at eighteen he packed his bags and headed north on his motorbike to work on a farm. Denis soon made new friends and was made very welcome by the local Exclusive Brethren, many whom he already knew. He lived and worked for some time with an Open Brethren family. Although this was frowned on by the Exclusives, it was not forbidden back then, and Denis soon fitted in, becoming part of the family. He enjoyed the Christian conversation, and the lifestyle, which was very similar to what he had known at home. He continued to break bread with the Exclusives, but learned to appreciate the more relaxed atmosphere in this Open Brethren home.

The Exclusive Brethren had always believed in separation from the world but now, in the late 1950s, it was becoming absolute. No longer could members socialise, or eat and drink, with non-Exclusives. No matter how good a Christian a person might be, if they were not 'partakers of the same table', they were part of the world and needed to be kept at a distance. Denis held out as long as he could, but the day came when he had to choose between his job and his 'faith'. He had often visited his cousins in the Taranaki area — there were some nice girls there — so, leaving his job and his Open Brethren friends, he packed his bags again and headed south-west to work for his Uncle Harold.

It was now 1960 and Denis was twenty-one. He went to the meeting nearest to his uncle's farm and felt quite at home there because the Exclusive Brethren are a 'universal' fellowship and their meetings were the same wherever you went. He got on well with his cousins and there was a steady stream of lovely girls, all wanting a ride on his motorbike with their arms clasped tightly around his middle. But there were more and more changes to the Exclusive Brethren rules. Among other things, university education was out and belonging to any kind of association was out. These didn't affect Denis, but there was a new rule about young people not leaving home. He was told he had to return home to his parents' house until he married.

Young people were now being encouraged to work for Brothers wherever possible, and Mr Hamilton offered to take Denis on as a builder's labourer. Denis was happy; he loved building, he loved the Brethren and now he was ready to look for a wife, build a house and start a family of his own.

Denis's early life had prepared him well for his future among the Brethren. He was older than me, and obviously ready to settle down. Partly because he was older, he had experienced a different teenage life from the one I was going through. There were a lot of changes and tightening of restrictions around that time. New rules were being announced every few weeks. Many of the things that Denis had experienced, like leaving home and working in a different town, were not permitted by the time I was old enough to do them.

We were engaged for five months, after being friends for only two weeks. Denis and I were married in May 1962. I think I married him to get away from home, which was not a good reason to get married. Did I love him? How could I love him when I hardly knew him? Here I was, eighteen years old, and about to embark on the single most important experience of my life, but I didn't know anything about what I was letting myself in for. It all seemed so, well, strange, foreign and unreal, a life I hadn't been prepared for. I'd been infatuated with numerous young men, but I don't think I was ever properly in love. Nowadays, someone might suggest a book to read on the subject, but not back then; it just wasn't done, not for Brethren girls anyway. You found out most things by trial and error, by doing them. I had all the potential to be a capable, efficient and frigid wife with little or no propensity toward affectionate love and devotion. I just didn't know much about intimacy or how to love a man.

I am sure my parents loved each other and us children, but as in many Exclusive Brethren families, any show of affection had been strictly controlled. Older relatives have told me I was a very self-sufficient and independent child, not seeming to need much attention, affirmation or affection from anyone. I know that I desired so much more but didn't know how to ask for it. My early understanding of love and affection came from what I saw outside the immediate family and, later, storybooks filled in the gaps. I think I compensated for any lack of love by lavishing on my younger sister all the attention I craved for myself. Once I realised that she also needed my protection, I became more like a little mother to her. This responsible and somewhat pompous attitude no doubt alienated me further from those who would normally have met my own needs for attention and for protection.

However, I had always had the ability to find something good and worthwhile in almost any situation. I expected to get married, and would make the most of it. Marriage would just be another way of life but with different people, not necessarily any better or any worse than before. I was prepared to work hard and to be a good wife and mother, obedient and submissive to my new husband to the best of my ability, and would give all I had to our marriage.

Denis said he loved me right from the start. It took me a long time to understand that, but now I believe him. I liked him, I liked him a lot. I knew I would be very happy with him, and I eventually learned to love him. At first it was only infatuation. He was very nice. I think I was in love with the kind way he treated me. I don't think you can be truly in love without getting to know a person. He wanted to get married as soon as we could arrange it.

I was eighteen, he was twenty-three. We were expected to get married young. Later, in the 1970s and 1980s, the Exclusive Brethren were marrying even younger than that. The girl might be only sixteen and the boy not much older. Long engagements were always frowned upon because a long courtship could lead to premarital sex, which was forbidden. I have heard that the average age for marriage has now been changed to twenty and the courtship period has been shortened to a few weeks.

For better or for worse, my life was about to change.

14

For better or for worse

A girl's wedding day is the most important day of her life, no matter what culture she is brought up in. Although it may be different now, back in the 1960s there were certain Exclusive Brethren wedding customs that had to be obeyed, like no long white wedding dress, no confetti, no music, no flowers and definitely no 'church wedding'. A church wedding conjures up all manner of romantic and traditional images, but these were missing from Exclusive Brethren weddings. I wanted a white dress but I was told to add some colour to it. Dad said that even a virgin couldn't be one hundred percent pure, and white signified purity. I compromised by stitching pink rosebuds to the ends of the belt of my calf-length white velvet dress and a small round of pink satin into the top of my white feather hat, and wore a pair of pale pink satin shoes.

We were married in the registry office of the local courthouse. Nowadays the Exclusives have their own marriage celebrants, and no longer use the registry office for the exchange of vows and the signing of the marriage certificate. I have since seen recent photos of brides in their long white dresses and veils who look no different from any 'worldly' bride you might see coming out of a church on the arm of her groom. I have heard, though, that they no longer have an engagement ring and no bridesmaid or best man, that they have a collection for the couple instead of wedding presents, and that a wedding is a local affair, which would mean that even close relatives and immediate family would not be there unless they lived in the same area. This does not mean that a boy can only marry a local girl, but it does mean that the boy's family, if from another locality, cannot attend the wedding. Weddings, like funerals, are now restricted to attendance by locals only, which sounds a bit unfair.

They are well aware of the problem of intermarrying and the effects of inbreeding on their future evolution. But, at the moment, distance is no problem for them as they are still allowed to use telephones and aeroplanes. They can choose a marriage partner from almost anywhere in the world, so long as they are Exclusive Brethren. They meet each other at Fellowship Meetings, and I have heard that, for a while, they used a book of photographs to make the initial match up!

They say that opposites attract, and you wouldn't find two people more opposite than Denis and me. Denis liked the Exclusive Brethren life. His family had been sincere Exclusives for as far back as their nineteenth century beginnings. He understood their doctrine and was more than happy to commit himself to them for the rest of his life. I, on the other hand, had not bothered even to try to understand them. I saw only the inconsistencies and the severe restrictions imposed upon me by family and Brethren alike. Although I had been breaking bread for a number of years, it was only a formality, expected of me upon turning twelve years old. I had learned how to conform to the rules but knew nothing of the heartfelt commitment experienced by Denis.

Denis and I had first noticed each other at Fellowship Meetings in Thames. I had met him before, several times, but this time was different. I saw him sitting up in the front of the room during the first meeting, and I remember thinking that the back of his head looked like a slice of burnt toast! He became aware of my presence during the break between meetings. Denis was ready to find a mate. He wanted a wife who had a happy disposition, and who would help him make beautiful and intelligent children! Some months earlier he had been to our home for a meal and he liked what he saw, and what he tasted even better. He said that he fell in love with the cook, although at the time I was sure that it wasn't my sunny smile but my beautiful older sister that he was after. At the end of the meetings that day, he sidled up to Dad and politely asked his permission to speak to me of his intentions. Denis did not speak to me at that stage, but Dad did.

'Ngaire, I want to speak to you, please,' he said, 'Denis wishes to "go out" with you. He will visit us in two weeks' time. In the meantime I have given him my blessing, and my permission for him to write to you.'

Some Brethren marriages may have been 'arranged marriages', particularly between older single people during the system days of the 1960s, but most are not. However, Exclusive Brethren marriages are very definitely subject to scrutiny and an indefinable kind of approval. In my case, once Dad had made his decision about the matter there was no way that I could go against him without a tremendous fuss. So I went along with it. As one of my friends pointed out to me, I could be happy with almost anyone. Denis, being over twenty-one and not legally needing his parents' permission, could marry whomever he wanted so long as she was an Exclusive. Nevertheless, his parents were disappointed in his choice because they had had an Australian girl picked out for him, and also because Denis's father had been involved with the earlier 'not crying out' fiasco. I guess I hadn't been fully forgiven and wasn't considered a good enough match for their son.

There are times in our lives when we make momentous decisions (or have them made for us), changing the whole course of our lives. It's all a matter of what you make of it. This was one of those times. In hindsight, it was the very best thing that could have happened to me.

After an exchange of several letters, Denis came to visit. He arrived on a Friday afternoon at the bank where I worked and we took a bus ride into the city. He steered me into a large jeweller's shop, and in no time at all we had chosen an engagement ring. Denis fished deep into his pocket for his chequebook and came up empty handed. He had lost it. Not only had he lost his chequebook, but also a cheque for two weeks' wages from his employer! This was the first of many similar scenarios over the years we spent together.

'Ngaire, what shall we do?' he asked. That was how I came to pay for my own engagement ring!

'Let's go and phone our families,' he said as he pulled me into the nearest telephone box.

'You asked Father if you could marry me but you haven't asked me yet,' I teased.

'I'll soon fix that,' he replied as he went down on his knees in the most cavalier fashion, right there in the phone box. 'Please will you marry me Ngaire?' Well, how could I resist him?

Wedding dates, cakes and dresses, and planning where we would go for our honeymoon, were becoming familiar topics of conversation in our house. Denis and I visited each other for the weekend, every two weeks or so for the next five months. Denis lived about two hundred miles away, and neither of us owned a car, so we travelled by bus. We set our wedding date for the beginning of May 1962 and, with family help, the dresses and cake were completed on time.

The Exclusive Brethren had no minister, priest or marriage celebrant so weddings took place (on a Tuesday) at the nearest Registry Office of Births, Deaths and Marriages, followed by a small home reception and a Wedding Meeting at the main city meeting room. After the registrar had intoned the usual words, 'do you take this man to be your lawful wedded husband . . . in sickness and in health . . . to love and obey . . . for richer and for poorer . . . ', Aunt Edna interrupted from the back of the room, 'You didn't say for better or for worse!'

'It's okay lady,' said the registrar, 'We don't say that any more.' I sometimes wonder if those few extra words would have made a difference to the future!

The registry office was near where my mother's parents lived. I had insisted on a change of venue from the usual registry office used by the Exclusives in our area, saying that I wished to be married at the same place as my parents had been. Mother's family could not attend the wedding because they were 'outsiders'. I thought this was very unfair, so I rang them from work, a few days before the wedding, and told them that if they were sitting on a certain seat in the grounds of the registry office at 2 pm on Tuesday, 1 May, I would stop and speak to them. Because it was a public place, my Grandparents would have had every right to be at the courthouse for the signing of the register, but so strict were the Brethren rules about separation from the world, no one dared to go against them. Any act of defiance is worse than the sin itself. I had deliberately defied the rules of separation, and if I were caught, the 'spirit of defiance' would be the more serious issue. After we came out of the registry office, I steered Denis toward the arranged meeting place, and there on the park bench, much to my parents' surprise, sat Grandma, Grandpa and two of my aunts. We stopped and chatted for a few moments before moving on. Unfortunately, there was no way that I could arrange for my mother's family to share the rest of the day with us.

The small reception was held at home, and then we all drove into Auckland city for the Ministry Meeting. At a Ministry Meeting, which on such occasions was adapted to serve as a Wedding Meeting, two or three Brothers — who felt prompted by the Spirit — would stand and address the congregation, one after the other. These messages were called 'words' or 'addresses' and two 'words' were usual, while three were definitely the limit. After three 'words' had been given, an elderly Brother rose to his feet.

'I just want to give the happy married couple a little word about love,' he said in a slow, halting voice. He was about to open his mouth to give us his pearls of wisdom when there was a stern voice from the side.

'We have already had three words and that's enough.'

The elderly Brother slowly subsided into his seat with his message about love undelivered. I often look back and wonder just what that message would have been and why I never thought to ask him about it later.

We were now husband and wife. For richer or poorer, that hadn't been important. For better or for worse, what a lot of life was summed up in those few words. In sickness and in health ... to love and obey ... How easy it is to live and to love when everything is going well, and how difficult it is when we encounter the downside ... poverty, sickness and worse.

15

No compromise

After our honeymoon, we returned home to collect up all my belongings plus anything else that Mum could spare. Because of some new directives from the MOG, Dad, making sure he was in line with current teachings, had been sorting through all my belongings. Most of my books were gone including all the books I'd won as school prizes, except for one encyclopedia and some cookery books. Any book that looked like a novel or a biography had been burned. Even books we had had since we were children, *The Beacon Light*, *Uncle Arthur's Bedtime Stories*, were gone, destroyed, burned. My dolls were gone, too, destroyed or given away to children in the neighbourhood. I was devastated but determined not to get angry about it; Dad was only doing what was best for me. I wasn't about to let anything spoil my new life. I had a future at last. I was free, or I thought I was!

We went back to Denis's hometown in the Bay of Plenty, and rented an old army hut on the edge of town. This hut was like a train carriage, perched precariously on sawn-off tree stumps. It consisted of three small-interconnected rooms with no passages. You walked into the middle section, the kitchen and dining room, turned left into the bedroom, and right into the lounge. The floorboards were not tongue and groove but had gaps between them so wide that a quick flick over the floor with a broom was all that was needed to keep it clean. The bathroom and laundry were in a small lean-to out the back that also housed Denis's motorbike and his carpentry tools.

An Exclusive Brethren woman is not permitted to work for money after she marries unless her husband, for some reason, is not able to do so. Denis went off to work every morning and I was left with very little to do to fill in the day. (Oh how I would long for this solitude and nothingness in a year or two.) It took only an hour at the most to clean and tidy the hut, and do the washing each morning. The rest of the day I would sew or spend some time in the garden. I knew I was expected to start a family as soon as possible, so I began making baby clothes right away. I was so disappointed when it took me two months to get pregnant!

We had no car, so off we went to meetings on Denis's Moby. Moby was a cross between a push-bike and a small motorbike and had a seat at the back for me. I would put one arm around Denis's waist and hold onto my hat and my handbag with the other hand. I was far too embarrassed to turn up at the meeting room on Moby, so Denis stopped around the corner and helped me off. I walked the rest of the way, tucking stray strands of hair under my hat and trying to look ladylike and dignified. We continued going to meetings on Moby until I was so pregnant that looking ladylike and dignified was no longer possible! Rather than adding a sidecar for the baby, we accepted the offer from Denis's father of an old farm truck to use each weekend. It didn't matter to me that we had no car. I couldn't drive. Dad didn't believe in women driving cars and so I still had to learn. This wouldn't happen for another four years.

The Brethren meetings I now attended followed the same format as those I had been used to in Auckland. I already knew all the people there, including two large families of my aunts, uncles and cousins. I often walked into town to visit them and other Brethren families. I didn't have a lot to do with Denis's family. I don't think they liked me very much. I soon found friends among the young married women in the meeting, and life became more interesting than I had previously experienced. However, gossiping about other Brethren and bemoaning the continuing tightening of the rules, over numerous cups of tea, was not a very profitable pastime. Everyone knew everyone else's business and the free-for-all gossip sessions seemed to be part of Brethren life, especially for the women who often found nothing better to do with their time.

During the first few weeks of our married life, Denis was offered a share-milking job with one of his relatives in Taranaki. He was very happy building houses, but he wanted to give me a choice.

'Do you want to be a farmer's wife, or a builder's wife?' he asked me one day. I thought about it for a while and decided that to continue with building might be more useful. This was a good decision because within a couple of years the Exclusive Brethren farmers were told they could no longer live on their farms, but would need to move into the towns and cities. Most of them found it too difficult to continue working their farms while living in town so they sold up and looked for other work. Many Exclusive Brethren farmers decided that this was too much to ask of them so they opted to leave the fellowship rather than give up their land and the rural lifestyle they enjoyed.

Denis worked as a builder's labourer, and six months after we were married he started building us a new house on a section near the city boundary, subdivided off the farm where he grew up. One day as I stood and watched the foundations being laid, I had a bright idea.

'Why don't you bring the back corner of the house around this way a bit, put the house on an angle more to the sun? It would look more interesting, too, don't you think?'

Up came the profiles, trenches were filled in and they started all over again. This was Denis's first introduction to a life full of bright ideas, some good, some disastrous. Once the house was started, I had plenty to do, digging, planting, sweeping up builder's rubble, and suggesting little changes here and there as the building progressed. The house was finished enough to move in before the baby was born.

Most people who are old enough will remember the 1960s as the decade of free love, flower power, hippie culture and the emergence of a number of religious cults. For the Exclusive Brethren it was a decade of change, led by a Brother from New York. He took on the role of the MOG in 1959 and was their leader until he died in 1970. Using a quotation from the Bible, 'Come out from them and be ye separate', the MOG taught that association with the world was wicked. Everyone had to break off any private or business relationships with people in the world. No longer could we belong to any public or community service such as a library, insurance fund, business partnerships, associations, or anything else that involved membership of any description. By the time Denis and I were married in 1962, the MOG had already brought in the concept of complete separation, to the point of not even eating in the presence of anyone not breaking bread with the Exclusive Brethren. This became known as the 'eating matter' and was a stumbling block for many Exclusive Brethren. I hadn't worried too much about it up till then because I just did what Dad ordered. After I was married, although I was not expected to make any decisions because that was Denis's responsibility, I did have a fair amount of influence over him. One day my influence would land us in a heap of trouble.

The catch cry of the day was 'No compromise', and this was enforced in every direction. We soon learned that no compromise meant no choices, no alternatives and no tolerance. Although the rules had been tightened in almost every other direction, Brethren were encouraged to drink whisky, to 'free up inhibitions' and show we had nothing to hide. It was also a time when everyone was pressured to confide details of their own personal life to another Brother or Sister, under the guise of caring and sharing. This was meant to be a mentor system where experienced older people guided the younger ones. However, this often had disastrous repercussions when the person confided in passed the information on to someone else. Because it was fashionable at the time, all manner of dastardly deeds, both real and imagined or exaggerated, were confessed and brought before the Assembly for judgement. It was said, 'You are as bold as you are pure.' The way to purity was to confess all your impurity. Since most misdemeanors involved one or more other people, every confession implicated others. This gave rise to the practice of 'thorough enquiry' to ensure that neither party was lying or covering up, (which was regarded as worse than the original sin because it was deliberate). Many people were withdrawn from. If the sin was of a category requiring 'Assembly discipline' the guilty person was put out of fellowship regardless of any state of contrition, regardless of how far in the past the sin had occurred and regardless of family circumstances, sickness, senility etc.

It was rumored, in the early 1960s, that the MOG had a drinking problem, and for a short time the leadership was taken over by two Brothers from Australia. These Brothers were from a very bright family, and the more dominant one was a very capable management consultant and a radical thinker. He merged his fundamentalist Christian beliefs and his training in efficiency with the intention of creating an elitist ruling class. Life was a tightrope walk both mind-boggling and exciting, and in many ways, a step in the right direction — toward personal motivation. These few years later became known, to the Exclusives, as the 'System Days'. (The term 'systematised error' had been used to describe the degradation that had supposedly crept into all the 'other' churches.) During this time there was an emphasis on making money, even if it meant 'spoiling the Egyptians' — a term used by the Brethren for getting as much as possible from the world while giving as little as possible in return. (See Exodus 12:35–36.) The women were still not allowed to go out to work, but many of us encouraged our husbands to work harder! Efficiency, profitability and time management were taught in the meetings. We were told to keep a timetable to account for each moment of the day. The day would be divided up to ensure that each hour was used profitably and that there was ample time for reading the 'ministry' books, which are manuscripts of meetings presided over by the MOG or by other leading Brothers, and subscribed to by all in fellowship. Even though each day was highly structured, I rather enjoyed this phase. Life now had an air of excitement about it that alleviated the boredom, but there was always the fear that our world could come tumbling down around our ears if we so much as set a foot wrong or committed some offensive indiscretion. All this was rather similar to Hitler's early days of enthusiastic idealism.

Denis and I were projected suddenly into an even more stressful and chaotic situation only a few weeks after our wedding. Late one night we had a phone call from Mum. Dad had been withdrawn from. I took a bus north to Auckland the following day. My younger brother and my sisters had been moved out of the house and were staying with another Brethren household. If I wanted to stay overnight, I too would need to stay with someone else. There was a new Brethren rule: when a person was withdrawn from, they were referred to as a 'leper' and were expected to leave the family home. If they didn't leave, then everyone else in the house would need to leave or they would be 'shut up' in the house with the leper, and be treated as suspected lepers. This lasted until full repentance had been discerned and forgiveness and restoration to the fellowship had been granted. The household would receive regular visits from the priests who determined whether or not the leprosy was spreading or receding! These were fairly recent directives that, in the following decade, were to become even stricter and more crippling. I was permitted to visit Mum so long as I didn't eat or drink with her. She, in turn, was unable to eat and drink with Dad, even though they were both 'unclean'. She had to live, eat and sleep in a separate part of the house. Mum explained to me that Dad had been 'dealt' with.

I needed to talk to Dad. He and I had a secret and I needed to know if he had confessed. I had been told that he had not personally confessed to anything but, when confronted, had reluctantly admitted to some misdemeanour. I guessed that my name had not been mentioned or I would have heard about it. Knowing that his reputation meant everything to him, I didn't want to get him into extra trouble, but if he was eventually forced to confess I didn't want to be accused of 'covering up evil'. The 'right' thing to do was to expose him further and to allow God to work in his soul and bring him to full repentance. The fact that I, too, would then be in the spotlight and could be accused of 'encouraging' him was an inevitable consequence. I waited with Mum until late that night. Dad had gone out in the car for a drive, and we were very worried when he hadn't returned by midnight. At last he arrived, very shaken and looking very white. He had tried to end his life. He made us both feel so sorry for him that I couldn't bring myself to talk about a full confession. It wouldn't have worked anyway. Dad was always right, and very persuasive. He would have found a way to blame me and make people believe him.

I returned home the next day, my secret still intact. No one else knew about it and I didn't want to share it. I didn't know Denis well enough yet to confide in him. If I just kept quiet, nobody would get hurt. I told myself that I didn't need to say anything; Dad was in enough trouble without me adding my accusations.

In the 1960s there were a lot of public confessions in the meetings, about a vast number of different things, especially sexual immorality. It was really sordid listening to public confessions about private things. It was a kind of legitimised voyeurism, producing a confused mixture of holy resentment, fear and excitement. But it wasn't so amusing when it happened to our own family. A few months later the Brethren accepted Dad back into fellowship again.

Married life suited me. Denis was a wonderful husband who loved me unconditionally, and together we looked forward to the birth of our first child. In many ways I was still a child myself. I could cook, sew and clean the house, which seemed to be the most important things to the Brethren women, but this baby business was a bit scary. The baby didn't wait around until his new mum knew how to look after him; he arrived, in the middle of the night.

16

Let parenthood begin

Paul was born with a mass of jet-black hair and big dark eyes surrounded by the most beautiful long eyelashes just like his dad's. The nurse handed him to Denis to hold.

'Have his photo taken as soon as you get home,' she advised. 'He will have lost his hair in a few weeks.' He didn't lose it.

Paul was my parents' first grandchild. Dad's manufacturing business had steadily progressed from gym frocks, drill rompers and black school bloomers, to ladies' fancy underwear. Now that he was a grandfather, baby and toddler garments were added to the range. Paul reminded Dad of Noddy, a children's book character popular at the time, and so this branch of his business became known as Noddy Children's wear and remained a popular brand throughout the 1960s. This was great. There were always plenty of sample garments to try out, and Paul became the best-dressed baby in town.

When Paul was nearly five months old we had him baptised. All our Brethren friends and relatives were invited, and even my parents and brother and sisters came down from Auckland for the occasion. I moved the table into the lounge, and on it I arranged towels and a large tub to hold the water. I had already made the sandwiches and cakes to serve to our guests after the baptism service. Denis was busy setting out chairs and stools for people to sit on. Old Mr Carter, who would baptise Paul, sat down and we waited as people gradually came in. When everyone was seated, Denis filled the big tin tub with warm water. After making sure that the water was just the right temperature, I handed my precious bundle to Mr Carter. There were no christening gowns for Exclusive Brethren babies, so Paul was as bare as the day he was born and Mr Carter promptly sat him in the tub of water before he had a chance to squawk his disapproval at being handed to a stranger.

'Paul Thomas, I baptise thee in the name of the Father, the Son and the Holy Spirit,' said Mr Carter as he gently placed his hand over Paul's face to prevent him taking a breath. He was lowered under the water until he was fully immersed. Mr Carter handed Paul, who was by then screaming at top volume, back to me, and while I took him away to dry and dress him, the Brethren opened their Bibles for the short service that followed.

It was about a week later that I noticed there was something wrong with Paul. He had a fever and cried all the time, keeping us awake most of Saturday night. The Breaking of Bread on Sunday morning had recently been changed from eleven o'clock to nine o'clock, and I was glad to be going off early because I knew that someone at the meeting would be able to tell me what to do about my sick baby. After the meeting, the Sisters gathered around and advised us to go straight to a doctor, which we did.

'Take him home and put him in a cold bath,' said Doctor Sutton after a quick examination.

'What is wrong with him?' I asked.

'I'm not sure, but if his temperature was one degree higher I would put him in hospital,' the doctor added.

We took Paul home, and while Denis rocked him gently in his arms, I filled the baby bath with cold water. I was doing exactly what I was told; I didn't know any different. I took Paul from Denis and began to lower him into the cold water.

'Don't do it.' Denis hadn't spoken, but I was sure I had heard the words loud and clear. I hesitated, then I carefully placed the baby back on the warm towel and wrapped him up again. I was too young and inexperienced to know that I should have sponged him with a cool damp cloth.

'I will go and see the Plunket nurse first thing in the morning,' I told Denis. 'I am sure she will know what to do.'

I sat in a chair, and held Paul all through the night. The next morning, when Denis had gone to work, I put him in the pram and walked to the Plunket rooms.

'How long has he been sick?' the nurse asked.

'Since Saturday night,' I replied.

'Take him straight across the road to Doctor Donaldson's surgery. Tell them I sent you and that he should be seen immediately,' she urged.

Everything happened very fast after that, and before long one of the patients, who was waiting to see the doctor, was driving us to the hospital. Paul had meningitis and was not expected to live through the night. But he did live, and the same doctor who had prescribed the cold bath looked after him in the hospital. He humbly told me some time later that if I had taken his advice literally that Sunday, Paul could have died.

While Paul was in hospital, I became pregnant with Charles. Although Paul had no permanent damage from the meningitis, he was slow to walk, and for four months I had a baby on each hip while I tried to keep up with the housework. Two babies in fourteen months; no wonder I was always tired! By now there was a meeting every night of the week as well as three or four on Sunday and one or more meetings most Saturdays. It seemed as if Denis was never home. He worked late each day to get as much overtime as possible, then after a hurried dinner he was out of the house by seven o'clock for the evening meeting. Sometimes I was so tired I would leave Denis at home to look after the boys and go out to the meeting so that I could sit for a whole hour and do nothing.

It was hard to breastfeed a baby under these conditions, although I did try for the first two weeks. By the time Charlie was six weeks old he had developed intolerance to cow's milk. At the time, there were very few alternatives available, and he started reacting to all dairy products, including goat's milk. We took him to the Karitane Hospital in Auckland, where he stayed for two months while they worked out a special diet for him.

Life started to settle down at home, and we began to enjoy our little boys. Denis was very faithful in carrying out my bright ideas around the house. They usually consisted of some major alteration, such as removing a wall here and building something there, but each task was carried out with the utmost of care and attention, directed of course by me!

    It usually started something like this.
    'Denis, I've been thinking, why don't we . . .'
    'Oh, no! Not again! What is it this time?'
    All these bright ideas of mine cost money; money that we didn't have, and money that I was not permitted to go out and earn. I knew I could earn the money we needed, I just had to think of a way. I was made of very resourceful stuff.

    One day when I was folding the washing, I noticed the ever-growing pile of baby crawlers and stretch and grow suits; then I knew what I could do. Because 'Noddy' was an up-market brand there were often garments with slight imperfections tossed aside and given away. Dad was willing to give me some of these 'seconds' and, by contacting some of the ladies I had met at the Plunket rooms, I gradually built up a list of willing customers who passed the word along among their friends. I kept very quiet about my new venture, never advertising and never selling to Brethren women. It took a long time to save up for big items, but the extra money gave me a feeling of independence. I no longer had to ask for money for every little thing. Sometimes I had difficulty in explaining some new acquisition, but there was always a way around it. Denis didn't know the extent of my little selling venture, and before long I was into manufacturing as well, making extra garments to sell every time I made something for the boys. All this was very easy to hide.

    I had learned that by outwardly obeying the Brethren rules

I gained approval and acceptance and kept the priests (Brethren policemen) at bay, but if I wanted a more exciting life, a few broken rules was the way to go!

By nature I am an honest and straight-up kind of person and I longed for a life where there was no need for dishonesty. At the same time, I was a very practical person. There was no way I could be everything I wanted to be, so in order to succeed in one area, a compromise would be needed in another. I frequently sacrificed honesty to achieve goals that I believed were worthwhile. Many Exclusive Brethren rules were discreetly broken in the process, all for the good of the family of course! If Denis ever suspected me of leading a double life, he chose to turn a blind eye.

17

Double-dipped for good measure

We didn't have much of a home life. Denis worked long hours, leaving early each morning and arriving home tired in time for a quick meal before the evening meeting. Denis and I seldom spent time together during the day, and the boys only got to sit on his knee during meetings, where they had to sit still and not make a noise. Life was hard for all of us. A continuous round of meetings and sleepless nights led to frayed tempers and senseless arguments. I was tired, I was snappy with Denis and the boys, and I felt sick. I was pregnant again, and before Charlie turned two, baby Angela was born. Angela was as beautiful as her brothers with her long, thick black hair and black eyes. For two such ordinary looking people, we certainly knew how to make beautiful babies! Angela was not only beautiful, she was a good baby and was soon sleeping all through the night.

Before Charlie was born, a new rule had come in regarding baptisms. Babies had to be baptised a lot younger than four or five months as had previously been the custom. All babies were now to be baptised on a Monday evening before the Prayer Meeting, at about eight days old. Until they were baptised, they were not permitted to attend any other meetings. The baby was baptised at home, without the extended family present or any accompanying coffee or cake; then the whole family took the baby to the Prayer Meeting. After having my two boys, I was delighted to have a daughter; at least we didn't need to have her circumcised as the boys had been! The night of her baptism, we nearly lost her. Mr Hopkins, the elderly gentleman who baptised her, was not used to handling very small babies, not ever having had one of his own. When he lowered her under the water, her face was not properly covered by his hand and, to my horror, my precious baby girl breathed in some water. When he handed her back to me she was choking. I quickly turned her on her side and gently thumped her back until the water came up and she let out a cry. As I was about to wrap her up, Mr Hopkins took her off me again. He was very apologetic, but he would need to baptise her again because her little feet had not gone completely under the water! How hard it was to let him dunk her for a second time! Thankfully, not every baby gets double dipped!

I continued to supplement our income and my resources were increasing. With the arrival of a granddaughter, Dad added a new range of products to his manufacturing business. He went to Germany to look at lace-making machinery and, with the help of one of his brothers, set up an automated system for making lace, the first of its kind in New Zealand. As quickly as the many varieties of lace were being produced, I was thinking up ways to use the off-cuts. Dad also imported many beautiful fabrics for his lingerie range, and so I had a choice of materials to work with. My own children didn't need all the garments I was making so I offered them to a local children's wear shop. This led to several years of producing exquisite christening gowns and baby dresses for three shops.

I had worked out how to organise my time better, and although I was still very busy it didn't stop me from dreaming up new designs and spending all my free time at the sewing machine! I can still remember the first gown I made. I tried it on Angela, and it looked so beautiful with its fine pin tucks and lace, and the wee hat to match.

There was no personal choice about how we lived, just obedience. The strange part about it was the way we so compulsively followed the leader, without question. Asking challenging questions just wasn't done because this would show us up as doubters. Most of the time we weren't even told that we *had* to do things, we just did them at the mere suggestion, for fear of being put out of fellowship. The enemy gets the stragglers, we were told. We were given stern warnings from the MOG about asking questions. Nobody in his right mind would challenge the MOG because they would be put out of fellowship for doing so. The reason for the challenge was of no consequence because there were no valid reasons for challenging our leaders. We just obeyed the MOG, no questions asked, like the time we had to let our hair hang loose, and started wearing scarves instead of hats. Following this rule was a test of fellowship. All these little things were so small, petty and insignificant on their own, but they added up to power and control, particularly over the women. Even though at the time I submitted without too much fuss for the sake of my marriage, I hadn't taken too kindly to being bullied.

The MOG decreed that if a woman's hair was her crowning glory, then it should hang loose so that he and the rest of the men out there could see and admire it. It was one way of making sure that the women really did have long hair and were not just hiding behind an artificial bun or padded hair roller. It needed to be long enough to dry a man's feet. The act of drying a man's feet automatically brought the woman to her knees. If the men wanted their wives to wash their feet, then the women had to have hair long enough to dry them, like the woman in the Bible who washed Jesus' feet and dried them with her hair. I am glad Denis never asked me to do that, but there is no doubt in my mind that I would have done it, had he demanded it, rather than be labelled disobedient.

For some of the young girls the idea of letting their hair down was great because they had really beautiful hair which up till now they had to keep hidden. Imagine, however, the feelings of a grey-haired woman of sixty for whom a loose, free hairstyle would hardly be flattering. The humiliating part about it all was that we women had absolutely no choice. Regardless of what we were used to, from that point on there was only one hairstyle. Young or aged, let it fall free, as your crowning glory, and it must look as though it (and you) are ready to dry the washed feet of your husband! The world gaped at us, and we were acutely aware of this. We now stood out as being very different. In theory that didn't matter because we only existed to please the Lord Jesus and the MOG, not to please the world or ourselves.

The change from hats to scarves happened very soon after. I have my own tongue-in-cheek theory about that. I wonder if the MOG's wife had something to do with it. Maybe she saw how ridiculous we all looked with our dressy clothes and hats and our long straggly hair hanging down to our waists. Perhaps she wanted a more casual look for Brethren women of the 1960s, and so she suggested scarves. I believe a number of Brethren Sisters had already become trendy scarf wearers to outings other than the meetings. However, if a woman *was* responsible for the change she would have needed to be very subtle and make it look like it was the MOG's idea!

While I agree that scarves were better and more practical than hats, I was upset by the change. We had to conform — no option or choice. It worked a bit like blackmail. The Exclusive Brethren say that they don't tell people what they can or cannot do, but we all knew the consequences if we didn't jump when commanded.

After we were married, Denis was very disappointed to learn that I had never invited the Lord Jesus into my heart. In short, I wasn't a real committed Christian. I was only making an outward show. This was a real worry because all fakes ended up being caught out. I did and said all the right things in public, but Denis knew I didn't have it in my heart. What a blow for him. In spite of this, he still loved me unconditionally, and told me so, at least once a day for the next thirty years! How could someone love me so much? I certainly didn't love me. I didn't even like me! Denis was a man of very regular habits, and it became a ritual for him to pray for me every morning. He would set the alarm clock one hour earlier than he needed to start getting ready for work. First he read the Bible to himself for half an hour, and then he read it aloud to me. I would listen, without interruption, and try to make the right kind of noises without getting into an argument. This was followed by prayer for the family, the Brethren both locally and internationally, and especially for me that I would give my heart to the Lord Jesus. Being a very affectionate man, he always finished this ritual with a cuddle.

I respected Denis's feelings about the Exclusive Brethren style of Christianity. I understood his need for it, and his desire that I, too, would embrace it. For some reason it just didn't happen for me. I found their whole concept of Christianity confusing and irrelevant.

18

The Aberdeen ambush

I loved babies. Mine were special, all three of them. Looking after them was hard work, but I was young and fit. I loved to dress my little boys like twins, they were so alike and close in age. They looked so handsome in their Sunday-go-to-meeting clothes. Their little sister, Angela, looked as pretty as a picture all done up in a frilly dress and hat. I would take them to the meetings and show them off. With small children to look after, it was very hard to concentrate on the service. Sometimes Denis would take the boys up to the front row where the Brothers sat. If they made a noise, he would send them back to me. Paul was nearly five and had already learned to read simple books. He was very happy to sit on the front row and read, pretending to be one of the grown ups. Charlie was a fidget and often had to be sent back to sit with me.

'Mum, is the meeting nearly finished?' Charlie would ask.

'No, sit still, you'll wake Angela,' I said, gently rocking the pushchair.

'Let me, let me,' said Charlie, reaching out and jerking the pushchair, waking Angela. Mrs Hopkins frowned and put her finger to her lips.

'Shush,' she said, but her frown meant, 'Keep that child under control!'

Mrs Irving sent a packet of raisins along the row. By now Angela was properly awake, she wanted raisins too and there was only one packet. I took a cracker biscuit out of my handbag and handed it to Angela. 'Raisins,' cried Angela, throwing the biscuit on the floor, where it was promptly grabbed by Charlie and stuffed into his mouth. By now Angela was in a real paddy and I couldn't calm her. Other Sisters looked at me and then glanced towards the door. I gathered the children's things together as quickly as I could, bottle, books, pieces of broken biscuit, my hymnbook and Bible, and stuffed them into my bag. I went outside, and wheeled the pushchair along the road, Charlie running along beside me. No wonder I didn't understand what the meetings were about. I was always either trying to keep the children happy inside the meeting room, or I was walking the street outside. It was times like this when I knew that I had as many children as I could manage, and didn't need another one. It didn't take me long to learn that it was much easier to get pregnant than not.

Although Denis was a very kind and considerate husband, he knew his rights. Abstinence was not his strong point. We found it very hard to practise 'Vatican Roulette', the only form of birth control allowed by the Exclusive Brethren. And so it was that I awoke one morning knowing that the nausea I felt in the pit of my stomach was once again morning sickness. Months later, another little baby with big dark eyes and long black hair was added to the family. Benjamin had had difficulty coming into the world, and as the doctors worked with him, helping him to breathe, I sent up a prayer of thanks.

'Thank you, Lord. I now have four children, an even number, my family is complete.'

Benjamin was a very good baby, easy to look after, and had a placid personality like his dad. My life was getting busier by the day but I felt myself slipping further and further behind in my understanding of the meetings. How could I possibly teach my children about the Exclusive Brethren belief system when I knew so little about it myself, and cared even less? Why bother anyway? Children were no longer required to account for themselves before being included as members.

There was a time when all Exclusive Brethren children were expected to understand something about the church, and to be reconciled to God and through repentance know that their sins were forgiven. This usually happened by the time they had reached twelve years old, the age of responsibility. The rules had changed; maybe because so many young people were slipping through the net. Now the children were automatically regarded as members as soon as they reached out and grabbed the bread and the wine as it was passed along the row at the Breaking of Bread. Young Ben was already breaking bread at ten months old. His natural instinct to reach out for food had been rewarded by a lifetime membership of the Exclusive Brethren.

As was expected of him, Denis spent a lot of time reading the ministry books and going to meetings, and not much time helping me with the children or the housework. I became very resentful. We were expected to ask visitors home for dinner on Sunday nights, but we were not to do too much preparation on Sunday. This made Saturday a very busy day. It was the only day of the week that Denis could cut the lawns, do the gardening and tidy the outside of the house. There was certainly no time left for him to help me in the house. It was not unusual to host two families for dinner on Sunday evenings. I cooked a large roast with baked vegetables and all the trimmings, and topped the meal off with dessert. After the meal, Denis would entertain our gentlemen guests over a glass of whisky while their wives helped me to clear up the dishes and look after the children. In spite of my grumbling and the extra work, we both loved having guests home for Sunday dinner. Sometimes we would be invited back to their homes a few weeks later. This was our social life, and in many ways it was the best part of being an Exclusive Brethren.

At first the other Sisters at our meeting were quite friendly to me, but after a while I became wary of trusting them. I had to be very careful not to show too much of my radical, independent nature, for fear that Denis would be spoken to, by their husbands, about my behaviour. I became a bit aloof, chatting plenty about nothing, about safe things, but never getting too close to people. I knew I was dragging

Denis down. Denis was very well liked and respected by the Exclusive Brethren, but I was not. I felt excluded from conversations and anything I had to say just didn't fit in. On Sunday evenings, when our visitors had departed, I would wait for Denis to pull me up about something I might have said wrong.

'Ngaire, I would rather you didn't argue with people. If you can't say something agreeable, don't say anything at all,' said Denis to me one evening. I had been complaining about the amount of alcohol the Exclusive Brethren were drinking.

'But Denis, it is getting worse and worse. They didn't used to drink so much and now they are overdoing it.'

'The MOG has set us an example and says that alcohol is to be freely available in our homes,' said Denis. 'We must not go against what the Brethren are teaching. You know that if we refuse to serve alcohol, we might be withdrawn from.'

I was thankful that we were not able to afford too much alcohol, and apart from a small glass of wine or whisky before dinner each night, we saved what we had for visitors.

Although I tried to appear to be a good Exclusive Brethren Sister, I didn't fool everyone, least of all Denis. I didn't do a lot of praying in those days, but I did have one earnest desire. I used to hope that the MOG, now quite an old man, would die. I mistakenly thought that if he died, his reign of tyranny would be over and we could all go back to being reasonably normal people. His meetings had become increasingly incoherent and characterised by abusive and blasphemous language, due in part to an excessive consumption of alcohol both during and between meetings. There were whisperings going around that the MOG was an alcoholic, but if you were caught saying that you would be in serious trouble. One older Sister, who had had years of nursing experience, said that he had symptoms of alcoholism. She was promptly withdrawn from. The Brethren could do without career women who made smart remarks like that!

In mid-1970 we were in Auckland for Fellowship Meetings and heard that something scandalous had happened in Aberdeen, Scotland. The MOG was taking Three-day Meetings, and there were rumours that he had been found in bed with a young married woman. It was explained that this young woman, with her husband's consent, was 'ministering' to the MOG in his bedroom, at night, with the door closed. It was all very 'hush hush', and within a few days we were being told not to talk about it among ourselves. I was very curious and tried to find out more about it. Someone sent us a confidential letter, setting out the facts of the Aberdeen meetings. Denis handed me the letter to open, and watched me as I started to read it.

'Who is it from, love?' he asked, looking at it over my shoulder.

'Um, nobody in particular,' I mumbled as I tried to hide it from him. 'It's just a copy of a letter and a little booklet entitled *If We Walk in the Light*.'

'Can I read it after you? Or better still, you read it out loud.'

By this time I had read enough to know that Denis was the last one to appreciate this information. Denis believed explicitly in everything the Exclusives said and did, and would not question any of their beliefs. This letter would not please him one little bit. It described what had happened at Aberdeen and offered a copy of tapes, recorded at the Aberdeen meetings, where the MOG had apparently used a fair bit of incoherent and disgusting language, and had also been topping himself up with whisky during the meetings.

'Give it to me,' said Denis, glancing over my shoulder. 'It is best if we don't read this sort of thing. I am sure we will be told about it at the meeting tonight.'

'But Denis, the letter says that many of the Aberdeen Brethren have already left the fellowship because of what has happened.' My mind was ticking over fast. Maybe this was the lucky break I had been waiting for!

'We will not mention this again until we hear what our Brethren have to say about it,' said Denis as he tore the letter into little pieces and threw them in the rubbish tin. Denis was very late home that night.

'You must make a decision,' said Denis. 'We have been asked to pledge one hundred percent support for the Man of God or leave the fellowship.'

'Have you heard any more details? Do you know exactly what happened?' I asked.

'A letter was read out at the meeting, saying that what happened at Aberdeen was an ambush. The Man of God says it's God's way of sorting out the sheep from the goats.'

'How long do we have to think about it?'

'I have already pledged my support, along with the rest of the local Brethren. I think it would be best if you did the same.'

'Do I have a choice?' I asked.

'Yes, but if you go against him, you'll be withdrawn from,' said Denis in a very quiet voice.

Although I had been praying for the MOG's demise, I hadn't bargained on this. If I didn't pledge my support, I would be kicked out of the fellowship and Denis and I would be separated. This was when I knew that, after being married to Denis for eight years, I loved him too much to leave him. I gave my pledge. The MOG died in October that same year, and the leadership passed to another American.

Things didn't improve under new leadership. We had all hoped that the previous MOG's son would become the next leader. He was a compassionate and gentle man and was well liked by the Brethren, but he was evidently not the first choice as successor. The new MOG was a strong, hard man and continued to enforce all that had been set in place by his forerunner. He insisted that he be consulted and kept up to date with all Brethren business, including details of people's private lives.

Dad offered Denis a job managing one of his factories. The Exclusive Brethren had recently opened a meeting room in South Auckland, so we moved up there at the end of 1970. There was only a small group of Brethren, most of whom had been moved there from Auckland city.

19

Vatican Roulette versus the pill

Shifting to another town was rather a radical move for us. Shifting to another locality was not normal unless members were told to do so by the Exclusive Brethren hierarchy. A few days before we left, I had a visit from an elderly Sister.

'If you move away from here, you will be going against God's will for you,' she said. 'You will probably lose your children to the world or have a terrible accident, or get some incurable disease, as part of God's punishment.'

I didn't take much notice of her. That kind of talk was familiar and usually reserved for people who wanted to leave the fellowship. Guilt and fear were tactics used to threaten members into submission and compliance. I knew the feeling well. We were not thinking of leaving the Exclusives; we were only moving to a different locality. However, I knew, for I'd often been told, that God's punishment was swift and sure if we dared to be disobedient to His word. God hadn't told us we could go; but then, the way I figured it, he hadn't told us not to either. I didn't really know what God thought about it because I wasn't conscious of being on familiar speaking terms with Him. It seemed like a good idea to get away and make a fresh start without so many relatives breathing down my neck, wondering when I was going to produce the next baby.

I was always craving for something new and exciting (but not necessarily babies!). I loved changes, the more spontaneous the better. The Exclusive Brethren didn't actually forbid us to go, they just weren't happy about it. They were always very careful not to tell us what to do. They just told us what the consequences would be if we went outside of God's will. To me, this narrow path seemed like a knife-edge. I can remember my father-in-law saying that I had never had the 'Light of the Assembly' — that personal divine gift which enabled one to believe the distinctive revelations vouchsafed to God's chosen and, according to him, this was the reason I had so much difficulty behaving like a good Exclusive. By now some of our local Brethren were very aware of my discontent and joined with Denis to pray for me to receive the 'light'.

I had recently been in trouble again. For a while it took my mind off the desire to shift. One day near the end of 1970 I had been looking through the newspaper and found a knitting machine for sale. It was second-hand, very simple to use according to the advertisement, and cheap. I was a hopeless hand-knitter. It had taken me five years to make one small garment and, with four young children, a knitting machine would come in very handy. I talked Denis into taking me to see it. With my mind already made up, and the money in my pocket, I became the new owner of this fascinating piece of equipment.

This was fun. I was good at it. My children had the nicest jerseys, hats and mittens that I could dream up, and were much admired. Before long I had agreed to make a garment for one of the Sisters. This is where I came unstuck. I asked her if she could pay me a small amount for it, just enough to cover the cost of the wool! Oh, dear! You would have thought I had gone out and got myself a paid job or something else just as wicked! I was told that I should learn to be content with my husband's income, and besides, the knitting machine could become an idol!

I knew all about idols. They were the things that we thought too much about, things that we might worship more than God, objects of misdirected love and attention. I had already been in trouble for having an idol. Earlier on I had had a cat, just a little one, soft and cuddly, but definitely an idol! The MOG had made an edict that all pets were idols and were to be destroyed, given away, got rid of. Exclusive Brethren all over the world followed his example when he banished his family pet. My cat disappeared while I was in the maternity hospital. So I knew it was wrong to have an idol. If I wanted to keep my knitting machine, I would need to hide it under the bed until all the fuss had died down.

We eventually shifted north and rented an old house on a farm on the outskirts of town, and settled the older children into a school for the last few weeks of the year. Denis travelled to Auckland each day, working on sewing machine repairs and maintenance for Dad. It took a long time to make friends with the other Exclusive Brethren Sisters, but I had my own family not far away. I even visited some of Mother's relatives (not in the fellowship) who were living nearby. It had been many years since I had seen them. I didn't visit them often. In front of them I felt ashamed, not because I was breaking the Brethren rules, but because I belonged to a group of professing Christians who made such rules.

Early in January 1971, at the age of twenty-eight, I had a slight stroke while helping to shift into a house we had bought in town. I had a fleeting horrible thought that maybe the prophecy of something dreadful happening to us was already coming true. Fortunately the stroke was slight. After a week I had recovered enough to resume my normal household responsibilities. My blood pressure had been a problem for some time. Added to this was the very real possibility that the Vatican Roulette might let me down. Ben would be two years old that year, and there was every probability that baby number five could be conceived at any time. The last thing I needed was another baby, and my doctor tried some gentle persuasion.

'Mrs Thomas,' said the doctor, 'it would be better if you didn't have any more children. I want to prescribe the pill for you.'

'No,' I replied. 'I can't do that. It's forbidden in our church; Denis would never agree.'

'Would you and Denis want to risk your life, and leave your children motherless, rather than disobey the rules of the Exclusive

Brethren?'

'Please, can I have time to think about it?' I asked.

I went back to see him the next day.

'Do I need Denis's permission to take the pill?'

'No, Denis doesn't have to know about it. What he doesn't know can't get him into trouble, aye!' said the doctor with a knowing wink in my direction.

That's how I came to be on the pill, without Denis knowing anything about it. If he ever suspected, he didn't say.

The phone rang very late one night. It was my brother.

'Dad and Mum have been withdrawn from again,' he said.

'What about the girls?' I asked. 'Are they okay?'

'Pearl is shut up; I've spoken to her, but I think she will stay with Mum and Dad.'

I hate it when the phone rings in the middle of the night. It's usually bad news. Someone has died, or maybe there's been an accident, and for us, the very real threat that a family member or friend has been shut up or withdrawn from. Bad news always gets around very fast. It is necessary that we found out about these things very quickly because we might unwittingly ring that person or visit them, and then we, too, would be in trouble. We were surprised that Dad had been withdrawn from, and Mum. She was very loyal to him. For whatever reason, Dad's time had run out. My children found it difficult to understand that their Grandpa and Grandma were no longer able to visit them, or talk to them on the phone.

Sometimes Dad and Mum would drive past our house, when they thought we would be out at a meeting, and leave parcels on the front doorstep. There would be little gifts for the children, a cake, or a box of groceries for Denis and me. You see, it is very hard to suddenly break off ties with family, and sooner or later you feel tempted to visit, or contact them.

Because Dad was now under 'Assembly Discipline', Denis was no longer able to work for him. Denis decided to return to the building trade. There was already another builder among the Brethren in our area, so Denis thought it better not to start building on his own. Being in opposition to or in competition with a local Brother was wrong. Denis joined a firm of prefab builders in another town.

The months that followed were very stressful, and before long my sister Chris and her family were shut up, too. Chris and I were still very close, and although I knew I would be in trouble if I visited her, I had to find a way of seeing her without involving Denis. Denis was a soft and gentle man and very fond of my family. It would have been hard for him to forbid me to visit Chris, so it had to be done behind his back. It was time for some more creative bending of the rules! Several years before, I had picked up a short curly blonde wig from a second-hand store for the children's dress-up box. Now I pulled it out and tried it on. I struggled to get all my hair tucked in underneath, but eventually I had arranged it to my satisfaction. With the addition of a pair of dark glasses, my disguise was complete. I rang Chris and asked her to meet me in an old disused quarry not far from where she lived. I couldn't go to her house because some Exclusives lived in her street and they would recognise the car. I had packed a flask and some sandwiches for lunch. After we had eaten, Chris's children and Ben played together while we talked. The very act of eating together was the ultimate in wickedness. This was the first of several such adventures, each time getting a little more daring. I even went as far as visiting Mum. All this, of course, would eventually be held against me. But life went on.

Ben had been very slow to talk, but I could understand him perfectly well. He was just a good kid, not noisy like most other three year olds. However, when his speech didn't improve, I took him to a speech clinic.

'I'll give you this tape,' said the therapist. 'Let him listen to it and help him try to imitate the sounds.'

'I'm very sorry, but we don't have a tape recorder,' I explained to the therapist. We had sold ours some time ago when the Brethren had decided that prerecorded music was a no-no. I wasn't about to tell the speech therapist that we weren't allowed to have one in the house. I only hesitated a moment before thanking her gratefully when she offered me a loan of hers. That night, after explaining to Denis about the need for the tape-recorder, I had a brilliant idea. Denis wouldn't know any difference if I purchased a couple of music tapes to listen to during the day. The next morning, I put Ben in his pushchair and walked into town after taking the older children to school. At the music shop I was almost overwhelmed by the number and variety of tapes. Knowing I would have to be quick if I didn't want to get caught, I asked to see their range of instrumental tapes. I knew that tapes with words on were very wicked, but maybe music with no words wouldn't be so bad. I really wanted a tape of Maori songs but I remembered Denis's father saying they were the worst kind. Even though we didn't know the meanings of the words, there *might* be someone walking past the house who did understand, and some of those words just *might* be blasphemous. Well, you couldn't be too careful, could you? I decided on some classical music by Mozart and another of Strauss waltzes. I enjoyed the tapes, and when it was time to give the tape-recorder back, I hid the tapes away for future use.

It was early in 1974, when Ben was nearly five, before anyone questioned me about the fact that I wasn't pregnant. Denis came home from the Prayer Meeting one Monday night and dropped the bombshell. We were going to get a visit from the local priests. Priestly visits were carried out if and when the Exclusive Brethren were suspicious about something. 'Mr Bluett and Bruce Alexander are coming to visit us tonight, darling,' said Denis as he gave me a quick hug. 'They will be here in about half an hour.'

'What do they want?' I snapped. I had a sinking feeling in the pit of my stomach as I tried to recollect anything I might have said or done to upset someone. Perhaps I'd been talking too much again. We had already been spoken to about my habit of talking more than Denis. It had been suggested to me that I keep my social conversation down to within ten percent of Denis's. That was very hard for me. Now, let me see, ten percent of nothing ...

'Mrs Harris has confessed to giving you some contraceptive advice, something about digging in the garden at the right time of the month,' said Denis with a very puzzled look out the window. 'You haven't been digging in my garden, have you?' Such things had never been his concern. As far as he knew, we were still practicing Vatican Roulette. He was quite happy with the rhythm method of birth control, so long as it didn't involve abstaining for too long, but lately that hadn't been a problem.

'You don't seem to get pregnant so easily these days; have you been taking Mrs Harris's advice?' he asked, no doubt wondering whose garden I had been digging!

I tried to hide a smile as I thought about the little packet of tablets I had hidden in the bottom of my sewing box.

'You had better let me do the talking,' I suggested as I went to answer the doorbell. I led Bruce and Mr Bluett into the lounge, then quietly slipped out to put the kettle on for a cup of tea. Thank goodness the children were all in bed and asleep. I didn't want them to know that we were being 'visited'. The Brothers were waiting for me to return to the lounge before they started talking about the reason for their visit. I still wasn't sure what I was going to say to them. I didn't need to worry; they weren't interested in what I had to say.

'Denis,' said one of the priests, 'we are very concerned. Ben is four and a half and Ngaire is not pregnant again yet. What are you doing to prevent it?'

'Um, we have been using the rhythm method. I know that it hasn't worked so well in the past . . . but maybe God doesn't want us to have any more children,' Denis added hopefully.

'Mrs Harris has confessed to giving Ngaire some advice about terminating conception. What have you got to say about that, Denis?'

'You mean abortion?' said Denis in a shocked voice. 'You wouldn't do that, would you, Ngaire?'

'No way.'

'Have you been digging in the garden at certain times of the month, Ngaire?' asked Bruce.

'No,' I answered truthfully. 'The garden is Denis's responsibility. I'm far too busy with the children.'

'Denis, we suspect that Ngaire is doing something to prevent another pregnancy. We are reminding you that you are responsible for dealing with this matter.' They rose to leave, their cups of tea untouched beside them.

I didn't want Denis to be a policeman or a spy in his own house. That night, we talked long into the early hours of the morning. I told Denis about the pill and how I had been taking it for the past three years.

'You must stop taking it,' said Denis. 'We will try harder with the rhythm method; you know that any other type of contraceptive is forbidden.'

'I'll think about it, when I've finished the packet I'm on.' I was desperately hoping I could come up with some alternative by then.

The priestly visits continued. Sometimes it was Mr Bluett and Bruce; sometimes James Harvey filled in for one of the others. One day I dared to ask James why his wife wasn't pregnant. Their children were the same ages as ours. He mumbled something about his wife being too frail and delicate to have any more children! The fact that *my* health was at risk was not a consideration. Though I confessed to taking the pill I wasn't sorry for it. I was only sorry that I had been caught.

We had a phone call the next night, telling us we were now 'shut up'. The priests would visit us again. These visits were similar to previous visits except that the priests were now more poker-faced and serious. Priestly visits are based on Old Testament scripture. If the priests are suspicious of some sort of unconfessed and unforsaken sin, then they will visit that person to take a closer look. If the sinner is unrepentant, or appears to be hiding something, then that person is declared a 'leper'. Because leprosy is contagious, the whole house is shut up so as not to risk contaminating the rest of the congregation. This was how our whole family found themselves shut up early in April 1974.

My being caught taking the pill would have been enough reason for them to pay us a visit, but there must have been other things that worried them as well. For the life of me I can't remember what they were! When you are shut up, your whole life and thought processes come under review. The original offence becomes less important. We were not permitted to go to meetings, nor could we make any contact, personally or by phone, with any other members of the Exclusive

Brethren. We had no friends outside of the Brethren, and so we were isolated. We were so well educated by example in this concept that we submitted without question.

Denis went to work and the children went to school, but apart from that, we stayed in our house with the doors shut and the curtains drawn most of the time. We were in disgrace. Shame and humiliation were meant to bring us to a state of repentance. In spite of feeling guilty, ashamed, humiliated and afraid, I was starting to enjoy some aspects of being shut up! Denis was at home every night. We played chess with the older children, and Denis had time to talk to the younger ones before they went to bed. By the end of the week I was convinced that I did not want to go to a meeting ever again. Denis's face lit up when he answered the phone on Friday evening. It was Mr Bluett.

'The priests are coming to see us tonight. Please tell them you are sorry,' Denis pleaded. I knew he wanted to go back to the meetings. He loved the Exclusive Brethren lifestyle, and believed implicitly in their teachings. I loved Denis too much to see him hurting. He had had that hounded, dispirited look all week. I gave in, and we flushed the remaining tablets down the toilet. That night I promised the priests that I would not take the pill again.

The current MOG was consulted, and he agreed that we could be restored to fellowship and start going to the meetings again. Although it had seemed as though we had been shut up for ages, it was in fact only one week. When I heard the news of our restoration, I was so disappointed that I went into my room and cried and sulked. I could have done with at least one more week of rest and relaxation, but I knew Denis had had enough of the shame of being shut up.

We held a family conference. 'You know how you children are always praying and asking God to give us another baby. Well, now we want you to start praying that he won't. It is far easier to have a baby than you might think.'

'Please, Mum, we want another baby. I'll help you with the housework,' said Angela, a far-off motherly look in her eight-year-old eyes.

'Mum, we will help, too,' added Charlie.

'I could help you with the cooking,' offered Paul.

I was outnumbered. I knew it wasn't any use. In any case, it seemed as though Denis only needed to look at me in that special way of his and I would fall pregnant. He liked making babies and, within a few weeks, baby number five was on the way. I put off going to the doctor as long as I could.

'Mrs Thomas, this is very serious. If you had come to me sooner, I could have talked to you about alternative choices.' He wasn't very happy. 'Make sure you get plenty of rest and come and see me every week.'

20

Shut up, then shipped out

Paul threw his school bag in the corner. 'Hi, Mum, can I have some toast and lemon honey?' he asked, hungry as usual. He put the bread in the toaster, picked up his school bag, and headed for his room.

'Where's Charles? Didn't he come home with you?'

'Nup, couldn't find him.'

'Did you look?'

'Yes, Mum, I must have been the last to leave, I looked everywhere, and he wasn't there.'

The boys went to a school over the other side of town. Charlie had been late home before, but he'd turn up by teatime.

'Where's Charles?' asked Denis when we were ready to sit down to dinner.

'I don't know. I've rung the school; they suggested he could have gone home with one of the boys in his class.'

'Do you know the name of the boys he plays with, Paul?' asked Denis.

'It could be Gary; his grandfather owns the picture theatre. Charlie plays with him sometimes.'

Charlie had been asking why he couldn't go to the pictures, so now I put two and two together. Once we knew where to look, Charlie wasn't hard to find. I suppose some children have a propensity for running away from home, and this was the first of many occasions when we would be out there, searching the streets for one or other of our offspring who wanted a taste of freedom. Later that evening, after Charlie had been found and brought home, we sat down with him and talked about the many reasons why we had boundaries. Denis explained to him that picture theatres were dens of iniquity, sinful places where God would never show his face. All manner of wicked things were flashed across the screen, and the language used by the actors was blasphemous.

'No matter how tempted you are, you are never to go into that place,' warned Denis. 'Now we will need to decide what punishment you will get.'

'Denis, please don't hit him,' I pleaded. There must be some better way to make him remember to come straight home from school.

'You're too soft, Ngaire, but I will leave it to you to come up with something. I want him dealt with tonight,' he added.

The children's cousins were coming to visit us the next day. Our boys loved playing with Rick. We had lived next door to them for several years before we left the Bay of Plenty. Rick was a year older than Paul. I knew that the most effective punishment I could mete out to Charlie was to prevent him from playing with Rick the next day.

'Tomorrow you can stay in the sewing room all day while the others play.' I thought that was a fair enough punishment and Denis agreed. They were only coming for the day and it would be hard for Charlie to stay confined to one room for five or six hours.

The next day, all went according to plan. When Jenny and her family arrived, Charlie was sent to the sewing room. The sewing room was a small room off our bedroom. It had once been a porch but, because it was on the cold side of the house, Denis had enclosed it. Now it contained a small bed, a sewing table, and all the creative sewing junk that had accumulated over the years. After lunch, the children asked to go to the park. It was several streets away but the older children promised to look after the younger ones. Mr Bluett's backyard backed on to the park. He was outside mowing the lawns when he noticed the children playing. They ran to the fence when he called them.

'Where's Charles?' asked Mr Bluett after he had chatted to the others for a while.

'Charlie's been naughty,' offered Angela.

'Shush,' said Paul. Charlie and Paul were the best of mates and he didn't want anyone to know his brother was in trouble.'

Mr Bluett turned back to Angela. 'Where's Charles?' he asked again.

'He's in the sewing room and he has to stay there all afternoon.'

Before the children arrived home there was a knock on the door. It was Mr Bluett.

'I want to speak to Charles, please,' he said as he marched through the dining room, through our bedroom and into the sewing room. By the time we caught up, he was asking Charles why he was being punished. I didn't hear his answer but Mr Bluett turned to us.

'You ought not to have punished him.' Turning to Charles he said, 'Run out and play with the others, I want to speak to your parents. As Charles left the room, he turned and thumbed his nose at us as if to say, 'Ha, ha, I won!'

'You ought to be ashamed of yourselves,' Mr Bluett said to us. 'It's your fault if he felt the need to run way. You should take the responsibility for this on yourselves.'

Maybe Mr Bluett was right. Perhaps we should have analysed the situation more carefully to determine just why Charles had run away. At the time, I thought that the punishment had fitted the crime. By isolating Charlie from the family, we were disciplining him in the same style the Brethren disciplined us. Charles was a hard child to discipline, harder than any of the others. He had the ability to turn everything to his own advantage. By interfering, Mr Bluett had undermined our authority as parents.

Charlie thought it was a huge joke. I now wish I had let his father give him a jolly good whacking instead!

The fact that I was pregnant again was now a visible reality. I was busy knitting baby garments on my knitting machine. One day I took a garment into a shop to find some suitable buttons. The man behind the counter handed me a pamphlet. A knitting machine instructor from Auckland was going to spend a day teaching in the shop. I was invited to drop in while she was there and watch her at work. This was very tempting but a bit risky. To shop for wool and buttons was one thing, but to fraternise with outsiders was definitely not done. But surely there would be no harm in stopping by for a few moments just to watch, I reasoned with myself. When I arrived on the day, I was told that the venue had been changed because of the number of interested people, too many to fit in the small shop. The knitting machine had been carried across the mall and into the back of an upstairs café. Ben was with me, and he amused himself with some other children while I talked knitting, and babies, then more knitting. I had many questions to ask the demonstrator and had taken along some samples of my own work. I stayed all day, and it wasn't long before I was sitting at the machine and showing the others some things I had worked out for myself. These people were full of admiration. I wasn't used to being praised for something I enjoyed doing. The demonstrator tried to persuade me do a course with her to train me to teach people to use their machines. She said I was a natural born teacher. I kept saying no, I couldn't, I wasn't allowed. She didn't understand. The next time I went into the shop, the man behind the counter had a note for me from the knitting machine distributors. They were offering me free training and a generous remuneration for my services as a teacher. This was very tempting, and I succumbed. I had fallen in love with the beautiful new model of machine that the demonstrator had been operating. I wanted one. I don't know how I thought I was going to get away with it, but I did. I went to Auckland for training, taking Ben with me and always returning before the older children came home from school. Now I had to do some negotiating with the man in the shop. If he wanted me to teach for him, there was no way I would do it in the shop. He was puzzled by my insistence. He agreed to rent the back of the upstairs café, once a week, on Monday afternoons, for two hours. I knew I would be safe up there, away from the prying eyes of the Exclusive Brethren. They wouldn't catch me up there; eating in cafés or restaurants was forbidden. They didn't eat any food prepared by 'unholy hands'.

It was strange and unreal at the beginning. A friend told me recently that I used to sit with my head down and my hair hiding my face! I soon got used to it. I was leading a double life and I liked it. It was so nice to talk to people on the outside; people who valued and appreciated what I was doing.

Ben came along with me until he started school. He never told anyone where we went every Monday afternoon.

The winter of 1974 dragged on. I was pregnant, sick, tired and disgruntled. The effort of organizing the family to get to the meetings, especially at six o'clock on Sunday morning, was more than I wanted to cope with. Oh, how I longed to just stay at home and sleep! The number of meetings on Sundays had increased to four, and although I was not expected to go to all of them, Denis and the older children usually did. We usually invited people home for dinner, so although I was not at a meeting, I was still busy preparing the meal. Sometimes we would have a glass of wine before dinner during the week, but on Sundays we had whisky. Whisky was the preferred drink of the MOG, and we were expected to serve it to guests. I didn't like whisky, not just because I was pregnant; I just didn't like it and was usually able to avoid it.

One Sunday evening we were invited out for a meal. The man of the house handed around the whisky and, as usual, I politely refused it. However, this time my refusal caused offence. I was invited out to the kitchen on some pretence, and before I knew it, I was being questioned about my refusal. I was accused of having something to hide! It was generally thought that whisky loosened the tongue, and to refuse it was damning evidence that I had some secrets I wasn't revealing. It certainly wasn't my pregnancy I was hiding! The whole scenario was so stupid. Hadn't I already been reprimanded several times for talking too much? Now I was being told I should open my mouth and let my mind spill out! I drank the whisky. I didn't want my host to have to speak to Denis about my tardiness. From then on I determined that alcohol would not loosen my tongue!

I always found it hard to get four children dressed and ready for a meeting at six o'clock in the morning. Now that I was pregnant, it was almost impossible. By the time I had dressed all the children and, due to morning sickness, had thrown up several times, I was exhausted. One Sunday morning I was up during the night to one of the children. The clock on the kitchen wall said four o'clock. I was tired and I wanted to sleep in, just this once. I very quietly switched off the alarm clock on Denis's side of the bed.

It was nearly seven-thirty when we awoke to a loud knock on the front door. The morning meeting was over and the 'attendance officer' had arrived. Denis answered the door. He came back and slumped onto the side of the bed, his head buried in his hands.

'I can't believe it, I forgot to set the alarm last night,' he wailed to me. 'He didn't believe me. He insisted that we slept in on purpose!'

Oh, dear! We were in trouble, and it was all my fault, again! The next meeting was at nine o'clock, and because Ben was sick, I kept him and Angela home with me. Paul and Charlie were grumpy.

'Why do we have to go out when Angela doesn't have to?' whined Charlie.

'Charles, put your shoes on and hurry up,' said Denis.

'I'm not going,' said Paul.

'Yes, you are. Come on boys, you can tie your shoelaces in the car. We'll stop at the dairy on the way home. I'll buy you both a chocolate fish.'

They were already late when they got to the meeting room.

'Give me the keys, Dad, I'll lock the car up,' said Paul. But instead, he jumped back into the car and locked all the doors. No amount of persuasion or remonstrating through the glass would convince Paul to open the door. Another car had pulled into the car park, and Denis didn't want to make a scene. He grabbed Charles's hand and marched him up the steps and into the meeting room.

I looked at the clock. Denis was home early. It was only nine-thirty. Denis came in. His face was a pale shade of grey, and he was on the verge of tears.

'We've been shut up again,' he said with a quiver in his voice.

'Just because we missed the meeting this morning?' I asked.

'No, there's more to it than that. They said I was not being head of my house and that I didn't have proper control of my family.'

I put my arms around him. I loved him so much. I couldn't let them blame him. He was such a good Exclusive Brother. I thought back over the twelve years we had been married. His favourite saying was, 'righteousness is doing one right thing after another.' This is what he believed and this is how he lived. I hated to see him so upset, and all because of me. I knew the Exclusive Brethren loved and respected him. Maybe they even pitied him? It was unfortunate that he had drawn the short straw when he married me!

'It's all my fault, Den,' I sobbed into his shoulder. 'Let me explain to them. Let me tell them I'm sorry.'

'It's no good, darling; we will need to wait until the priests visit us on Monday night.'

It was the beginning of August and the weekly priestly visits were about to begin again. Guilt and fear were raising their ugly heads as I contemplated my future. I was torn between my love for Denis and the children and my growing desire to leave the fellowship. I had had a taste of the real world. Ordinary people had included me in their conversations, praised my abilities and wanted to be my friends. Had I not experienced this, I may well have been content to stay within the strict confines of my prison walls. However, something learned cannot be easily erased. I could see that I had been brought up with blinkers on. I lay awake most of that Sunday night, thinking, turning over in my mind the events of the past few months. I thought of all the things I wanted to say to the priests when they arrived the next night. I would tell them . . . No, I couldn't tell them anything; they wouldn't listen. I only had two options. I could dress myself in the proverbial sackcloth and ashes, grovel and snivel, say I was sorry and promise once more to try harder. I was a good actor. I could pull it off. The second option was to tell the truth. I preferred to tell the truth, but I was afraid that if I gave the Exclusives any reason to withdraw from me and not Denis, then I would lose Denis and the children. They would be taken from me and I would never see them again. It was like a game of truth and consequences. Whatever I did I would lose. As I tossed and turned that night, and many other nights, the most sensible thing I came up with was to wait, be patient and keep my mouth shut.

The weekends were the worst. When you have been used to going to meetings every day and for most part of the weekends, you miss it. It is like going from the ridiculous to the sublime. It was spring. The garden, house and section needed sprucing up a bit. We threw ourselves into a flurry of work to keep from going batty. We sanded and painted the windowsills where the old paint was flaking off. We raked and hoed and planted the vegetable garden. Even the garage received some much-needed attention. We didn't know how to sit and relax. To do nothing was a sin; to enjoy doing nothing was even worse. We started to explore the countryside. We would get up early, pack a picnic lunch and drive off to some remote piece of bush or stream. The children loved it. Denis and I felt guilty because we both knew that we should be sitting in a meeting somewhere. We never ventured far, and we always made sure we were ready and available for the inevitable trouncing at the weekly priestly visit on Monday evenings.

The children began pleading with us to take them away somewhere for the school holidays. They logically reasoned that because we couldn't go to the meetings, we could go somewhere where there wasn't a meeting. Up till now, if we went somewhere for the holidays, it was always to a place with an Exclusive Brethren meeting close by so as not to miss a single meeting.

'Please, please can we go to the snow?' Charlie begged. 'Gary's grandfather takes him every winter.'

'Ooh, yes, let's go to the snow,' said Angela, 'I can make a snowman.'

'But it's spring; all the snow will be melted,' said Denis. He sounded disappointed.

After a few phone calls confirming that indeed there was still snow on the mountains, we made enquiries about renting a caravan for a few days. The whole family was excited. Our first real holiday with no meetings! We could go wherever we wanted. We checked out the caravans and chose one that would comfortably accommodate our family.

'Do you want to hire a television as well?' the lady asked.

'No, thank you,' replied Denis before I had a chance to accept. I had seen a small radio-tape recorder in the top drawer and was glad I'd kept the tapes I'd bought earlier in the year.

'Don't forget to take some old tyre tubes, they're good for sliding on, or some strong plastic rubbish bags,' called the lady as we were about to drive away.

We were packed and ready to leave on Friday afternoon, when Denis remembered something.

'I had better go and ring Mr Bluett and tell him where we're going.'

'Why do we need to tell him everything we do?' I objected. 'What if he says we can't go?'

Mr Bluett didn't forbid us to go, which surprised us both.

It is easy to take pleasure in the simplest of things. We had been deprived of the enjoyment of nature for so long, and now we saw the world in a new light. Although we lived in a beautiful country, we had not fully appreciated what God had created for our enjoyment. Enjoyment was almost a dirty word. If something is enjoyable, it is certain to be wicked! We had a great time, slipping and sliding and sloshing through the melting snow on the sides of the road. We took our time, enjoying the feeling of not having to rush to be on time for a meeting. We finally stopped at a camping ground with a natural thermal swimming pool. This would be our base for the next week. We went up to the mountain and played all day and then home to the caravan at night. We relaxed in the hot thermal pools in the evenings, and listened to my tapes while the children slept. And sleep they did. They were so happy and full of fun. If only life could always be like this. But all good things come to an end.

We had missed one weekly visit from the priests but arrived home in time for the next one. We were happy and glowing and ready to give them an account of the most marvellous holiday you could possibly imagine! They were not impressed.

'We are very disappointed in you, Denis. You know the Brethren don't go to tourist resorts.'

'But I told you we were going. You didn't say we couldn't.' Denis had been so happy before they arrived; now he looked defeated and sad again.

'We don't tell people what to do, or not do,' replied Mr Bluett. 'It's your choice. You chose to go, and take your family, to such a worldly place. If you had asked us if you could go instead of telling us you were going, then I would have pointed out the wickedness of it.'

'I am so sorry,' said Denis. 'I thought that because we were shut up, and because it was the school holidays, it would be okay.'

'That's the trouble, Denis, you don't think. You let Ngaire do your thinking for you and she sets you on the wrong path. It is the narrow path that leads to salvation and you are not keeping to it.'

They continued for some time, talking about my lack of subjection and insubordination to Denis. As Eve, in the book of Genesis, had deceived Adam and caused him to sin, so had I deceived Denis and made him do something he didn't really want to do. It was always my fault.

The weekly priestly visits soon fell into a regular pattern. The priests, usually two of the three, would arrive at nine o'clock on Monday evening after the Prayer Meeting. They would, of course, refuse the offered cup of tea; maybe they had already consumed a glass of whisky before the visit. Sometimes they would sit there for ages without saying anything, just staring at us with long mournful faces. I was always glad that the children were in bed by then, although I suspect the older ones sometimes listened at the door.

After a while, one priest would clear his throat and start the interrogation. They usually spoke to Denis first.

'Denis, you are grieving the Holy Spirit, and the beloved Brethren. The Bible says that a man should be head of his house, and you are not. What have you got to say for yourself?'

'We are working through that issue.'

'You're on very shaky ground, Denis. You need to take a firm stand against iniquity in your household.'

After they'd finished with Denis, they would start on me. Most visits lasted for several hours. Some sessions went on longer than others. At times, one priest would doze off to sleep, leaving the other to interrogate us! It is very difficult now to remember the exact words they used or the details of their concerns about us. It seemed as though they were desperately searching for incriminating evidence and wanted a report on every tiny detail of our lives, although they appeared to believe only half of what we told them.

Every Tuesday morning, after Denis went to work, I carried out a little ritual of my own. I vacuumed the floor and the seats the priests had sat in, washed down any surfaces they might have touched, sprayed air refresher around the room, and rearranged the furniture before closing the door to that room shut for the week. I never entered the room again during the week if I could avoid it, and before long the whole family followed my example. After my cleansing ritual I would sometimes take Ben with me to a neighbour's house for a forbidden cup of coffee. She had befriended me when she realised that we were no longer going to the meetings.

At times, being shut up was sheer mental and emotional torture. It was meant to be. It was designed that way. You knew that you would not be accepted back by them until you not only agreed with all the accusations, but hated yourself for having sinned — or at least had convinced them that this was so. The big problem was that I had a happy knack of turning any situation to my advantage. I looked for new opportunities around every corner, and there were plenty of corners. I suppose the priests had our best interests at heart. I believe that they wanted me to 'get right' so that we could all go back again into the fold, submissive and contrite. There was never any question about whose fault it was. I knew, and they knew, that up till this point I was the problem — I was simply not good Exclusive Brethren material. I was scheming and devious — they couldn't trust me. The flip side was that I couldn't trust them either because they came between my family and me. I was sure of one dreadful fact: if they could pin something on me and not on Denis, then we would be separated. However, I believe that the priests *did not want this to happen*. They gave me so many opportunities to submit and repent. They almost succeeded. We later received written apologies from these priests.

21

Judge, jury and executioners

Now I'm coming to the hard part. It isn't hard to remember what happened, but it is hard to express the trauma and the emotional torture we went through at the time. This was the second major crossroads in my life. Like my marriage to Denis, this was a dramatic change of direction that would alter a whole family's future. Although for years a lot of the guilt remained, it was more the guilt of being the winner, because in winning, I had made Denis the loser. Now I know we were both winners.

I take full responsibility for what happened. I'm a proactive person, and because I was given ample opportunity I could have procured a different outcome. I've always been the strong one and was well aware of the consequences of not submitting fully to the idiosyncrasies of the hierarchy. Just knowing that Denis would find it difficult to take his share of the responsibility made me even stronger. Sometimes I felt that the priests were primarily visiting me and that Denis was taking the role of an innocent but concerned onlooker. I expect they realised or suspected that he was a victim of circumstances. I certainly tested their boundaries. I wasn't exactly trying to be withdrawn from; what I really wanted was justice and compromise. I'm a great believer in compromise. I like to look for the best alternatives and outcomes, to work things out to suit everyone. I could have continued in there for Denis's sake, if only I could have had a little more freedom for myself.

I didn't dare tell the priests that. Compromise was a dirty word to the Exclusives. 'No compromise' was one of their absolutes. They didn't want a watered down or workable solution, they wanted complete capitulation. A Bible verse, Revelation 3:16, supported this attitude. 'Thus, because thou art lukewarm, and neither cold nor hot, I am about to spew thee out of my mouth.' This may be appropriate for people who have a black and white attitude to life, but personally I appreciate the various shades of colour found in the broad spectrum of human differences.

I wasn't of a mind to go out and do anything drastically worldly, but I did enjoy mixing with interesting and broad-minded people. Those knitting-machine classes on Monday afternoons gave me the strength and boldness for the priestly visits in the evening.

Two priests, with serious poker-straight faces, would arrive at the door — after the prayer meeting — at about nine o'clock at night. Denis would usher them in and we would all sit looking at the floor till an atmosphere of judicial solemnity pervaded the room. Only then were they ready to begin their inevitable questioning. They tried to wear us down. They tried to catch us out on something, dragging up juicy gossip from twenty years earlier. They went over our lives like forensic investigators. Anything we had ever done or said might be dragged up and discussed, to see if we had a self-condemnatory assessment of our past borderline conduct. The visits continued for about three months. It seemed like a long time, but I have heard that that is about average.

I'm surprised they didn't excommunicate me a lot sooner. If they had, I think they could have held on to Denis. But generally it's the wife and children who remain with the Exclusives, not the other way around. The women are less likely to stray. I have often thought it was a man's world in there, that the men have it pretty good because the women have been conditioned from birth to be submissive and obedient to the men, but now I know that it's just as hard for the men.

If a man is head of his house and is loyal to the fellowship, then his wife is subject to him and does what she's told. If not, then the man must be lacking in some essential quality. That expectation creates an enormous responsibility for both partners, and carries a load of guilt when it can't be fulfilled. There have been cases where the husband and children have remained with the Exclusive Brethren and the wife has left, but they are in the minority. The Brethren don't usually want wives who aren't submissive, or men who can't control their wives, because then the man is not the 'head of the house'.

I'm often asked if it's true that the Exclusive Brethren *try* to split families, but I'll give them the benefit of the doubt and say that is not their objective. Nevertheless, they don't hesitate to rather hurriedly put someone out of fellowship who has transgressed, whether or not they are repentant. They then give that person 'priestly service' towards repentance, assuring them that this will bring about speedy restoration as soon as repentance is witnessed. Whether temporary or permanent, a 'divided household' is just one of the costs of striving for a pure fellowship. In my opinion, there are significant parallels between the Exclusive Brethren system and Hitler's Nazi Germany. The Exclusives want a pure Assembly, untainted by the evils of the outside world. I think the Exclusives genuinely believe they are God's chosen people. The Exclusives prefer complete families, but in any case, they always want the children to remain with them. They want salvation for the children, even if the parents are lost.

Even though I disagree with many of their principles, I sometimes feel myself react when people ask me if the Exclusive Brethren are really Christians. They zealously strive to be worthy Christians, according to their restricted understanding of the Bible. I might talk (and complain) about my life with the Exclusives, but I also want to defend their rights to believe what they like as individuals. I am loyal to them when other people make unfounded criticisms, while I still acknowledge their cruelty towards many former members. From our earliest memories we were conditioned to see ourselves as the select group, chosen to maintain the real and perfect truth of true Christianity, and the true calling of the church. All other branches of

Christendom were considered more or less degenerates. We expected to be misunderstood because we were favoured with a special revelation. To have this heritage questioned as 'unchristian' still revives in me all those ingrained arguments. This loyalty to their culture may sound as if I'm contradicting myself, but what we learn as small children often stays with us into adulthood. I understand the evolution of their thinking.

At one stage they almost succeeded in bringing us back into the fold. I had said I was sorry for everything. There wasn't any real reason for them to withdraw from us. I think at that point we could have been accepted back. I know that in my mind I had decided to give up my worldly ways and be a good Exclusive Brethren 'Sister', even if just for Denis's sake. All along, Denis was stereotyped as being worthy, and I as being different. Because of this, it was difficult for him to take his share of responsibility for our problems. It was always easier for me to make the changes rather than expect him to.

It was the middle of October and we had been shut up for almost three months. We were all under a tremendous strain. I was six-months pregnant and my legs were swelling. I was put on bed rest with the warning to Denis and the family that I was to have no stress or worries! My doctor had a word with Denis.

'If you can't use contraceptives after this baby is born, I would strongly advise that one of you has an operation to prevent further pregnancies. Think about it.'

We did think about it. We talked about it. The simplest thing was for Denis to have a vasectomy. He didn't want to go ahead with it, so it would have to be me who had the surgery. But there was a big problem. We knew the Exclusives wouldn't allow it for either of us. Denis made a suggestion.

'We could go out of fellowship, have your tubes tied after the baby is born, then we could go back in again!'

'What a good idea, Denis.' I was one step ahead of him. Denis must have been very naïve, or have had some serious misgivings to have even allowed such a thought. However, I knew the real reason behind Denis's thinking. He didn't like abstaining and an operation for me would fix that for the future. My mind was also working overtime. Once we were out we might like it. If not, we could go back in again. However, if we did like it, we could stay out! Denis genuinely thought a short spell on the outside was a good solution, and I supported him, suspecting that once we were all out, wild horses wouldn't drag us back.

It didn't quite work like that. You don't go to the Exclusive Brethren and say, 'We're leaving for a while, we might come back some time in the future, after we've attended to some private and personal matters on the outside.' There was no such thing as leaving on amicable terms — we could only leave on their terms, not ours. The Exclusive Brethren *always* expect to hold the initiative. I knew that if we told them we were leaving, they would come up with something to gain control, and they did. They got in first. I believe that they had contacted the MOG for further instructions. One Monday evening near the end of October they found our Achilles heel.

Denis was a very thoughtful and considerate but hot-blooded man, and I — like a good subject Exclusive Brethren wife — had promised him that, within reason, I would never deny him his conjugal rights except under extreme circumstances. The Bible says, 'The wife has not authority over her own body, but the husband; in like manner, the husband has not authority over his own body, but the wife. Defraud not one another . . .' 1 Corinthians 7:4–5. When questioned on the subject of intimacy, Denis confessed to being sexually adventurous at times — within the marriage, of course. We both believed that whatever went on between the sheets, in the privacy of our own locked bedroom, was our own business, but they didn't think so. We were a very normal couple, and his conjugal rights were proving to be more fundamental than his beliefs! Because we knew they were looking for dirt, and because it was expected of us, Denis made a confession. We weren't doing anything drastically wrong, but the priests declared otherwise. One of them said, 'We always knew there was *something* wrong with you, Denis, we just didn't know what it was, and now we know.' I think that around about that time the MOG decided that being shut up wasn't humbling enough as it was, so he brought in a new rule: No sex allowed for couples while shut up! The priests hit us with it. They put restrictions on us! But Denis was a hot-blooded man and his conjugal rights were important to him!

We tried to abstain, but you know what it's like when you're told not to do something: that's the very thing you want to do. Can you just imagine them coming back the next week and asking the delicate question: 'Did you? Or did you not?' It might sound funny now, but at the time, even though we had precipitated the crisis, it was very serious stuff — no laughing matter. When the priests came to see us the next week, they didn't stay long. Only long enough to ask the dreaded question: 'Did you . . . ?' began one of the priests.

'No,' said Denis. 'No, we didn't.'

Denis had told a lie, and I was astounded. I had never known Denis to tell a lie, and for the thirty-three years we were together, I never knew another occasion. Denis was basically a very honest and truthful person. He told me once that 'A lie was never told, unless to gain credit where credit wasn't due'. I couldn't believe that I was hearing him deny what we had done, something that was entirely our own business. Rather than give him away, I left the room. I slipped outside, hoping the cool spring air would soothe my anger. I wasn't angry with Denis. I was angry because I felt violated. The priests knew that they had to find our Achilles heel and they had succeeded. Their car was parked outside our gate, on the verge, facing downhill. In my anger, I went to the car and tried to push it down the hill. Fortunately, the hand brake held. Fortunate, too, that my neighbour was observing me from her kitchen window, and by guiding me into her house for a clandestine cup of coffee she prevented me from doing anything drastic.

The priests left soon after. When I returned home, Denis was slumped in his chair. We talked for a long time that night.

It was Tuesday, 31 October 1974, the morning after the night before. Denis rang one of the priests and confessed to him that he had lied. We waited for the inevitable repercussions — another visit, maybe? Denis came home from work that afternoon to the news that Charlie had run away, again. He had told Paul that he wasn't coming home until we had sorted something out. The boys were now ten and eleven, and old enough to know that their lives were being turned upside down. Although they were always in bed when the priests came to visit, they knew that their parents were in trouble. Denis and Paul were out looking for Charles that night when the call came, after the Tuesday night Ministry meeting. The Exclusive Brethren had found their mark and they acted swiftly. It was one of the priests. He wouldn't speak to me. He wanted Denis. He rang back later.

'Denis, we are sorry, but we can no longer walk with you and Ngaire.'

'What about the children?' Denis asked, his voice shaking.

'They will be spoken to in due course but as yet they've done nothing wrong, so are still in fellowship with us.'

'What were the charges laid against us?'

'You are charged with lying. Ngaire is charged with being contentious and rebellious,' was the reply.

It was over. We were out.

It's hard not being able to see friends and family who are still in the fellowship. I would love to see my brother again before one of us dies. I miss him. We were close in age and got on very well together. After all these years I'm still hurt by the unjustified invasion of personal privacy, and the stigma of being referred to as 'wicked persons', doomed and far removed from the saving grace of God.

There was something totally unfair and one-sided about the whole process. There was no denying that in their terms I was contentious and rebellious, but I would use other words like enthusiastic, innovative, creative and energetic. The charge against Denis was unjustified. Denis was not a liar. I believe they took unfair advantage of him in their desire to be the victors. They couldn't just accept the fact that he ultimately chose to support me. They should have allowed us to go with dignity; instead they found a convenient way to solve a problem that was becoming an embarrassment to them. They wanted to find something wrong with Denis to justify their predetermined actions. All they could really find was that he was not being head of his house in the way expected of an Exclusive Brethren. It was their way of saying to Denis, 'If you can't deal with Ngaire then we have to deal with you both,' and being 'dealt with' meant being withdrawn from. They said that he was at fault because he was not being the head of his house, but ultimately I still got the blame because I was not submissive enough. They withdrew from us when we weren't there to defend ourselves, but even if we had been, there would have been no defence. In my opinion the Brethren Priests became judge, jury and executioner because they were expected to present our 'case' to the Brethren as a complete package — signed, sealed and delivered, with no further questions asked.

I remember in former times when a person under Assembly discipline could, and was expected to, go to their own Assembly meeting and account for himself or herself. This provided some level of check against unfair charges. Now people aren't given that opportunity, and as a result the Brethren have years later had to review cases where people were quite unfairly put out, often by priests who are now themselves under Assembly judgement. By then it is usually too late and the victims want nothing more to do with the fellowship. Even so, the Brethren would seldom admit to being at fault or that there was something fundamentally wrong with their practice, which is, to all but themselves, clearly contrary to Bible teaching.

I'm not sure what they said at our Assembly meeting. It would have been something like 'we have visited Denis and Ngaire, and we find them unrepentant of the matters we laid upon them. We are sorry to report that we can no longer walk with them'. There may have been a scripture read from the Bible, perhaps something like: 1 Corinthians 5:5 (referring to a sexual sin): 'to deliver him to Satan for destruction of the flesh, that the spirit may be saved in the day of the Lord Jesus.' I don't really know what was said. We were not told. I can only guess from what I remember of other people's Assembly meetings.

Several years later, when so many things went wrong, we wondered if we had been cursed. The way we were treated is typical of their treatment of hundreds of families worldwide, many of whom suffered much worse than we did.

Life on the outside was tough, very tough.

22

Life on the outside

I am always amazed how so much meaning can be taken from so few words. Once we were told we were withdrawn from, we knew exactly where we stood; no one had to spell it out for us. It was an unwritten code. The Exclusive Brethren would no longer recognise us if they saw us in the street. No friendly wave or smile, no words exchanged. If they saw us walking along the street, they would cross to the other side. It was as if we were already dead and stinking. We in turn would honour this code of conduct as faithfully as they would. We knew that our only contact with them, be it friend, family or fellow Brother or Sister, would be if and when we repented and asked to return to the fellowship. They would wait, and hope for us to grovel, and any forgiveness meted out would be purely at their discretion. Until then, we would be looked upon as wicked people, not fit for a place in the Kingdom of God as they knew it.

We were all acutely aware of the consequences of leaving the Exclusive Brethren. We had been taught from a very early age that if we turned our backs on them we were worse than all those evil people in the real world. Although they didn't actually say so, we believed that unless God granted us repentance there was grave doubt about our salvation. Although we were taught that once saved we were always saved, if we turned our backs on the 'Truth' it was doubtful that we had ever been saved at all, and any righteousness in our lives up till then had been in vain. We believed that God was most disapproving of people who turn their backs on the light because they are worse than those who have never received the light.

That first night, after the children were in bed, Denis and I sat and held each other and cried — well, I cried and Denis tried not to. The fearful magnitude of what we had done had hit us. All the time we were shut up, we felt as if we were in limbo, waiting, almost in a dream from which we would eventually awake. Now we were on the outside, raw, vulnerable, scared and on our own. No one would guide or help us. We had been 'delivered unto Satan'. Our immediate reaction was to capitulate and do everything within our power to get back to that safe, familiar place where, indirectly, everything was decided for us and we had no individual choices. It is only now after all these years that I fully appreciate the extreme sacrifice Denis made when he decided to stay with the children and me. It would have been so easy for him to return to the fellowship at that point, alone, and become a national Exclusive Brethren hero.

For the first few weeks we lived much the same way as we had for the previous three months, except that the priestly visits had stopped. In fact, if anything, we were more isolated and secluded than ever. We lived in fear of emerging into the outside world. We had been told, many times, how bad it was. Now we had to go out there and face all those wicked people. Having been taught so much about separation from evil, we instinctively kept away from others who had suffered the same fate. Any contact with other 'exs' would jeopardise our chances of restoration in the future; we might also make it difficult for them to return to the fellowship. We had been taught that everyone who was withdrawn from was striving to get back in as soon as possible.

In spite of contacts I had already made I felt like an alien from a different planet. We didn't know what was expected of us. We didn't know how to behave in a normal society. It was like coming out of prison, after a long stretch, into a world we knew nothing about, a world that had progressed far beyond our understanding. During those first few days and weeks, even I wanted to go back into the safe protective custody of those who controlled our entire existence.

We were not aware, at the time, of the devastating effect all this was having on the children. We were so screwed up by our own hurts that we didn't see what was happening to them. The older ones suffered the most. They were eight, ten and eleven years old. They were at a stage of their development when they were learning the rules of social behaviour. Suddenly the rules changed but nobody told them how to adjust to their new life. They were old enough to know the severity of our predicament, but not old enough to understand how we got into it, or how we would adjust. Everything we had taught them came tumbling down around them. Their trust in us as parents was being tested to the limit. It never entered our heads to seek counselling, either for our children or for ourselves. The Exclusive Brethren would have seriously frowned on such a thing. I wish we had known how to explain our predicament to the children in a language they could understand.

Years later, Angela told me about the nightmares she suffered. 'The nightmares started that night. I thought we were going straight to hell. I didn't want to go to sleep because that's when Satan would come and get me. I tried to stay awake. I must have slept because I felt myself slipping down, down, down, through a dark tunnel into a cavern filled with dancing flames. Before I reached the sea of fire, I woke, screaming. These nightmares recurred, in varying intensity, for a very long time.'

Meanwhile, Denis and I were having nightmares of a different sort. We were continually on edge; trying to turn chaos into some semblance of order. At times it all got too much for us and we found ourselves succumbing to 'worldly' temptations. One Saturday evening my sister Chris, who had left the Exclusive Brethren before us, invited us for dinner. During the drive to her house, we had a family discussion.

'Chris says they've hired a television set,' I said quietly to Denis.

'Well, we're not going to watch it,' he replied.

'Then we'd better tell the children now. We don't want to make a fuss when we get there.'

'Boys,' said Denis, over his shoulder to the children in the back seat, 'we're coming home straight after dinner. We don't want you watching the television. Do you understand?'

'Yes, Dad.'

We hadn't been to Chris's place for ages. We had always enjoyed their company, and Denis just loved her roast dinners. After the meal, we sat around the table and talked, telling them what had happened during the months when we were shut up. After a while I looked around and noticed that Ben and Angela and their cousins were missing. Growing bored with grown-ups' talk they had quietly slipped into the lounge and were sitting cross-legged on the floor in front of the TV.

'Come on, children, it's time for us to go,' said Denis.

'But Dad, we only just got here,' wailed Angela. 'Please can we just watch this one programme?'

'It's a good one,' said Chris, 'an English comedy about an old man and his young friend.'

We stood for a while and watched the opening scenes of *Spring and Autumn*. We watched as leaves danced on top of a clear stream of water, which tumbled over stones in time to the music.

'It's beautiful,' I breathed softly. 'How can they make it look so real?' I had never seen anything like it before. It was only black and white, but still it was magic. Before long, we were all sitting down, absorbed in the story of a special relationship between an old man and a boy, and marvelling at the realness and aliveness of the unfamiliar English countryside. It seemed to finish all too soon, and Denis was trying to move us on.

'The next one's an Australian serial about a part-Aborigine detective called Boney,' said Chris. 'You'd like this one, Denis.'

'Please, Dad,' pleaded Charlie.

'We'll go home after this one. We promise,' added Paul.

'All right,' said Denis. I could tell he was getting interested.

We stayed. The younger children fell asleep on the floor. The rest of us sat hypnotised by the sounds and the movement on the screen. *Boney* was followed by a Western. My eyes were sore and my head was aching, but still we stayed. The actors were using guns, and people were getting killed! All manner of dreadful things were happening. It looked so real. We were very quiet on the way home. That night, Denis and I couldn't sleep. Every time I shut my eyes I could see the guns, hear the gunfire and feel the pain. The next day we went fishing at Manukau Heads with Mum and Dad. They didn't know about the television. None of us mentioned it, but we all moved round like zombies through lack of sleep and over-stimulation. Although Mum and Dad had been out of fellowship longer than us, they still lived like Brethren and expected us to do the same. They would have been horrified had they known how worldly we had suddenly become.

It wasn't long before we had grown accustomed to the worldly pleasures of television, and had a TV set of our own. This process of being seduced by television had its funny side. But the flip side was that because we had watched it against our earlier convictions, our consciences told us we were no match for the Devil and we were already slipping into worldly ways just like the Brethren said always happened. We had to live with this guilt and confusion. Now that one fence was down, were any boundaries going to remain, or was our family going to be a walkover for the Devil?

During those first few months, we still thought about going back before we got 'hooked by the world'. Denis still wanted to go back. He didn't say much, but I knew he was missing the Brethren, and the meetings. I know he didn't feel rejected by God, but he felt that God was displeased with him. He couldn't see that maybe it was God's will that we were on the outside.

I will never know, for sure, whether initially Denis made contact with the Exclusive Brethren priests or whether they approached him first. He told me years later, after many more visits with them, that the priests could not understand why we had never asked to return to the fellowship. All I know is that there was a meeting between them one night, and I believe Denis told them that he was finding it difficult living on the outside and wanted to return.

'Ngaire, I have spoken with the priests,' he told me.

'What did they want?'

'They told me that my right place is with the Assembly. Quiet submission to the Assembly judgement, and diligence to learn the lesson involved, would see the household back in line with the truth and fellowship happily restored. They said that I know the right thing to do and so I should do it.'

'Does that mean that you should leave me?' My voice was shaking.

'That's what it amounts to if you won't submit,' he answered, wrapping his arms even tighter around me. 'But I would be required to do it properly; morally, physically and legally.'

'What do you mean by morally, physically, legally?' Those three words held a sinister threat.

'It means that you or I would have to move out of here and have no contact with each other. It would also mean that we would need a legal separation before I could break bread with them again. The priests say that it's the only right way.'

'Do you want to do that?'

'Yes, darling, I do want to go back, but I love you. I love the children too much to take them away from you, and I love the little baby you are carrying. I want to be there when you give birth, and forever,' he added simply. I could see that Denis was under unbelievable pressure. I knew that we were going through a crucial period where firm decisions had to be made because the Exclusive Brethren would be relentless in their pursuit of their so-called 'righteousness'.

'What about the Bible, Denis? Doesn't it say somewhere that the only ground for divorce is adultery?'

'Yes, but the Brethren only require a legal separation. They haven't said anything about divorce. I'm not going to divorce you; I'm sure that would be wrong. The Brethren don't agree with divorce, only separation.'

I knew how hard this was for Denis. Because it is important to the Exclusive Brethren that the children remain with the fellowship, Denis would have been expected to fight me to retain legal control of the children. He loved the Exclusive Brethren, and I am sure they had always held him in high regard. They had separated from him only because they believed it was the right thing to do in the circumstances. They always hoped that we would repent and return as a whole family as soon as possible. I was the problem. I think Denis and the Brethren eventually accepted the fact that I could and would keep him out of the fellowship indefinitely. We had been married for twelve years, and that night I felt overwhelmed by his love for me. This man loved me unconditionally. He loved and needed me so much that — with a little gentle persuasion — he was prepared to give up the Exclusive Brethren for me! I knew without a shadow of a doubt that I loved him, too — too much to let him go without a fight.

Although I was glad that Denis wanted to stay with me, I was angry with the priests for suggesting otherwise. I wrote them a letter. I told them that if they dared to set foot inside our property again, to talk to Denis or the children, I would call the police. This was no idle threat; I meant every word of it. I was behaving like a wild animal protecting her litter. Of course, they took no notice of me. I was only a woman and, as such, was held in disdain. They just arranged to come when I was out or they met Denis elsewhere.

The priests continued to visit him about every six months or so for the next twenty years, and you can be sure that none of these visits were for social reasons. They had only one thing in mind: to see if anything had changed that would allow Denis back into fellowship with them. They probably felt duty-bound to provide some spiritual nurture and comfort to Denis in his difficult circumstances. He was seen to be suffering 'governmentally'. He was seen at heart to be one of them, while I was not. I have very little knowledge of the real nature of those visits, apart from the fact that they assured him that they were praying for me to 'get right', but I do know that he remained faithful to me for the rest of his life.

Victoria was born early in 1975. She signalled the dawning of a new life for us. Before I left the hospital, I had my tubes cut and tied. Vicky was to be our last child. Like all the others she was beautiful; with long dark hair, big dark eyes and long black eyelashes. I wanted to do something for Vicky that I had never been able to do for the others. I wanted to breast-feed her. It wasn't that the Exclusive Brethren didn't believe in breast-feeding; there just wasn't the time to do it. Our lives had always been too stressed, too busy to sit and relax. I was sure that, with all the extra time I had now, I would be able to do it. However, by the time I had left the hospital she was on a bottle. I found an advertisement in the local newspaper and contacted the ladies at La Leche League who were offering help and support for breast-feeding mothers. They were so nice. They were my first real social contact with the outside world, and they went out of their way to help. I think they were surprised at my tenacity. This was something I was determined to do, and with their help I eventually succeeded. For some reason, Vicky was not able to suck properly. For five months I pumped off my milk ten times a day and fed it to her from a bottle. At the same time I was trying to get her to take it directly. I almost gave up. Then it happened. It was in the May school holidays and Denis had taken the older children away for a few days. I fed Vicky water from a spoon for two days until she was very hungry, then at last she latched on. I went on to breast-feed her for nearly a year. It seems now to be such a small victory, but at the time I knew I was doing something quite unusual and special. I had also proved something to myself.

23

Learning a new culture

I gradually made friends on the outside, and one in particular stands out from the rest. Her name was Helen. Vicky was only a few months old when I met Helen at the Meremere drag-strip one Saturday afternoon. We were sitting on the grass watching the stock-cars racing.

'Hello, Ngaire,' she said, dropping to the ground beside us. 'I'm Helen, one of the ladies in the knitting class.' I recognised her then. I was a little apprehensive. Helen was smoking! Her language was what the Exclusive Brethren would call rough, coarse, even a little blasphemous at times! In fact, Helen was everything we had been taught to avoid! With a heart of gold, she was a self-professed collector of lame ducks, and she became my best friend. I turned to Helen for instructions when I didn't know how to react or cope, or when I needed a sympathetic ear. She taught me to look in the mirror and like what I saw there.

Life on the outside was difficult. We were gradually learning how to behave in public. I know that sounds strange, but I think anyone who leaves a cult or a strictly controlled group would experience similar difficulties. We had to learn a different way of life in the same way as people who immerse themselves in a foreign culture. One of the problems was deciding how much of the former lifestyle was of value and what could be dispensed with. Although we wished to keep a high standard of values for our family, we no longer had arbitrary rules to live by. We were unused to making discretionary decisions. When in fellowship, we heard warning accounts of how quickly Brethren who leave the fellowship give up their standards and are seduced by the world and its pleasures. We wanted to show ourselves to be strong and not let that happen to us.

We had a way of dressing and speaking that other people laughed at. We used 'Brethrenisms' — words and expressions that other people didn't understand in quite the same way we did. There were so many life situations where we just didn't know what to do. One of the big challenges was how to discipline our children effectively.

Previously, we knew only how to say 'No'. In fact, we were often too strict. When the children asked, 'Why not?' we had said, 'Because we are Exclusive Brethren and we don't do that.' The Exclusives had power and control over us, and we in turn treated our children in the same way. Our (self) discipline was extreme, and at times severe, yet so simple, so automatic. It is just so easy to say no without having to think. For one's conduct to be regulated by obedience and submission was then of highest value; to be regulated by love or respect was rather suspect. Now that we were cut adrift from the whole authority hierarchy we had very few in-house rules that we could depend on. We were floundering, full of uncertainties. We wanted to give the children reasons for our decisions. For example, Charlie's friend Gary invited him to his birthday party. Gary's grandfather, who owned the picture theatre, had arranged seats for them to watch the latest children's film. We wanted to say no because that was the easiest response, the one we were familiar with. But why? We needed a reason for saying no. How did we know if the film was suitable for a ten year old? We didn't. We needed to find out, but how? We looked at the advertisement in the local paper. That didn't tell us much. We had nothing to *measure* anything by; it was beyond our limited experience. It wasn't so bad when the children were young: a children's film was probably okay, but how would we know about such things as they grew older? We did learn, but the learning was painful.

It took me a long time to realise that people were not 'out to get me', or wanting to find fault with every little thing I did, or wanting to lure me into wickedness. It took a while to understand that other people just wanted to be helpful. I had been used to a painfully authoritarian regime where constant disapproval seemed to be normal. I was still on the defensive, just waiting for someone to pounce on me and find fault. I expected it to happen; I was always waiting for some kind of criticism. One day I had a phone call from the headmaster of Paul's school.

'Mrs Thomas, I would like you to come and see me, please,' said Mr Smythe. 'I want to talk to you about Paul, about the books he's reading.'

My heart sank. Apprehension set in immediately. I quickly tried to remember the titles of his latest books. 'What's the problem? Has he done something wrong?' I asked.

'No, no, nothing to worry about.' I think he sensed my anxiety.

I was relieved, but deep down inside I felt fearful that Mr Smythe was going to find fault with me somehow. I was so used to being in the wrong. This simple summons unnerved me. I had joined the local library and because Paul loved to read I often handed books on to him when I had finished reading them. I racked my brains to recall if I had taken any books home that might be considered unsuitable. Our reading had been so restricted as Exclusive Brethren. Now I was starting to be more adventurous, but I couldn't help feeling guilty in case I had inadvertently given Paul something to read that was inappropriate. I needn't have worried.

'Are you aware, Mrs Thomas, that Paul has been reading *King Solomon's Mines*?'

'Yes, I remember reading it when I was at school. When I saw it in the library, I wanted to read it again. I let Paul read it when I'd finished. Have I done something wrong?'

'No,' he hurriedly reassured me. 'When you read it you were probably in high school. I was surprised that Paul was reading and understanding it at such a young age. He's a good reader, so try to keep him interested in books, and give him a wide variety of subjects to choose from.'

Vicky was a real family baby, and the older children had kept their promise to help me in the house. I began looking round for something interesting to do. Even though I had five children to look after, life was so much more relaxed than the hectic life we had been living before. I needed a challenge.

'Denis,' I said one night after dinner when the children were in bed. 'I went to see the man in the sewing shop today. He asked me if I was ready to start teaching again.'

'Are you sure you can cope with the extra work? What about Vicky?'

'I can cope. He said I could take Vicky along, too. Other mothers will have children; we'll organise a crèche. I might even start teaching at night.'

'Sounds okay. If you're happy, go for it. I'll help you as much as I can.'

'He said the business is for sale if we know anyone who is interested.' I said tentatively. 'I wondered if we could buy it.'

'How much?'

'He didn't say. Perhaps we could both go and see him tomorrow. I've already told him that you enjoyed repairing sewing machines when you worked for Dad.'

It was the middle of 1975, and by the end of the year we had bought ourselves a business. In hindsight, this proved to be the very best thing we could possibly have done. For the first two months, Denis worked in the shop, learning the trade from the original owner. Poor Denis, he was so scared of the customers at first. As soon as someone walked in the front door, he would disappear out the back!

Very few Exclusive Brethren owned retail shops, and we could see why. The hours were long. Late nights and Saturday trading meant more time away from the family. Taking Vicky with me, I helped in the shop during the day while the older children were at school. I continued teaching knitting and sewing classes in the evenings, while Denis stayed home with the children. It was hard work but we enjoyed it.

The four older children were technically still in fellowship with the Exclusive Brethren. They had not been withdrawn from because they had not done anything wrong, yet. Paul and Charlie were, by now, twelve and thirteen — old enough to know that it would take something quite serious to warrant being withdrawn from. If they got into trouble with the police, that should do it. Better still if they could annoy the Exclusive Brethren at the same time! One night, they went down the street near the meeting room, looking for full bottles of milk to pinch. They lined the bottles up on the meeting room steps, stood back a little and fired shots at them with an air rifle. Ping, ping, ping. One by one they broke the bottles, spreading glass and milk all over the steps. One of the Exclusive Brethren Brothers, living near by, caught them.

'Are you going to take us to the police station?' one of the boys asked hopefully.

'No, I'm taking you to your father.'

That plan hadn't worked; better try another one. A while later, they broke into another Brother's garage and stole a carton of the Exclusives' preferred brand of whisky. After taking the whisky home, and hiding it in the back of their wardrobe, they took a few bottles to school and shared them with their classmates. One of the teachers caught them and made them pour the remainder down the drain.

'Are you going to report us to the police?' they asked.

'Not this time. I'm going to report you to your father,' said the teacher, and he did.

Once again their plans were thwarted. They would try again some years later, with more serious consequences.

Denis usually took this sort of thing quite calmly. He didn't rant and rave, or shout, or thrash the living daylights out of them. He handled most situations well, but at times he seemed almost detached, as if it wasn't happening. This sort of thing was very tough. At times like this they didn't seem to be our children, and in a way they weren't because they were a product of an abnormal upbringing. I usually got quite emotional when the children misbehaved. I took it all personally, with lots of recriminations, blaming myself; if only I had . . . and all that sort of nonsense. In fact I felt guilty about a lot of things. I knew that I should let Denis go. I knew he was unhappy. The boys were playing up and we didn't know how to handle it. I thought maybe if Denis took them back to the Exclusive Brethren they would settle down.

I went through a period of deep dark depression. I was overloaded with stress. I decided to leave him. I planned it for weeks. I didn't want Denis or the children to know that I was going to leave. There were so many things I had to do first. The deep freeze was huge, and it would need to be full. I baked the family's favourite foods and packed them into the freezer. It was autumn, so I bottled countless jars of Denis's favourite preserves. The pantry was filled with jars of beetroot, peaches, pears, strawberry jam and lemon honey. Denis was a hopeless cook; he would need all these things to help him get through the first few weeks until someone else could help him, or until the Exclusive Brethren found him another wife. I know that sounds a bit irrational; Denis couldn't marry again without a divorce so my imagination must have been working overtime! But don't laugh, it wasn't funny at the time. I was dead serious. I had it all worked out in my mind. Vicky, of course, would come with me. She didn't belong to the Brethren because she had never been baptised by them. The other children would probably stay with Denis. I washed and ironed and folded and stitched until all their clothes were ready. Then I set about making a few new dresses for Angela. She would miss her shorts and jeans, but she wouldn't be able to wear them when she returned to the fellowship.

Although Denis had seen me crying into the sink several times, I was very careful not to make him suspicious, just fobbing him off with remarks like 'It's probably PMT.' I mustered all my strength to appear as calm as possible in front of the family, but inside I was a mess. At last everything was ready and the day I had planned to leave had arrived. I went to see Helen. I needed somewhere to sleep that night, and for a few days until I could sort myself out. I explained that I would need to look after the children until Denis came home from work, and then I would slip away. She seemed a bit doubtful about my plan but she said there would always be a bed for me at her house.

It had seemed easy enough when I was planning it in my head, but carrying it out was a different matter. It was the ultimate sacrifice for the man I loved, but I didn't really want to go. The car was packed and Vicky was sitting in the back. I locked the car doors and started the engine ready to slip out before I lost my resolve. Denis appeared in the doorway, saw the car packed up and knew immediately that I was leaving. I will never forget the look on his face as he desperately tried to get the car doors open. Tears streamed down my face when I saw him move to the back of the car and dare me to run him over. Helen was very pleased not to have a house guest that night.

Denis was a very affectionate man and he loved me very much. Although he had tentatively thought about leaving me and returning to the Exclusives, the possibility that I might leave had never occurred to him. We talked that night, kissed and cuddled then talked some more. Denis explained that being out of fellowship was devastating to him but not having me beside him would be worse. There was still that one point where he couldn't agree with the Brethren. Denis believed that the Bible did not support a legal separation between husband and wife unless one of them had been unfaithful to the other.

I wondered why the Exclusive Brethren expected a legal separation. Couldn't we just live together and let Denis go to the meetings? No. The MOG had made that quite clear. It had to be a physical, moral and legal separation before Denis could attend any meetings and break bread with them again. He wasn't prepared to do that, and he said the priests wouldn't put pressure on him to do that because they wanted a 'whole' household.

Years later, Paul told me what I think I have always known: if Denis had gone back, then he and probably the other boys would have willingly gone back, too.

Angela and Ben started attending a Sunday school class at the Baptist Church. Paul and Charlie didn't want to go, and Denis and I were not ready for church just yet. We continued our ritual of praying and reading together, every day, with the family. Denis read to me each morning, still praying faithfully for me to give my heart to Jesus, as he had done consistently for the past fifteen years. His prayers were answered at eleven o'clock on Thursday morning, 26 August 1977. I was staying with some friends in Whangaparoa for a few days, and I had picked up a little book off their bookcase called *God's Truth Made Simple*. I sat on a wooden seat at Little Manly, overlooking the Whangaparoa Harbour looking towards Auckland. I read that little book from cover to cover. When I had finished reading it, I held it in my hands while I prayed to a God that I had heard so much about, but whom I had never met. I turned the book over and reread the title. *God's Truth Made Simple.* It did seem simple; very simple. All I had to do was believe. I stood and turned toward the trees on my right. I saw what appeared to be an image of light. This was the first of many encounters with a deity I shall call God. I have always had difficulty differentiating between the three parts of the Christian God, but at this point it didn't seem to matter. I sensed a voice, which I think came from somewhere inside me, saying: 'Come, follow me, I'll show you the way.'

I knew that God had spoken to me. I heard myself replying, 'But if I follow you, you will lead me back to the Exclusive Brethren.' Although I instinctively wanted to please this 'God Vision', and I had been taught that the Exclusive Brethren were God's chosen people, going back to them was by now the last thing I wanted to do.

'No,' the voice said. 'I have other work for you to do. I want you to talk to people about me while you are teaching them practical things.'

'What will I talk to them about?' I asked.

'To start with you could talk to them about the weather: it belongs to me, and most people want to talk about it sooner or later. That will be your cue.'

'Okay, God, you've got yourself a deal.'

'There's one thing I want you to do first.'

'What's that?' I asked, thinking that surely this time God would suggest that I go back to where I had come from.

'Throw your cigarettes into the water,' God said very gently, 'and the lighter.'

I had first tried cigarettes because I thought it was cool. I had been smoking for only about two months and I didn't like it much anyway. I didn't mind giving them up! I stood and threw the whole packet into the sea, followed by my cigarette lighter. I returned to my friend's house and rang Denis at the shop.

'Denis, I have just asked Jesus into my heart.' It was so simple. No need to understand everything. No bells and whistles. It was just a feeling of a private contract between God and me. Denis was so pleased. He had prayed for me every day that I might give my heart to the Lord. I felt sorry for Denis. He had been so faithful for so long. Now that I had changed at last we were no longer within the fellowship that he loved so much. I battled with this for ages. I wanted to do the right thing, for Denis, for the children and for me. My first thought had been that I would need to return to the Exclusives, but I had found something bigger and better. I had previously thought that you couldn't be a *proper* Christian unless you were breaking bread with those who had the Light of the Assembly. Now I had my doubts about that. The more Christians I associated with on the outside, the more the Exclusive Brethren lifestyle lost its Christian significance. I was meeting people who had made a real and personal choice, not had a choice made for them by others.

I started going along to the Baptist Church with the three youngest children. It was a long time before Denis joined us. One Saturday evening I went, with several other Baptist women, to a meeting at the Baptist Tabernacle in Auckland. It was a cold, wet and blustery night — the kind of night when every sane person should be snuggled up in front of the fire with a mug of hot chocolate. It was definitely not the kind of night for going to a Christian meeting, if you had the choice. I had the choice, and I wanted to go. So, obviously, did hundreds of others. I looked around the crowded room at all those happy faces; faces of people who had given up a quiet night by the fire to attend this meeting. 'This is amazing,' I thought. 'All these people are here because they want to be here, not because some attendance officer might come and ask questions if they weren't!' I felt the same thing the following summer when I was sitting in another church overlooking the sea. The day was hot and sticky, just the right kind of day to lie on the beach and soak up the sun. But inside this church were hundreds of worshippers, singing, praying, praising God, and *enjoying* themselves. These people were for real. Even the teenagers were joining in. Another phenomenon I found was women's Bible study groups. Women gathered in large and small groups to talk to each other about the scriptures, and to pray. They prayed for one another, for people who were sick, for our nation and for the world. And they prayed for me. I was hesitant at first, but after a while I joined in with the discussions and found that I had something worthwhile to contribute.

The spark in my heart grew. One day, I saw two Exclusive Brethren Sisters cross the road before they reached our shop and walk along on the other side. I had an overwhelming desire to rush out to them, throw my arms around them and tell them at last I understood. I now loved God and I loved them, too. I checked myself in time. There was no way that they would have responded to my exuberant greeting. They would have remained as poker-faced as always. The realization that they would not be able to understand or accept my conversion as real confirmed my resolve never to return to them.

The phone rang one evening, and I recognised the voice. It was one of the priests. Knowing how much I resented the Exclusive Brethren keeping in touch with him, Denis reluctantly admitted that he had told them they could visit the next night while I was at a Parent Teacher Association meeting. The priests wanted to speak to the children. I had wondered how long it would be before they started to put real pressure on them. Bother, the PTA meeting would take about two hours, and although I had told them never to come to the house, just for this once I wanted to be home when the priests came. Although they visited Denis regularly, they always came when I was out, or Denis would meet them somewhere on his own. Instead of ringing the police as I had threatened, I agreed they could visit. I had something else in mind.

I got Paul and Charlie together to help me form a plan. I wanted to tape the conversation. I knew the priests wouldn't come into the house; they would talk in the front entrance with the connecting door shut. Paul and Charlie set up the tape recorder and microphone so that they only needed to flick a switch at the right time and the tape would start recording. I asked the boys to ring me at the school as soon as the priests arrived. I wanted to arrive home while the priests were on the doorstep, knowing full well that I would be shut out of the conversation if I were inside the house. I had no personal desire to speak to them, or listen to them for that matter, except that I imagined they were after my kids!

All went according to plan. The boys set the recorder going, rang me at school and then stood around in the front entrance while the priests talked.

'Mum's a Christian now,' said Charlie proudly and enthusiastically to the priests.

'No, she's not,' answered one of them. 'We will know when your Mother becomes a Christian.'

'How will you know?' asked Charlie, slightly deflated when his news was not accepted.

'She will let her hair grow long again, she will stop wearing trousers and she will ask to come back into the fellowship,' they explained.

It was about this time that I turned up. I walked up the path to the front door and stood to one side. Unfortunately, the priests were not prepared to say any more in my presence. I listened to the tape after they'd left, and laughed at their criteria for me becoming a Christian. It was all about outward appearances, nothing about the change I had made in my heart. I was glad that God didn't care what I looked like!

I don't like to say 'I became a Christian' because I am aware that so many 'Christians' will want to claim this special experience to confirm their own particular concept of what it means to be a Christian. My experiences were unique, deeply personal, compulsive and related to a stage in my spiritual growth. They were an experience with God that I don't connect with any particular church following. My conversion was none the less very real. I had changed. I developed a hunger and a thirst for spirituality. I read and studied the Bible in several different translations and many other books about the Christian way of life. I bought audiotapes of Christian songs and especially loved the *Scripture in Song* chorus collections. I was like a giant sponge, joining Bible study and discussion groups and absorbing spiritual qualities from other people. At last I was living a full, productive and meaningful life.

Denis was thrilled with the change in me. I was drawing on his knowledge of the Bible, and for the first time in our married life we had a common interest in spiritual things. I had become softer, more compassionate towards the Exclusives. I understood them better; I had more empathy with them, and in my heart I was ready to forgive them.

That very special day in August 1977 would be the beginning of my remarkable working relationship with God, but it didn't lessen a mother's heartache when her children continued to be in trouble with the law.

24

You've got to take your medicine

Vicky sat on the broad kitchen window sill with her little feet resting on the bench. She had a tea towel in her hand and was drying the unbreakables. I was crying into the sink, depressed, worried and maybe even a little crazy. I had woken up that morning with a strange phrase rolling around in my head. 'Nail up the doors and windows, nail up the doors and windows.' I tried to shake it off but it kept coming back, repeating itself over and over.

'Mummy, Jesus can make you better; but you still have to take your medicine.' She was not yet three years old but had an uncanny understanding far beyond her age.

I cried even harder. Her profound statement reminded me of the scripture old Mr Bates had given me years ago: 'God, slow to anger, and abundant in goodness and truth, keeping mercy unto thousands, forgiving iniquity and transgression and sin, but by no means clearing the guilty; visiting the iniquity of the fathers upon the children, and upon the children's children, upon the third and upon the fourth generation.' (Exodus 34:6–7 Darby.) It seemed as though the Exclusive Brethren predictions were coming true, Satan was attacking my children. I had looked out the kitchen window that morning and I just knew that the boys had been out during the night again. The shop van had been parked in a slightly different position to where I had left it the previous evening. I had suspected for some time that Paul and Charlie had been sneaking out at night after we were asleep. This time I felt confident enough of the facts to be able to ask them about it. When challenged, they said they were out in the dark catching eels in the creek. Although I knew they sometimes went down to the creek at night, I didn't believe them this time. Something was going on and I meant to find out what. I dried my tears, finished the dishes and dressed Vicky. We were going out.

In the back of the van I had found a pair of shoes. They didn't belong to our boys and I knew they hadn't been there the night before. I had an idea they might belong to Steve or Joe, Paul and Charlie's best friends. Joe's house would be my first stop. The dog barked loudly as we walked up the path towards the house. I knew Joe's mum. We often had coffee together, talking about our children and trying to keep one step ahead of them.

'I wouldn't mind a dog like this one,' I said, remembering the strange message and wondering if maybe we needed protection. 'He makes plenty of noise when visitors arrive, doesn't he?'

'Yes, he's a good guard dog, barks at every little noise during the night. Sometimes I have to yell at him to be quiet.'

'That's what I need. I wonder if he would bark if someone was leaving the house.' I laughed, but I was deadly serious. Nail up the doors and windows. Did that mean someone was going to break in, or was it the other way round?

Without mentioning the message, I told my friend about my fears that the boys were up to no good, and showed her the shoes.

'Yes, they're Joe's, and they're damp. He must have been with them.'

'We don't know if they are up to something; maybe they *were* just catching eels.' I was trying hard to convince myself. 'Maybe I'm overreacting.'

As we left the house, I glanced back at the dog. I wondered where I could get one. I had a heavy feeling of impending doom. Something was about to happen, and I had to stop it. The feeling stayed with me all day. After lunch I drove to Auckland city to pick up Sue. Sue was my cousin, and she was staying with us for the weekend. She was fifteen, the same age as Joe and a little older than Paul. I think she fancied Joe. She often spent weekends with us, and Joe was a frequent visitor, especially when Sue was there.

It was a Friday afternoon, 4 November, a day I'll never forget. I had been aware of God's spiritual guidance for several months. I had learned the art of conversational prayer, and so I talked to God all the way into Auckland that afternoon. I told him about my heavy feeling and about my concerns for the boys. I often talked to God like this. I don't think I always expected answers. It was good just having a sympathetic ear.

'Nail up the doors and windows,' He said. I turned my head. Did I hear a voice, or was I imagining it? It was that same message again.

I listened. I could hear it again and again. Nail up the doors and windows. Nail up the doors and windows.

'You look worried. What's the matter?' asked Sue on the way home. I told her about the message. 'I didn't hear anything,' she said.

All the way home, the message continued. I could hear it in the noise of the tyres on the road. I could hear it in the wind. Maybe Vicky was right. Perhaps I needed to take some medicine to make me better, or even worse perhaps I needed some time in a mental hospital. I was not only depressed I was going crazy! I was not my normal happy self that evening. The uneasy feeling continued; so did the message. Nail up the doors and windows, nail up the doors and windows. 'Okay, God, I'm listening!'

There was a knock on the door that night. It was Joe. His face looked white.

'I've just seen an accident on the corner. I talked to the police. I had to describe what happened. No one was badly hurt but it gave me a fright,' explained Joe, his teeth still chattering.

'I'll ring your mum and tell her I'll bring you home after you've had a hot drink,' offered Denis.

I had a sudden urge to talk to Joe about God. I went on and on, preaching to him, asking him questions. I asked him if he knew Jesus who had died on the cross at Calvary to save him from sin. 'Joe, what if you had been involved in that accident tonight? Would you have cried out to Jesus for help?' All the children sat there listening, with their mouths open. They knew I had started believing in God, but in a very quiet and conservative way. This was a very different Mum to the one they usually knew.

'Come on, Mum, that's enough, he gets the message,' said Paul, slightly embarrassed at my outburst.

'I'll take you home now, Joe,' said Denis quietly.

'What was all that about?' Denis asked me later that night. 'I've never heard you go on like that before. Poor Joe, he wondered what had struck him.'

'I don't know, Denis, it just came out.' I tried to explain to Denis about how I was feeling, and about the message I'd been receiving all day. He was very kind and patient. He put his arms around me and gave me a hug.

'I loved it when you got all fired up like that. I was proud of you for what you said, but seriously, I think you might be overtired. Why don't you take a break for a while? Take some time off with Vicky and spend a few days doing nothing. I can manage the shop.'

'I might,' I sighed. I was busy. I worked hard at the shop, teaching classes and taking my turn at the counter. I could do with a break. But now my mind was in turmoil. I needed to make sure my family was safe from whatever it was that might happen. I had a feeling that Sue was in danger too. She was a guest and I needed to protect her. I needed some way of being alerted to any unusual comings or goings within the house. I tied things to a long piece of string: a tin jug, a wooden spoon, the eggbeater, some tin mugs, anything I could find in the kitchen that would make a noise when they clanged together.

'What are you doing?' asked Denis.

'I'm going to tie this end to the girls' bedroom door like this; the other end I will tie to our door,' I explained as I added more things to the string. 'That way I will know if they leave their room in the middle of the night because all these things will clang together if someone opens the door.'

'You don't have to do this,' said Denis. 'They will be all right, nothing is going to happen.' He gave me a reassuring smile.

'I have to be sure. I want to nail up all the doors and windows, too.'

Denis gave a big sigh; he was such a patient and loving man. 'I'll help you then, but I don't want you to go hammering nails into our new front door.'

I knew that Denis was only humoring me. He didn't really believe anything would happen, but he went along with it. He went out to the garage and brought in his toolbox and some nails. We had an old house with seven doors to the outside, not counting the front door. Denis nailed them all up, the windows too. Our house was like Fort Knox, except for the front door. That could be locked from the inside. No one could get in. But I was still worried because someone could get out.

'Come with me,' said Denis. 'We are going to kneel down in front of the doorway and pray. "Our dear God and heavenly Father, we are mindful of your promise to protect all those who call upon the name of your Son Jesus Christ. We ask for your protection this night, for our family and for our house. In the name of the Lord Jesus, Amen." Everything will be all right,' he said. Denis led me to bed and carefully tied the other end of the piece of string to our bedroom door, leaving it slightly ajar. We talked for a few minutes, prayed once more, switched off the light and settled down for the night. We didn't wake till the phone rang early the next morning. What follows is the gist of what happened that night, pieced together from what Paul and Charlie told us as they solemnly sat on the end of our bed.

Around midnight, there was a knock on the boys' bedroom window.

'Come on you guys, get Sue, and hurry up.'

'We can't open the window; go around to the front door.' They said this several times and finally made themselves understood. Charlie and Paul, still in their clothes, slipped out of bed, went to the front door and opened it. They stood just inside the door. Outside were their three friends: Joe, Steve and Craig.

'Come on, you said you'd come with us,' said Joe.

'We can't, Mum's gone crazy. She thinks something dreadful is going to happen. She'll probably come out and catch us any minute now,' said Paul.

'She's nailed up all the doors and windows,' added Charlie.

'Come on, don't take any notice of her, she's gone potty.'

'No,' said both boys. 'We're not coming, neither is Sue.'

'Okay, suit yourselves, if you want to be wimps,' they called, as the three older boys walked away.

It was very early the next morning that the phone rang. It was Joe's father. One of the boys answered the phone.

'Is Joe at your place?' his father asked.

'No, he's not here. Let us know if you can't find him.' The boys were worried. Joe's father rang back a little later.

That's when Paul and Charlie came into our room and sat on the bed. 'Something terrible has happened,' they explained. 'Joe's dead.'

Gradually, during the day, we were able to piece together the events of the night. The whole thing was planned, and had been for days. Joe, Paul and Charlie, their two friends and Sue, six of them, all young teenagers, were going on a joy-ride. They planned to steal a big and powerful car from a market gardener, visit some girls, and hopefully take them along for the ride. That was the plan, and that's what they did, but only three boys went out that night. After a brief visit to the girls, the boys decided on their way home to try the car for speed. They drove through a cutting, going faster and faster. The car was going too fast. They couldn't slow it down in time to make the corner. The car flew over the fence, rolled over, and over, and over, and landed in a paddock. It was after one o'clock in the morning. The driver was okay, just a few cuts and bruises, and a bit shaken. The boy in the back seat flew through the window and broke his back. Joe, in the front passenger seat, came off worst. By the time help arrived, Joe was dead.

This was the first time any of us had come so face to face with death. The whole family went to church the next morning. We were mourning the loss of a young friend, but humbly thankful that our own sons and cousin had been spared.

This was an incredible experience. I have read about people receiving messages and premonitions of disaster, but I found it hard to believe that this kind of thing actually happened — especially to someone as down to earth as me. It didn't save Joe's life, and I'm sorry and puzzled about that, but glad that my own children were safe. I felt very humble. I knew then that God had spoken to me. It was almost as if God had been preparing me for it for months.

It was more than intuition. I may be wrong, but it was like God was talking to me, warning me, wanting me to do what I was told, even to the point of making a fool of myself. I had never experienced anything like that before. I felt as if God had chosen me, set me apart, taken me out of the Exclusive Brethren fellowship for a reason. I felt that I had a destiny, a special purpose in life. It was almost, you might say, supernatural, like a miracle. I don't think the Exclusives ever had that kind of experience. If they did, I didn't hear about it. This was a different kind of spirituality; more real and practical, like a two-way working arrangement.

The accident made a difference to the boys' behaviour for a time, but the effects wore off after a while. I remember the boys painting their bedroom wall and including a graveyard scene featuring a headstone with Joe's name on it. Yes, it did affect them for a while, but they soon started playing up again.

Because my experience was something quite alien to Denis, he was awed by the possibility that I'd genuinely received a message of some kind. He believed me because he had always loved and respected me, even though he sometimes found it hard to understand my way of thinking. We now had more in common, and something very special to share together. He felt that God had indeed spoken to me, and he was delighted with the changes in my attitude, but he didn't really understand the intense spirituality of it.

Denis was very conservative, in the traditional, fundamentalist Exclusive Brethren style. He believed in the Holy Spirit, but not in the 'baptism of the Holy Spirit' — miracles, speaking in tongues, divine intervention and all that sort of thing. He accepted that supernatural things did sometimes happen, but he didn't understand or expect them. The Brethren had drilled it into us that these supernatural occurrences had to be 'signs and wonders of the Devil' because they were outside the Brethren belief system, and also, of course, outside their understanding.

Life got harder. I began to wonder once again if perhaps the Exclusive Brethren predictions of disaster were right. Everything they had warned us about seemed to be coming true. Honestly, our lives were a mess. At least my Christian faith was growing. I didn't really understand it all back then, but I was very receptive. I believe it was all part of my personal spiritual journey. The following year I was baptised at the Baptist Church.

I had already been baptised by the Exclusive Brethren when I was a baby because the Exclusives believe in household baptism. A baby is baptised upon the faith of the parents. Now I wanted to be baptised as a believer. It was my choice, not theirs.

My parents weren't at all pleased. They didn't accept my recent conversion either, nor the fact that I was going to a church. They believed that I had been converted at twelve, when I began to break bread with the Exclusives. I tried to tell them that that wasn't real, but they didn't believe me. Although Dad and Mum were out of the Exclusive Brethren fellowship, they still held most of their old beliefs. After being withdrawn from, they had been accepted into fellowship with a small group who were a breakaway fellowship of people who had rejected the MOG's behaviour at Aberdeen. This little group still held on to most of the Exclusive Brethren teachings, and so believed they were upholding the truth while the Exclusives had been deceived by the Aberdeen event.

There are confusing grades of wickedness involved here. The very worst, in the Exclusive Brethren opinion, would be the various breakaway groups such as the one my parents had joined. That's understandable; they had set up a separate table — Brethren-speak for starting a new group or fellowship. The next worst are the Open Brethren because their fellowship had supposedly begun with compromise. They were regarded with disdain rather than as serious rivals — even though that split occurred about one hundred-and-fifty years ago, in the mid-1800s.

Even joining the mainline churches like the Baptists, Anglicans or Methodists is not an acceptable thing to do. The Exclusive Brethren don't have much time for other Christians, and seem to be less condemnatory of ex-members who don't go anywhere. All mainstream churches are stereotyped as pathetic, wishy-washy, orthodox, degenerate versions of Christianity. They are seen as having quenched the Holy Spirit, who is now only free in the Exclusive Brethren fellowship. Of course, being baptised by the Baptists, or any other denomination, only compounds their disapproval.

Family life didn't automatically get better just because I had changed. It got worse.

Charlie ran away again. He was fourteen, and this time he was gone for three months. We eventually found him picking fruit in an orchard in Nelson. He was determined not to return to school, so we left him there. Charlie was a hard worker. He was physically very fit and soon earned the respect of his workmates and employer. He passed quite easily for the sixteen years that he told them he was.

He eventually returned home, but we no longer had any semblance of control over either of our teenage sons. Those Exclusive Brethren predictions were like a curse. I won't go into the one hundred and one things that teenagers can do to bring their parents to their knees. We experienced them all. Nevertheless, I would like to tell some of those stories, like us becoming very young grandparents, and having two sons in prison at the same time.

25

The next generation

Charlie and Paul often brought friends home, mostly boys and occasionally a girl or two. There hadn't been any talk of anyone special, but then, parents are usually the last to know these things.

'Mum, can I invite Lisa home for dinner tonight?' Charlie asked one morning.

'Sure, who's Lisa? Have I met her?' I asked.

'No, you've not met her yet. I'll bring her around tonight. You'll like her,' he added.

'How old is she?' I asked. Charlie had had lots of girlfriends but this one sounded more serious.

'She's older than me — about fifteen and a half, I think.'

'We'll look forward to meeting her. I'll cook a roast.'

'Mum, you'll be careful what you say to her, won't you?' he cautioned. 'And don't let Dad put her through the third degree either.'

After dinner that night, Charlie, with his arm around Lisa, broke the news.

'Mum, Lisa and I are going to have a baby.'

Just like that. My mind went into hyper-drive. How did this happen? When? Where? Oh, no! These two are only children themselves and they're going to have a kid of their own! How would they cope?

How would I cope? How would Denis cope? What would my Dad and Mum think? And what about my brother Daniel? And the Exclusive Brethren, if they ever got to hear about it, what would they think?

'Why did you have to spring this on me so suddenly? Why couldn't you wait a few moments and tell your father at the same time?'

'Mum, you know how Dad goes on about things. We were hoping you could tell him for us,' said Charlie.

I was sick of being the go-between. It was always my job to smooth things out between Denis and the children.

'Denis, please come here,' I called. I grabbed Lisa and Charlie by the shoulders and turned them around to face Denis as he walked in the door. 'Charles and Lisa have something to tell us.'

'Dad, Lisa and I are going to have a baby,' Charlie repeated.

'Do your parents know about this, Lisa?'

'No,' said Lisa, looking at the ground.

'Get in the car you two. Paul, look after the children please, your mother and I are going out.'

Lisa's parents were as shocked as we were.

'They'll have to get married, of course,' said Denis after Lisa and Charlie had told her parents.

'No way,' said her mother. 'I think it would be best if you took your son home. We want to talk to Lisa on her own.'

When we got home, Charlie disappeared into his room and shut the door. It was no use talking to him, I thought; better to wait until tomorrow.

The next day Lisa came to see me. I was teaching a craft class in the Salvation Army Hall, so she sat and waited for me to finish. When the class was over and everyone had gone, Lisa helped me to clean up.

'Mrs Thomas,' she said, 'I'm scared.' I was, too, but I couldn't tell her that. We sat in the car and talked for a while. 'Mum says that I can't go home till I've had an abortion. She's made an appointment for me at National Women's Hospital this afternoon.'

'How are you going to get there? Is she going to take you?' I asked.

'No. She said I have to go in the bus, by myself.'

'You can't do that. I'll take you. But first I'll need to find someone to pick Vicky up from kindergarten.'

I organised that, then stopped to give Denis the message that I would be late home, and hurried home to put on a stew for the family's dinner. It was a forty-minute drive to the hospital in Auckland, plenty of time to find out what the story was.

'Do you want to have an abortion, Lisa?'

'I don't know. I don't know what they'll do. I only know that I can't go home till it's done.'

The poor kid, I thought. I couldn't expect her to go through this on her own. I didn't know much about abortion myself, but I knew Lisa would need some support. When I thought about it, I was a bit shocked that I was actually driving her to the hospital in the first place. Maybe I had been too hasty. I should have talked to Denis, or someone from the church. I remembered the time when my doctor had suggested an abortion to me, but it hadn't been an option I wanted to consider. The Exclusives didn't teach us much about the subject — only that it was sinful. Come to think of it, I can't remember hearing of any Exclusive Sister ever having had an abortion. If they did, they wouldn't admit it or they would be withdrawn from quick smart!

I parked the car at the hospital and we followed the directions Lisa had written on a piece of paper. We were told to sit in the waiting room till the doctor was ready to see us.

'Come with me, Lisa,' said a nurse. She led her down the passage and into a side room. I wondered if I should go in with her. No one suggested it so I just sat there idly flicking through a magazine. After a while the doctor came out.

'Are you Lisa's mother?' he asked.

'No, I'm the mother of the baby's father. Lisa is carrying my grandchild.' I don't know why I said that. It sounded as if I was proud of the fact. He led me into his office and I sat down beside Lisa.

'Lisa is past the time when we consider it safe to do an abortion,' he said. 'If we did an abortion now, we would be killing a baby that, if it had been born premature, would normally have some chance of living.' He proceeded to tell me exactly how it would be done.

'You can't do that. Come on, Lisa, let's get out of here.' I took her arm and started steering her toward the door.

'Mrs Thomas, I can't go home if I don't have an abortion.' I was amazed at how calm Lisa was. I was the one getting upset.

'Well, you can come and live with us then,' I offered.

'Sit down, Mrs Thomas. We need to talk about this,' said the doctor. 'If you are willing to look after Lisa for a few months, and if her parents agree, we can arrange temporary guardianship for her under your care. Near the end of her pregnancy, she could go into a special home where they look after young pregnant women. She could stay there for a while after the birth to get used to looking after the baby. You'll need to think about whether Lisa should keep the baby. There are always plenty of people wanting to adopt.'

It seemed like the best solution. I took her home with me. One more teenager in the family wouldn't make much difference. That night Denis and I talked about it.

'I wish you wouldn't make these decisions without talking to me first. I'm the head of the house and I have a right to decide who lives here.'

'I'm sorry, Den.' I had done it again — rushed headlong into something without thinking it through properly. 'I didn't know what else to do. I couldn't leave the poor girl there. I wanted to help. What would you have done, Den?'

'It's okay love, I would have done exactly the same as you,' he admitted. 'We'll manage somehow, although it won't be easy having Charlie and Lisa both here under the same roof.'

'I hadn't thought about that. What about after the baby comes? The doctor said something about adoption.'

'That won't be our decision. Charles and Lisa will need to decide that. Don't let's worry about it yet; there's plenty of time.'

Lisa and Charles decided on adoption. The baby just didn't seem real at first. However, by the time Rebecca was born, there was no way any of us wanted to part with her. I would have added her to my own family rather than have someone else take her away. Lisa and Rebecca stayed with us for several months, and then Charlie and Lisa rented a house so they could live as a family.

26

An upside-down world

It was all very well for two young teenagers and a baby to set up house, but finance was a big problem.

Charlie had a job, but not enough to pay the rent, power and food bills for the three of them. What they needed was a windfall of some sort, by fair means or foul. Charlie talked to Paul and together they worked out a plan. They decided to hold up a dairy. It was a daring plan, straight out of a television drama. They wouldn't hurt anyone; just frighten them into handing over some cash. It looked so easy on the television. Charlie was working for a friend of ours, a farmer. They 'borrowed' his shotgun. Paul and Charlie worked on it in the garage, sawing off the end to make it easier to hide. They needed help, someone with a car. Who better than their cousin Rick. They set off hitchhiking, with the gun wrapped in newspaper at the bottom of a duffel bag. They hadn't seen Rick for a while. He was still nominally an Exclusive Brethren but he had a keen sense of adventure and daring. It wouldn't do to knock on the door and ask for him. They would need to hide, and hope they could attract his attention somehow. They didn't have to wait long. Rick agreed to slip out after his parents were asleep and meet the boys at a motel in town.

The motel owner showed Charlie and Paul to a small unit near the road. By the time Rick arrived, they had hidden the gun, still wrapped in newspaper in the duffel bag, under one of the beds. They left the motel and went to look for a likely place to rob. Up to this point everything was going according to plan. They had decided where the robbery would take place and now they needed to work out a plan of action. They had only just returned to their motel room and closed the door when two policemen confronted them. One of the policemen was holding the gun, no longer in the duffel bag. The motel owner had become suspicious when two young teenagers, joined later by a third, booked into the motel for the night. As soon as the boys had left, he searched the rooms and found the gun under the bed. He had called the police, and here they were, confronting the three lads with the evidence of their planned escapade.

At the preliminary hearings at the local court, Rick was released into his parents' care, while Paul and Charlie were remanded to Mount Eden Prison to await sentencing at the High Court in Auckland. It's no fun sitting in a courtroom watching the guards escorting your sons in handcuffs. At times I felt detached from it all; rather like watching a horror film but not wanting to believe it was happening to us. In due course, the judge sentenced them both to three months in a prison for young offenders, on a charge of conspiring to commit an armed robbery.

When I write about it now it sounds like something out of a storybook. I don't remember it being so amusing at the time; I probably did more crying than laughing. Lisa and baby Rebecca came back to live with us while the boys were in prison. We went down to visit them several times, taking Lisa and the baby.

It was humiliating for us having two sons in prison. What would the Exclusives think? Denis was very upset, but he handled it well. He was always very supportive. This wasn't the first time the boys had been in trouble with the law, and it wouldn't be the last. Denis was always there for them, sitting through court hearings, bailing them out, and always lamenting the fact that he wasn't a good enough father, which of course wasn't true.

I often wonder why they got into so much trouble. It's not as if we weren't good parents, but even as I say that I realise that good parenting means different things to different people. I should have learned a few lessons from my own teenage years, but no, I let my children make the same mistakes. I remember old Mr Bates's scripture in Exodus; in a nutshell it means 'you have to be responsible for the consequences of your own actions.' Like a lot of other loving parents we kept rescuing our children, bailing them out, making it too easy for them. We had a lot to learn about tough love.

The boys seemed to have no social conscience — at that stage I suppose we weren't much better. In the fellowship, a child learned that survival depended on what you could get away with. We had never taught them how to interact with society, or how to accept responsibility for themselves and their actions. We were only just beginning to learn this for ourselves. But we were adults, mature enough to work out an acceptable way to behave.

Prison was good for Charlie and Paul. They loved it. I believe it was a very positive experience for both of them. They went in with long, thick, curly 'Afro' hairstyles, and came out with neatly trimmed hair, a style that they have kept to this day. That wasn't the only change, of course. They liked the discipline. They both earned reduced sentences for good behaviour but chose to stay for the full term. They enjoyed the exercise programme and often earned an extra dessert at dinner for completing the daily cross-country course ahead of the rest. The army-like discipline was something they understood, and after their prison experience they were both very eager to join the army. Ironically, because of their police records they were not permitted to do this. Yes, I think they would admit that prison did them a lot of good, although that didn't stop them from getting into more trouble.

So, at last, Paul and Charlie had earned a dishonourable discharge from the Exclusives. It was a shame it had to happen that way. I often wonder if their earlier attempts at petty crimes against the Brethren were what started them off.

There were some added problems. The older boys received a lot of attention, and the younger ones resented it. Copycat behaviour ensured the desired attention, and there were times when I wanted to 'divorce' the lot of them. It was very nice having such a close-knit family of young teenagers, but it had its obvious drawbacks, and for a while there we had all four of them acting out in some form or another. Someone advised us to let the older boys go their own way and concentrate on looking after the younger ones. This was not an option for us; all the children needed our love and care. We knew this and did the best we could to act in responsible ways.

Our position was a little different from the children's. We adjusted very well to life outside the fellowship because we were in control of our own lives at last. We called the shots, made our own choices, and fixed our own mistakes. The children had been taught a certain way of life; then, when we left the Exclusives, life changed without them knowing why. We didn't realise that we needed to teach them how to adjust to those changes. I don't think we handled the situation very well at all. We were so focused on our own personal adjustment that we lost touch with the rather different struggles the children were going through. This intensely difficult phase of our lives lasted for about ten years.

Vicky was a lot younger than the other children, and her reaction to what was happening around her was quite different. When Paul and Charlie went to prison, Vicky was in her first year of school. One day she drew a picture that said it all. She drew lots of people on a large sheet of paper, and then she drew a small person upside down in the middle. Well, that's how the teacher explained it, but Vicky kept turning the picture the other way up. 'I'm the only one standing on my feet in an upside-down world,' she said. That was very typical of her.

Vicky was never a member of the Exclusive Brethren because she wasn't born when we left. All the older children had social problems to some degree. They seemed to attract more trouble than the average kid. They will probably grapple with the effects of those years of conflict, turmoil and pressure for some time. Vicky was different. It was almost as if she was protected from that.

I have often thought about what we could have done differently. Given another chance, I would be more concerned for the children than for myself or Denis. We were adults, we understood better. The children were developing and the trauma stayed with them. That's something I reflect on with sadness. We were too preoccupied at the time to realise what was happening. Maybe other ex-members could have helped us to adjust, if we had let them. We didn't know very many, and Denis discouraged me from contacting others apart from family. There was always the mindset that it might undermine their chances — and ours — of ever being restored to the fellowship. At that stage we still saw ourselves as wicked people. We even believed that other people who had been withdrawn from were wicked. We had been very well instructed in the art of making negative judgements.

I would also be a lot more careful about criticising the Exclusives in front of the children. When we first came out, I said a lot of things against the Brethren. The children only heard about the bad things. We didn't say much to them about all the good and positive things. Denis and I had our memories, probably as many good ones as bad, but we didn't talk much about the good times, or share them with the children. Consequently, they were more disparaging of the Exclusive Brethren than they might have been had our conversation been more balanced. This was mostly my fault.

I was quite convinced that we had been cursed, and eventually Denis began to feel the same. At the time it seemed the only reason for so many things going wrong, one after the other. I'm sure the Exclusive Brethren don't believe in placing curses on people. I'm not even sure if you can put a curse on someone unwittingly. I think they would be horrified at the thought. They might imply that disaster will befall you, but they don't actually say it.

Some years after we left the Brethren, we were given a book to read about curses and blessings. The author pointed out that some things are 'spoken into' our lives so that we believe them. Then, when something negative happens repeatedly, it is possible that a curse is the reason. We were desperate. At first Denis wouldn't believe it, but by the time we had had our four oldest children expelled from the local high school, he went to the pastor and elders of the Baptist Church and asked for help. We had been out of the Exclusive Brethren for about seven years by then, and the situation was getting worse and worse.

We had a meeting at our house and invited some people, including the pastors of two other local churches, to come and pray with and for us. We asked God to break the curse, if it existed. The occasion, rather like a cleansing ritual, lifted the curse from our spirits. This had a flow-on effect to the children. We noticed a difference almost immediately. One by one, the children changed. It may have been a natural growing-up process, but Denis and I genuinely felt that the curse had been lifted. In practical terms that is what had happened. The older boys had been withdrawn from by then, which helped to relieve the pressure. Ben and Angela were withdrawn from several years later.

I'm not sure what the criteria were for withdrawing from girls and young women, except that it was often the outcome of any hint of sexual misconduct. Angela would have been in her early twenties before she came to the attention of the Exclusive Brethren priests. By that time Paul, Charlie and Ben had already been withdrawn from. Because the priests had visited Denis regularly, they thought they knew everything about our family. I dare say Denis was expected to report to them if the circumstances of any of the children changed. I know that at the time Angela was doing all the things a normal twenty-one year old would do and was very involved with the Youth Group of the Baptist Church. For whatever reason, the priests wanted to talk to her, so they asked Denis for her address. At the time she was renting a room in Remuera, in the house of a couple and their young daughter. Two (male) priests visited Angela unannounced one Saturday morning. They walked up the steps to the front door and rang the doorbell. The owner of the house answered the door and the priests asked him if they could speak to Angela. She was looking after Vicky and her friend's baby, for the weekend. She arrived at the door with the baby balanced on her hip. The priests took in the scene at a glance.

'Your father didn't tell us you were married,' said one of the priests in surprise.

'Oh! I'm not,' said Angela with equal surprise.

The priests turned on their heels, grimly and purposefully

descended the steps, and walked away. They obviously thought that she was an unmarried mother, living in a de facto relationship! As usual they had jumped to their own conclusions, had asked no relevant questions, did not discuss the matter with Angela or us and had established no facts. In their opinion Angela and her landlord were committing adultery! They dealt with her summarily in the 'normal' sanctimonious and pompous Exclusive Brethren manner by withdrawing from her at the next appropriate Assembly meeting.

The way the priests interpreted the scenario with Angela is, on the surface, amusing storytelling stuff and the type of behaviour we had learned to expect from this group. Angela was very pleased to be disassociated from the Exclusives, but this story, like many others, is also very serious because it shows that things are not always what they seem or what they appear on the surface. The Exclusives may sincerely believe they alone have the 'mind of God' and are acting 'righteously', but playing God and interfering with other people's lives and relationships is nothing short of criminal, especially when it involves serious false accusations, permanently alienating partners who love each other and separating children from parents. If this book does nothing else, I would want it to persuade these people to look at the devastation they have caused in the lives of thousands of families worldwide. I hope that one day God will grant the Exclusive Brethren repentance and the grace to say they are sorry, honestly and sincerely, to the thousands of people they have so cruelly mistreated. This would mean that their behaviour towards those they have rejected would have to change dramatically.

For our family, life on the outside gradually improved. One by one the children grew out of their propensity to produce grey hairs on the heads of their long-suffering parents and turned their energies to more adult pursuits of adventure. In spite of the dire warnings we had received, all our children have grown up to become good and responsible people. Some of them married and had children of their own and amazed us with their ability to bring up their own families with all the finesse and expertise that seemed to be lacking in our own efforts.

I realise that the good times far outweigh the difficult times, and the hard times have helped me appreciate the love and understanding of family and friends. Because life on the outside was so difficult to begin with, we all tried extra hard to adjust. I have a God-given ability to love life and to make the best of any situation and, once I had thrown off the shackles of Exclusive separatism, nothing could hold me back. The past twenty-five years have been years of intense personal growth. I have been like a giant sponge, absorbing a wide range of interesting experiences that most people only dream of. I conjure up ideas, and then look for innovative ways to carry them out, believing always that if something is worth doing, I will find a way to do it.

Buying a retail business during the first year on the outside was the very best thing we could have done. We loved the personal and social contact we had with so many interesting people, and it gave me an opportunity to develop the teaching talents I had been blessed with. We rented a shop with a large open upstairs room that I used as my classroom. I taught a wide variety of handcraft, cooking, knitting and sewing classes, to adult students. Over a period of about fifteen years this grew into a business of its own and became independent of our retail shop. I regularly taught groups of home-schooled children, and their mothers, in arts and crafts, and for several years — in my spare time — I taught in the home economics department of the local high school.

Because of the problems we had had with our own teenagers, we set up a series of practical and innovative classes for parents, based on the Tough Love programme popular at the time. This led on to discussion groups on motivation and self-esteem and other confidence-building courses. I was always aware that I was untrained for this type of work, but it had evolved out of personal experience and developed into a valuable community project.

I will come back to my story a little further on. During the 1980s and 1990s, we heard more and more disturbing reports of dictatorial mayhem from within the ranks of the Exclusive Brethren. The power and control of the MOG and his henchmen had become unbearable for some members, and others were constantly afraid of repercussions from seemingly innocent remarks and actions. In the past few years I have personally interviewed many ex-Brethren and have documented some of their stories.

27

Other people's stories

I have heard so many almost unbelievable stories. Every person who has left the Exclusive Brethren will have a story to tell, and many of them will be very similar. The following stories are about a few of the people who found themselves under Assembly discipline during the 1980s and 1990s. By searching for 'Exclusive Brethren' on the Internet you will be able to read many more. There are some cases where families were split up that would be fairly typical of what was happening worldwide, while other stories are unique. Teenagers with an independent spirit have always found Brethren life difficult, and many of them have found themselves outside the gates, alone.

The MOG began applying separation to relationships and physical circumstances during the 1960s. At first he was very careful to prevent undue interference with marital relationships, but once it got on a roll there was no stopping him. Separation from all things undesirable ended up taking precedence over the holding together of relationships. I think that the Brethren genuinely tried hard to keep families together if at all possible. However, not all couples were so fortunate.

I want to tell you about an elderly couple I'd known since I was four years old.

Ray and Edith were separated by the Brethren in the mid-1970s after being happily married for twenty-five years. I spoke to Ray recently, and he told me that he still loves Edith very much, even though he has not been able to have any contact with her for the past thirty years. He told me a sad little story. Ray, by now a very elderly gentleman, was always on the lookout hoping to catch a glimpse of his wife. He sometimes hung around the local shopping mall, just in case she happened to be there. One day his patience was rewarded. He saw Edith emerge from the store with her trolley of groceries. He knew he must not speak to her, but he was so thrilled to see her; he still loved her and he just couldn't stop himself. She saw him as he walked eagerly towards her. She panicked. Leaving the trolley of groceries where she stood, she turned and fled, through the mall and out to the car park. Ray didn't follow her. It was no use. He had wanted to put his arms around her and tell her he still loved her. He says there is a big gaping hole where his heart used to be, but he looks forward to being with her in heaven.

The idea of separation being moral, physical and legal was a fairly new concept back in the 1970s, but Ray's story is typical of many others from around the world. There are many elderly people now living sad and lonely lives, waiting and hoping for opportunities just to catch a glimpse of former spouses, children and grandchildren. The sad part about it is that in many cases the Exclusive Brethren children and grandchildren are not even told that these people exist. Separation is the price the Exclusive Brethren pay to maintain the purity of the fellowship. It is accepted as God's way of testing those who were true to this great calling to be God's chosen people.

The need to 'keep a clean place for the Lord' is central to the Exclusive Brethren charter, and means absolutely no association with evil; thus the legal separation. Those who woke up to the fact that you can't beat the system either kept quiet or simply left the fellowship and suffered the pain of being totally cut off from all they had ever known. A legal separation was necessary if either husband or wife persisted in standing by personal convictions. They had to condition themselves to think the same if they wanted to stay together and remain in fellowship. Harry and Rose had always supported each other, but later found they couldn't agree to differ on even the smallest issue because that would be compromise.

Harry had been having serious doubts for some time. It was his discontent with superficiality that made him a misfit. Harry came from a family who spurned mere conformity. He took life seriously, took the Bible seriously and found a profound beauty in it all. As Exclusive Brethrenism became more and more a matter of compliance and conformity, so Harry became a misfit. He was one of the last Exclusive Brethren in New Zealand to attend university, and even back then he was, by Brethren standards, a bit radical, a nonconformist, but none the less, a very genuine chap. He met and married Rose when they were both in their late twenties — rather late in life under Brethren standards — and together they had several children in quick succession. He enjoyed the excitement of the 'system days' of the late 1960s but, like many other people, his doubts loomed large during the 'Aberdeen ambush' in 1970. Harry and Rose didn't always think the same on some of the more important issues, and Harry began to find maintaining double standards depressing. Among other things, he didn't like preaching on street corners or doing 'priestly service' — his sympathies were often for the accused. He felt like a hypocrite, believing one thing while outwardly conforming to something different. He eventually resolved that if he were cornered and questioned he would be honest. It wasn't long before he was challenged over some trivial matter which resulted in him and Rose being shut up, and their children being taken away and cared for by other Exclusive Brethren families.

Removing the children from the 'contaminated' home, and repositioning them in the homes of Brethren friends or relatives, worked rather like a hostage system: 'We [the Exclusive Brethren] have got your children; you had better get right with us if you want them back!' Harry was prepared to listen and consider but was not about to get down on his knees to beg and grovel for mercy, but after two months of regular priestly visits, which resolved nothing, the family was unexpectedly reunited and restored to the fellowship. The priests had reached a stalemate but reported that Harry had had a conversion. Harry struggled to believe it was him they were talking about and so received his 'release' even more disillusioned than ever. He suspected the priests had simply decided to back off, maybe on the advice of the MOG. It was all a farce.

Rose had shared some of Harry's concerns about the Exclusive Brethren system, but not enough to stand by him when they were once again shut up after Harry expressed a different point of view from the Brethren. The children were now accustomed to and accepted the barbaric practice of being sent to stay with other families. A few months later Harry was withdrawn from with the hope that acceptance of discipline would result in recovery.

The Exclusives adhere strictly to their code of separation, even between husband and wife when one of them is under Assembly discipline. Harry and Rose had been living separately in their house for several months. Rose used the main part of the house, while Harry accepted exile to the spare bedroom and the adjacent lounge, which could be closed off from the rest of the house. Harry's meals were brought to him on a tray three times a day. The children visited their mother during the next three months, and occasionally their father.

One morning Rose told Harry that she had been thinking about their situation and had come to ask him to agree to a legal separation. A week later the papers were signed, and Harry was expected to leave the family home immediately. He moved into a small room behind his office. 'Don't make yourself too comfortable,' he was told, repentance could soon see him restored to the fellowship and back with his family.

They were legally separated with no provision for Harry to see the children. Harry left the family home to Rose and the children, who were immediately reunited. Rose's bottom line was loyalty to the Brethren, and although Harry later implored her many times by letter to seriously consider what was going on, she remained adamant. Some years later he divorced her because the marriage was no longer a reality.

It seems so unfair. He should at least have been allowed to see his children, so why didn't he fight? That's the extent of the power and control that the Exclusives have over their members, and ex-members. Very few people fight them — mostly because of fear.

Mind control by a religious group is a very insidious thing. It takes away individuals' faith and self-respect, giving the group the power to manipulate them. Maybe Harry should have marched into his house, taken Rose by the arm and the children by the scruff of their necks, and said, 'I'm head of this house and you're all coming with me, OUT!' I know some husbands who did just that, but not Harry. He was a kind and considerate husband and father who wanted only the best outcome for his family. Like many others in his position, he humbly accepted the possibility that he was in moral darkness and that the Exclusives' action was justified. To fight for his rights would diminish any prospect of restoration, while obedience, he had been assured, would bring about speedy reconciliation — a reconciliation that the priests suggested was a definite prospect.

It's very expensive to wage a legal battle against a system with almost unlimited finance and a determination never to be beaten. It's hard for individuals to fight when they know they can't win. And if they do win some legal rights, their battles have only just begun. The Brethren make access to children as difficult as possible. For Harry, the idea of an ongoing battle was unacceptable. It would achieve nothing. Better to leave them in peace and let them make their own choice. Later two of his children left the fellowship of their own accord.

I recently spoke to Harry's son Brad. I wanted to know how he felt about his father, and what he had been told during this intensely disruptive period of his life. I sensed that reconciliation between father and son had been hesitant and slow, but that the relationship has now been healed. 'I loved the guy,' said Brad when I asked him. 'He was my dad. He used to take us to the beach, and do important boy things with us like fishing and tramping in the hills. Memories of these practical occasions are special and will stay with me forever. I missed him, but there was a certain exhilaration and notoriety about having the family divided and in the spotlight. This added excitement to a rather boring life, but that soon wore off.'

The children wanted to get back home, to have their father back in his familiar and rightful place with the Brethren and with the family. 'Every time we asked how Dad was getting on, and when he would be recovered, we were fobbed off with all manner of excuses till we stopped asking. What was the use? Because we were our father's sons we were under constant observation. All our behaviour had meaning.' Brad, the youngest of the three who were staying with their uncle, was a bit stroppy, causing his host family a mite of trouble and anxiety. Brad, not long before Harry was withdrawn from, insisted on being reunited with his mother, even though this meant being shut up again. Within a few years he had left the fellowship himself.

Not all stories end like this; there have been some winners with 'happy-ever-after' stories. I'm thankful to say that although most ex-Exclusives have varying degrees of difficulty adjusting to life on the outside, many make the transition very successfully and go on to live very happy and fulfilled lives. After listening to Wayne and Andrea and recording the following true story, I have written it as I pictured it from their descriptions and without any exaggeration. If anything, I have omitted many facts that could be even more incriminating to the priests who inflicted so much unnecessary and senseless pain and stress on this family. I have used some typical, but fictionalised, dialogues to help give you the feeling and atmosphere of their struggle. I'm going to enjoy telling you this one because Wayne and Andrea were winners — eventually.

28

If you love her let her go

Wayne and Andrea had a simple Brethren wedding in her parents' home. His brother was the Best Man, but no other members of his family were there. He was sorry his mum and dad couldn't come; his mum would've loved to see Andrea all dressed up and looking so pretty. But this was a typical Exclusive Brethren wedding of the time, and only his brother was permitted to attend. His parents and his other brothers and sisters were not. An Exclusive Brethren wedding was by now a local affair, attended only by the Brethren who lived in the area.

She came and stood beside him, as nervous as he. Although he'd seen her on numerous occasions at Fellowship Meetings, they'd only officially met a few weeks before. He'd had his eye on her for a while but, once he had made his intentions known, the wedding arrangements were made very quickly. Although there hadn't been too many opportunities to be alone together to get to know each other, they had a lot in common, both having being brought up with Brethren values.

The ceremony began. The marriage celebrant, an Exclusive Brethren elder, read the vows and Wayne and Andrea said 'I do' in reply. They signed the register, right there in her parents' lounge, with his brother and her sister as witnesses. Later, neither of them could remember the actual wording of the ceremony, but that didn't matter; they just wanted to be married. After the reception they attended the usual Tuesday-evening Ministry Meeting, the meeting considered by the Exclusive Brethren to have the most suitable format for a wedding.

Wayne and Andrea were both born and raised within the Exclusive Brethren fellowship, as were their parents and grandparents and great-grandparents before them. They understood the tenets of the church they belonged to, and lived according to the rules. They taught their three children to love, honour and respect the Brethren, especially the MOG.

Wayne and Andrea had been married for nearly six years when they experienced a short period of marital disharmony. Andrea embarked, briefly, on an indiscretion. All was confessed and forgiven between them, but *the Exclusive Brethren would need to be told.* Periodically, the Brethren have bouts of 'Confession Madness', when members are required to bare their souls and confess all, sometimes publicly, and more often than not, with dire consequences. It was said that 'unconfessed sin is unforgiven'. In this case, forgiveness by the Exclusive Brethren was not forthcoming, and so Andrea, after being visited by the priests, received the ultimate punishment. She was withdrawn from. Wayne and Andrea sat around the kitchen table that night after the children were in bed. They loved the Brethren. They would do everything required of them to facilitate Andrea's speedy return to the fellowship.

'What will we do, Wayne?' Andrea's face was streaked with tears. They were tears of remorse, of fear and of apprehension. There was little she could do; it was Wayne's decision. He was looked upon, by the Exclusive Brethren, as being the most responsible for their plight.

'I don't know, I really don't know,' he said, sitting with his head bowed and shoulders slumped. 'I don't want to leave you, Andrea, I love you.' He choked back the tears as he reached out to clasp her hand in his. 'But we must do whatever is necessary to get back into fellowship.'

'If you leave me and return to the fellowship, they'll expect you to take the children away from me, you know that. They'll insist on a legal separation. I don't know if I can stand that.'

'Yes, I suppose they will. I wouldn't want to do that to you. And the children, they need a father and a mother. No, Andrea, separation is out of the question, but I expect the priests will come and see us soon; they always have the last say.'

The priests came the next night. The priests would never tell them exactly what to do. They would hint about something, and if Wayne and Andrea got the message, it was up to them to do something about it. 'A moral, physical and legal separation might facilitate a speedy recovery,' was the underlying message.

'We want to return to the fellowship,' said Wayne, 'but we're staying together.'

'Then you will be shut-up,' said one of the priests.

'You know what that means, don't you?' The priests looked at Andrea then back to Wayne. 'You understand that you will remain separate from one another in your home, you will not attend any meetings or contact any Exclusive Brethren members, even your families? Do you understand that there is to be no sexual intimacy between you, no eating together and no leaving the house together for any reason?'

'Yes, we understand.' Wayne and Andrea both nodded their heads in agreement. They understood that this was the way of the Exclusive Brethren; they had seen it happen to others, many times before.

'And do you understand, Wayne, that you are not to associate with worldly persons, or go to any worldly places? You are still one of us, and the position of the Assembly needs to be maintained.'

'Yes, I understand.'

The priests returned regularly, every two or three weeks, to speak to them both. They were probing for signs that the leprosy might be spreading. After about three months, they had reason to believe that Wayne **had** breached several of the Exclusive Brethren rules. He had been seen downtown with his wife, and he'd taken the children to some stock-car races, a fact that he reluctantly admitted. If he genuinely 'belonged' to the fellowship he would never do anything — even in these circumstances — that he would not do if he were in fellowship.

This lapse had placed his sincerity in question. In March, Wayne, too, was withdrawn from for making a mockery of the Exclusive Brethren — for making them look silly.

Wayne and Andrea had left behind all their extended family and friends. The children missed their friends, too. The whole family had, except on a few isolated occasions, kept themselves separate from the 'world', and so had not made any friends on the outside. They loved the Brethren, they believed in their teachings and they wanted to return to the fold as soon as possible.

Although Wayne and Andrea were now both withdrawn from, their children were only shut up. Theoretically, although they lived with their parents, the children still 'belonged' to the Exclusive Brethren fellowship. This gave the Exclusives the right to keep some sort of contact with them. For twenty-one months the family tried to be reconciled with the Exclusive Brethren. The elders, however, did not feel able to recommend them being restored. By the end of 1991 they had lost heart and felt frustrated by the 'vacuum' in which the family was being required to live. It seemed that they had a simple choice: either they waited until they were accepted back into the church to which they had belonged all their lives, or they could reject the church and join the outside world.

They initially chose to do all they could to get back into the church. Wayne embarked on another round of confessions, which were not accepted by the elders because he didn't show enough remorse. However, they did take some notice of Wayne's confessions. As a direct consequence, they approached Andrea and indicated that on the basis of the confessions Wayne had made, it was the elders' view that *she* should separate from *him*! Indeed, the only prospect of her and the children being allowed to rejoin the church would be *if she separated from Wayne, morally, physically and legally!* The Exclusive Brethren were now trying their same old tactics, only in reverse.

Wayne and Andrea still wanted to get back to their families. They still thought that the Exclusive Brethren was the only true church. How could it be anything else with such a horrendous price tag? There was always the possibility lurking in the background that one's inability to satisfy the priests was because God hadn't granted repentance — making that person a hell-bound reject. The act of rejecting the priests would seal that state of never being granted repentance. It was a vicious circle.

Wayne had the courage to tell the elders that his view was contrary to their own. To do what they asked was against what he had read in the Bible, and against his own conscience. Saying this didn't help at all because it is a very serious offence to challenge the priests. It showed a lack of humility. A challenge is a threat to them. Consequently, it made the elders even more determined to entice Andrea and the children back into the fold. Wayne, worried about the number of times the elders contacted Andrea by phone when he was at work, arranged to have their phone tapped. He overheard them telling her that if she and the children didn't return to the fellowship, then one of the children might die — a common scare tactic used by Exclusive Brethren worldwide.

The Exclusives arranged for Andrea to obtain legal advice to bring about a formal legal separation. She was advised not to go along with Wayne's proposal to attend marriage guidance counselling because 'the marriage was made in heaven' and the situation therefore was not capable of being addressed by temporal, or worldly, means. The church offered to pay for the legal costs and made it clear that they required Andrea to obtain a formal Separation Order and a division of the matrimonial property *before* they could contemplate her being fully readmitted to the church. In line with Exclusive Brethren practice, church members were encouraged to make gifts and donations to Andrea '*for standing for the TRUTH*'. By Christmas 1991 the marriage was over.

The court gave Andrea custody of the children, but the Exclusive Brethren made it difficult for Wayne to get visiting rights. He could only see the children once a week for a couple of hours, at his parents' house. This must have been difficult for the grandparents, too, because they had to watch their son as he talked to his children without talking to him any more than was necessary. Wayne was a good father and would have liked to spend more time alone with his children.

The elders approached Wayne at work one day and told him

that because they hadn't required him to hand over his house and business to his wife, they in turn expected him to give the Exclusive Brethren full rights to the children! Although the Exclusive Brethren acknowledged the orthodox legal rights of the father as set down by the court, they indicated that they considered this right to be overridden by the 'rights of God' and that the church would be the 'final court'.

For a while it looked as though the Exclusive Brethren had won. All over the world, similar scenarios were being repeated. Several, in fact far too many, families suffered the same fate. Usually, the wife and children remained with the Exclusive Brethren, while the husband found himself on the outside.

One day, near the beginning of 1993, Wayne had a message from Andrea. She wanted Wayne to visit her at home.

Wayne nervously looked up and down the street before knocking on the door. 'You can't be too careful,' he thought to himself as he patted his hair and straightened his jacket. 'There might be some Exclusive Brethren heavies hiding in the bushes ready to pounce. This might be an ambush,' he muttered to himself as Andrea opened the door.

'Come in, Wayne,' said Andrea, grabbing his sleeve and guiding him into the house that the Exclusive Brethren elders had helped her find. 'Take a seat in the lounge while I put the kettle on.'

Wayne glanced around the room at all the familiar things that used to be in the house they had shared together. His own house, the one they should be sharing together, was cold, lonely, quiet and empty. Wayne slipped into the kitchen. He reached out toward the most beautiful woman in the world, his wife, so close, so desirable. Andrea turned.

'No, Wayne, don't,' she cautioned. 'I just wanted to talk to you. Oh, bother!' She said as the back door opened and in walked two Exclusive Brethren priests.

'Wayne, get out of this house immediately, there is a separation order in effect and you have no right to be here,' said one of the priests.

'My wife invited me here to talk things over,' explained Wayne. 'Seeing as you're here, perhaps we could talk about your interpretation of the legal effects of the separation.'

'We have nothing to say to you. You are trespassing in your wife's house. Please leave at once.'

Wayne could see that Andrea was in no position to contradict the priests. The situation was getting out of control. He could be making life more difficult for her by arguing with them.

'Okay, I'm leaving,' he said. He smiled and waved to Andrea as he walked away, determined to meet with her again before long. Wayne and Andrea arranged to meet secretly a few days later. It soon became apparent to them both that they were still very much in love and wanted, above all else, to be together with their children.

'Please come home, I miss you,' pleaded Wayne.

'I want to, very much, but . .' Andrea knew that the Exclusive Brethren priests would try to stop her, somehow. 'Let me organise a few things first; it will only take a couple of days.'

'Okay, but be careful. Don't tell the children yet, and make sure the priests don't find out. They might try to take the children away.' Wayne was only too aware of the heartache some of their friends had been through recently when they left the children with their Exclusive Brethren grandparents while they 'got themselves right'. Unfortunately, when they decided to stay out of the fellowship, it had taken several years of fighting through the courts to get their children back.

Andrea packed up their belongings and secretly started shifting them back home. Finally, the car was packed for the last time, the children were buckled into the back seat and they were ready to go.

The Exclusives tried to stop them, but by this time Wayne and Andrea had had enough. They decided to move their family to another country.

Because Wayne and Andrea are no longer members of the Exclusive Brethren church, their families who are still in the fellowship are forbidden to have any contact with them. The children do not see either set of grandparents, or aunts, uncles or cousins. Shifting to another country has made it easier for the whole family. They have made new friends, and memories of the old life are fading. The children are thoroughly enjoying participating in 'normal' activities, watching television, listening to music, playing in local sports clubs and joining in with school activities such as using computers and video aids in the classroom.

Wayne, Andrea and the children love their new life. They go to church when they feel like it, join their neighbours for a barbecue at the weekends, and enjoy a wide range of activities and experiences that were previously denied them. But most important of all, they are a 'whole' family who are free to think for themselves.

29

Peace reigned at last

I have told you only a few of the things that coloured our lives during the first ten years on the outside.

There are many more stories I could relate, but, as in every family, some of those stories are not solely mine to tell. Some time in the future my children may wish to tell those stories for themselves.

During the next decade, from the mid-1980s, a gratifying change came over the family: the children grew up and became responsible adults. Because the four older children were close in age, some of those changes seemed to affect them one after the other in quick succession. As a family we came out of the slough of despair and into a life full of adventures that were far less destructive than previously. Our children had always had loads of character, and a huge potential for productive, interesting and creative lives. We had learned at last that a balanced approach to tough-love was the best strategy for bringing up a family. Because Vicky was so much younger than the others, she benefited from our experience, and life for her and with her was so much easier than we anticipated.

As the children matured, so did the relationship between Denis and me. We had more time to spend together without the constant need for surveillance of marauding teenagers. We could relax and enjoy each other's company, and learned to love each other in a way never experienced before. After twenty-five years of marriage we reaffirmed our vows in a moving ceremony, on a day that also included Paul and Judy re-enacting their wedding vows, which they had sung to each other at their wedding a few weeks before, and the celebration of Angela's twenty-first birthday.

Being a grandparent is the highlight of being parents. I would recommend it to everyone. I remember something very special that Charlie said to Denis when his second child was born. 'Dad, if any one of your children have given you only a small fraction of the pleasure this baby is giving us, then you should consider yourself richly blessed.' And a remark by Ben, 'Dad, I want to find a wife who will help me bring up our children the same way you and Mum have brought me up.' These comments and others like them, from all of the children, have a very special place among my memories.

The privilege of being with some of my grandchildren during their birthing was an experience I will treasure for life. On each occasion I knew the baby's name and, along with the parents, I was able to talk to them and encourage them as they were being born.

Life was good. We sold our shop, built a new house and became sales reps. Denis and I both worked for the same companies, some of which we had sold products for in the past. Because we were job-sharing, we worked hard for three days each week and enjoyed four-day weekends. Vicky was the only one at home by then, and after much thought we decided to offer a home to my father and mother.

At first this wasn't easy for me. Along with Dad came the inevitable memories of our past life among the Exclusive Brethren; he was still very much a Brethren at heart. When I was growing up I stereotyped my father as typical of Exclusive Brethren because Dad's authority and the power and control of the Brethren seemed to be synonymous. But, as in any community, personalities vary widely. Nevertheless, I can see that the Exclusive Brethren system fostered in him the characteristics that typically lead to abuse. The hypocrisy, keeping up appearances, sanctimonious responses, the intellectualising of reality and denial of personal wrongdoing were strands of his pattern of abuse. He had a clever mind, which allowed these idiosyncrasies and blatant irregularities, and in this sense I think he epitomised the Brethren system. I had long since forgiven him for past indiscretions — even though he was still in denial — and during his last few years I enjoyed a relatively relaxed friendship with him. As it happened, he lived with us for less than a year. He died in 1990.

Mum died three years later. As children we each accept our parents as they are. My perception of Mum was that she was almost a non-person, quiet, submissive, dutiful and it seemed to me that she had no mind of her own. She was loving and caring to us children, but listless and lacking the inspiration and creativity that is so vital to a healthy home life. Only after recent years of soul searching have I been able to recast this tragic figure. I can recall her funeral service at which I heard surprising stories told by her family and others who knew her when she was younger. She came from a good stable hard-working family who were well known and respected for their social and unselfish involvement in their rural community. I will not speculate on what attracted her to my father, but her committal to him and his Exclusive Brethren belief system must have been a profound mixture of the strange beauty of total yielding and the supreme sacrifice of her own self. I can only imagine her inward battle not to succumb to admitting her disillusionment. Her readiness to share with us children her vision of the divine plan and apocalyptic end time concepts indicates that she genuinely found an anchor there to balance the bewilderment and turmoil of her contemporary reality. In hindsight, I think she must have had an inner strength of character that most people failed to notice. I still have many regrets that I did not get to know and love my mother better. I could have made her last few years much happier but I was too 'busy' and left most of her care to my sister Chris. It is only recently that I have begun to understand that she had been a victim of the Exclusive Brethren regime, in a community that offered no support system or understanding for the less fortunate among them.

I can't end my story without telling you a little more about the last few years that Denis and I had together.

The priests continued to visit Denis off and on for twenty years; right up till a few weeks before he died. He had never talked much about it to me, although I usually knew when they had been to visit him. I objected strongly at first, but after a while I felt safer. The Exclusive Brethren might have retained part of his heart, but he chose to live with me, not with them. I know Denis eventually grew to like his life on the outside.

Denis was a person who was born to be Brethren. I no longer feel guilty about keeping him out because he probably could have gone back to the Exclusives if he had really wanted to. He loved me, and I loved him. We had a right to be together. For years I had taken the blame for the family being on the outside, ostracised and cut off from what Denis believed was the only true church. I no longer feel that way. I no longer take all the blame. We were in it together. Near the end of his life, he began to see that the Exclusive Brethren teachings were becoming more extreme. I have the highest respect for Denis for standing firm to his conviction that any attempt to drive a wedge between us — to split our family apart — was not right. I honour him for that.

In 1992 we rented out our house and moved south to live for a year as caretakers in an empty prison at the foot of Mount Ruapehu, in the Tongariro National Park. This was to be the most beautiful place in which to experience the solitude and serenity of being close to nature, and to each other. Denis fulfilled his long-time dream of once more working on the land and caring for livestock. In a short time he accumulated a varied assortment of animals and proudly watched them flourish. The old prison fire station became a cosy home for a family of pigs, and Cody the sheltie pup learned to herd the sheep and calves in the paddock in front of the house. I turned the prison chapel into a craft room and invited the local people in for classes. We went for long daily surveillance walks around the empty prison houses, through the native bush, along the streams and back across the paddocks. It was an idyllic lifestyle, but it eventually came to an end.

After we moved to Taupo, at the beginning of 1993, we knew Denis was sick.

30

Goodbye, my friend

I sat by Denis's bed, holding his hand, waiting for him to wake. He lay on a high bed in the Intensive Care Unit of the Rotorua Hospital, surrounded by machines that clicked and hissed as they monitored his breathing, his heartbeat and his blood pressure. He looked so small among the various tubes and bottles with their steady drip, drip, drip slowly pumping in the fluids necessary to keep him alive.

'Would you like to help?' asked the nurse on duty. She could see that I needed something to do, so she picked up the tube that was replacing blood lost during the operation and curled it into the palm of my hand and placed my other hand over it.

'The warmth of your hands will help to warm him,' she added. Already I could see the colour coming back into his face.

When we took him to the hospital the day before, he had looked so well, so accepting of what he was about to face, confident that the surgeon would be guided by God to remove all the cancer that had invaded his lower bowel. Now, after a four-hour operation, he didn't look so good, and the tears trickled down my face as I waited for someone to tell me what they had done to him back there in the theatre. At last the surgeon arrived, a man of few words who came straight to the point.

'I was bitterly disappointed to see so much cancer in Denis's liver,' he said. He explained that they had done a pre-operation scan the day before and had found what they thought was a tumor in his liver.

'Liver cancer?' I asked.

'Yes, we knew about the liver yesterday, and were able to confirm it during the operation'. He went on to explain that the bowel operation had gone well; he was confident that he had removed all the cancer.

'What can you do about his liver?' I asked.

'Nothing,' he replied. 'Let him get over this and then we'll talk about it.'

I was absolutely stunned. When the surgeon turned and left the room, my mind filled with a thousand and one questions, the first one being: does Denis know that he has cancer in his liver? I returned to his side and once more took up the coil of tube from the drip. This was the only thing that I could do for the moment as nurses quietly worked around us checking pulse and blood pressure and melting into the background, while I wept.

Denis and I had been married for thirty-one years. I was fifty and he was fifty-four, far too young to die. There was a time when he wanted to die. I remembered back to the time when we left the Exclusive Brethren. Denis was so torn between his love for them and his love for our family and me that he saw dying as his only way out. I'm not aware that he ever tried to do anything to hasten the event, but he often spoke about dying as a release from the situation he had found himself in. I had heard of several suicides in New Zealand and others overseas. They were Exclusive Brethren men who were pressured beyond the point of endurance. While I had had no real fear of this happening, the possibility was disconcerting. At the time I had recognised Denis's talk of death as metaphorical. Now it was fast becoming a reality.

One afternoon, while Denis was still in Rotorua Hospital, I received a phone call from one of the priests who had 'visited' us twenty years before. I knew they had regularly kept in touch with Denis in the past, but I'd not heard anything from them for several years.

'We would like to visit Denis in hospital, if that's all right with you,' he said very kindly and politely. I asked him to wait for a moment and handed the phone to our son Paul.

'I think Denis would like to see you,' said Paul, 'but I'd rather you didn't upset him by talking to him about going back to the Exclusives. He is a very sick man.'

'Thank you, Paul. There will be two of us. We will be there to see him at three o'clock tomorrow afternoon. We would appreciate it if we could speak to him alone.'

'As long as you keep the visit short and don't preach at him, then that's okay.'

The priests did visit him. I was tempted to be there at the same time; I felt fiercely protective, but I waited till the evening to visit Denis. According to Denis the priests kept to their side of the bargain; they didn't preach at him, nor did they bring up anything from the past. I believe it was a caring, kindly visit, and I thank them for that. He had other Exclusive Brethren visitors, too. One of Denis's sisters, and her husband, went to see him, taking with them a priest from their own meeting as a witness. The priest would have been necessary in case they inadvertently turned the occasion into a friendly, social one. Denis told me later that his sister and brother-in-law did put some pressure on him, but he thought it was for the benefit of the attendant priest. His sister told Denis about cryotherapy, a new treatment for liver cancer.

Death from liver cancer is usually quick, and the surgeon, when he spoke to us a few weeks after the operation, said that it would only be a matter of months, six at the most.

'Is there anything at all that we can do?' asked Denis. Even a man who once would have welcomed death was eager to hang on to life now that he was faced with the news that the end was near. 'I've heard that there is a doctor in Wellington who operates on the liver.'

'Yes, there is an operation where the tumor in the liver is frozen and removed,' said the surgeon. 'But it can only be done in a private hospital. It is pioneering stuff and very expensive.'

It was when Denis decided to try to raise the money for the operation that I knew at last he had come to terms with the Brethren's decision to withdraw from us back in October 1974. *He no longer wanted to die.* It had been a difficult twenty years. Denis had kept much of his stress to himself, and this had, no doubt, hastened and stimulated the onset of cancer in his body.

We went to see the surgeon in Wellington. He was very hopeful of the operation being successful, but he pointed out to us that it would only be buying time; how much time, he couldn't say. We had to decide the value of a life. Surgery was scheduled for October. We went home to raise sixteen thousand dollars to pay for it.

It is at times like this that we learn about true friendship. Family and friends rallied around and, by October, the money was in the bank. Two-thirds of his liver was removed during the operation. A shunt was put in place through which chemicals would be injected, if necessary, to kill any stray cancer cells. Regular blood tests eventually showed that the cancer had returned. The chemotherapy shunt, which we had hoped never to need, was activated. After the first week the shunt failed to function and was removed.

There is so much I would like to tell you about our last year together, but I've got a lump in my throat and my eyes are misting over. Everyone was so helpful and kind. I want to tell you about how hard people had worked to help us raise the money, and how brave Denis was. That wasn't the end, no way; Denis didn't give up, he still wanted to fight it. He asked the surgeon about another operation.

He'd already had two-thirds of his liver removed, but the liver grows again within about six weeks. This time the cancer was on the outside edge, easier to get at. We didn't have much time; we had to start fund-raising again, only this time it was harder.

Hard work is a great antidote for worry, and work hard we did. With family, and friends from the Apostolic Church in Taupo, we formed a fund-raising team called 'Operation Dollars for Denis'. Many people donated money — again. We did all the usual fund-raising things like cake stalls, garage sales and car washes. Because the second operation was less than a year after the first, and because we had only a few weeks to find another sixteen thousand dollars, we continued fund-raising for several weeks after he came home from hospital.

Our Christian friends stormed the gates of heaven on Denis's behalf. Friends from many parts of New Zealand were praying for him. We were right behind them, believing that God could, and would, heal Denis.

At the beginning of 1995, Denis felt better than he had done for years. He was back at work, part time, building and renovating houses. We bought a house in Taupo, and Denis spent hours in the garden. He drew up some plans to add a room at the back of the house — a large room, a suntrap, a space where we could sit and entertain our friends. He spent more time with his brothers, both out of the Exclusive Brethren fellowship. We were grateful that one of his sisters, still in the fellowship, continued to keep in touch with him. Denis looked forward to her phone calls and the occasional visit. When she told him about herbal remedies and introduced him to a clinic specialising in alternative medicines, we were surprised, not realising the Exclusives sanctioned such things. Denis took this new treatment very seriously, and began a programme designed to build up his resistance and to keep him in remission. He was so relaxed and happy. He stopped having regular blood tests because he wanted to enjoy each day without the threat of what the next test would show. Life was good. Denis was feeling well. We were both happily planning our future together, a future free from cancer. We had been encouraged by our Christian friends to believe that Denis had been healed by faith.

One evening in June, we were relaxing in the local hot thermal pools when I noticed his colour had changed. A dull yellow tinge was showing under the skin, no doubt heightened by the warmth of the water. I looked at his eyes. The whites were yellow. The doctor confirmed it the next day: Denis had jaundice. The cancer had returned, stronger than ever. I was devastated. What about his healing? Some well-meaning Christian friends told me that he was dying because I didn't have enough faith that he would be healed.

'Is this the beginning of the last three months?' Denis asked the doctor. He had been told earlier that, if it returned, the last stages of the cancer would take about three months. During this time he would probably suffer only a little pain, but would feel very tired.

'No, this is the beginning of your last few weeks. The cancer has come back with a vengeance,' was the doctor's answer.

Denis was with us for another eight weeks. The special quality of those two months was a celebration of his life, and those who had the privilege of sharing some of that time with us were enriched by the experience. I am very grateful to family members who recorded on video many happy, and sad but memorable, family occasions during those last weeks.

Nothing I could say in a few words would do justice to those last few weeks. It is such a short time ago, and the memories come flooding back. At the time it was like having almost completed an intricate, million-piece jigsaw puzzle with each small piece joined together with love. Some parts of the puzzle are hard work; others slip together with ease. Some pieces look as if they're never going to fit, but in the end there is a definite space left for them. Life is a lot like a jigsaw puzzle, and some are just too hard to finish, or time runs out before they are completed. Not everyone has the opportunity to complete their lives, but Denis did. When the end comes it's like taking a last look at the jigsaw puzzle before breaking it up and putting it back in the box. I'm reluctant to put it away; I want to see the puzzle completed, to put in that last little piece, and then frame it. This book is that frame.

Everything has an ending: a life, a story, a day, and then the sun rises again in the morning, and life goes on. This story, too, has an ending.

That day in June 1995, knowing the end was near, was the first day of the rest of our lives together. Denis intended to make the most of it. His first concern, as always, was for me. There were two things he wanted to do. One was to build the new room at the back of the house; the other, to arrange his own funeral. That first day, he made an appointment with the undertaker, and went to the District Council for a building permit.

'I have some plans here,' he told the man at the council, unrolling the papers. I want to arrange a permit so I can start building. How long will that take?'

'Six weeks.'

'I don't have six weeks,' said Denis, pointing to the whites of his eyes now heavily tinged with yellow.

'Start tomorrow; I'll look after this,' said the man as he took the plans from Denis.

The next step was to arrange to have the frame pre-cut and nailed. One firm said six weeks; the other promised it would be delivered within the week. He returned home that day and started measuring the ground for the floor. Four metres wide, and five metres long. By the time the frame arrived, the boys had helped him lay the concrete floor. With the help of his friend Lester, the framework was assembled and the building began to take shape.

Meanwhile, he began to plan his funeral.

'There's a very special poem I would like to have read,' said Denis one day while we were sitting at the table. Spread out on the table in front of us were hymn books, song sheets, his favourite book of poems and a note book in which he had collected poems, stories and sayings from a number of different places during his lifetime. He picked up the book of poems. It was old and well read when his uncle had given it to him years ago. Denis knew many of the poems by heart. He had read and recited them to the family many times.

'Which one would you like?' I asked, picking up a pen to record the title on our 'funeral service plan'.

'*The Last Words of JG Bellett,*' he said without hesitation. JG Bellett was a close friend of JN Darby — the founder of the Exclusive Brethren — and one of the original group who met together in Ireland in the early nineteenth century.

'Who will you ask to read it?'

'I'm going to read it myself. I'll read it onto a tape and you can give it to someone to play on the day.'

I wasn't very sure about this. He had asked me to help him plan a creative funeral, but . . .

'Come on, I'll need your help. See if you can find a new blank tape; I'll get the tape recorder.' He had a twinkle in his eyes. I think he was looking forward to speaking at his own funeral. For once he was going to have the last say!

We assembled the tape recorder and the microphone. He began to read.

> My pilgrim days are waning,
> The voice of Him I love,
> Has called me to His presence
> In my Father's house above.
> Long, long by faith I've known Him,
> But now I'm going to see
> The One that lives in glory,
> The Man that died for me.

His voice was so vibrant, alive, and so full of love for the man who had written the poem so long ago, and for the people who would hear it, maybe for the first time. He read through the nine verses. He was disappointed when he played it back. It was too long and something was missing.

'Got any ideas?' he asked.

'What about picking out five or six verses and playing some soft Christian music in the background,' I suggested.

'Good idea.' He chose a CD from the rack. 'Try playing a little bit at the beginning, then turn it down low while I read. Can you raise the volume and let it play a little between each verse?'

'Easy,' I said confidently. It wasn't so easy; we had to repeat it several times before we got it right.

'Put it away in a safe place until you need it,' he said. Denis slumped down into the sofa. He was tired with the effort of recording. He lowered his head and the tears began to roll down his cheeks. We had been through some tough experiences during our thirty-three years together, but I had seldom seen him cry. He patted the sofa and I sat down beside him. For thirty-three years he had always been there for me, lovingly enfolding me in his arms, soothing the hurts and kissing away the tears. Now it was my turn to comfort him. He had plenty to cry about: he was dying. But it wasn't his imminent death that was making him cry.

'I wish I'd been a better father,' he sobbed.

'You were the best, Denis, the best father that any child could wish for. You were always there for them. You were always so good when they were sick or in trouble, much better than me.'

Denis was crying also for his parents, and for mine. His mum and dad had both died within the fellowship, still believing to the end that Denis was a wicked person. He had been informed of his father's death after his father had been buried, and of his mother's death only an hour before her funeral, too late for him to attend. He had had great love and respect for his parents, and now, when his own life was waning, he regretted the aloofness that had been imposed upon their relationship.

We talked a lot during those last few weeks. Denis worked on the building, stopping often to lie down on the day bed in the lounge. At night, when he couldn't sleep for the constant itch of the toxins coming out through his skin, we talked. His favourite spot was a mattress on the floor in front of the fire. He loved the romantic glow of candles and the soft music. We talked of the past and made plans for my future, while I gently massaged his frail body. I loved him so much; it just wasn't fair.

'I want you to go to university,' he said one night. 'You've always wanted to go, and now you can. You've always wanted to write a book, so go to university and learn to do it properly.'

'I can't think that far ahead,' I answered. 'I just want to get through the next few weeks.'

'Are you afraid of what's happening?' he asked.

'I am very happy to nurse you at home. I don't want you to go into a hospital, but . . . ' I hesitated to say what I was thinking.

'But, what?' he asked.

'I'm not sure about the dying process,' I admitted. 'I don't want to watch you die. I don't think I could cope with that very well.'

'You don't have to be here, you know,' he said gently. 'I want all the family to have the choice. Some of the children might rather not be here either. I don't mind.'

'Of course I'll be here, darling,' I said, giving him a hug, and at the time I meant it.

During the next few weeks we had a steady stream of visitors. Friends came from all the different places we had lived, and all the different churches we had attended. They called to offer words of friendship and comfort. They themselves went away encouraged and comforted. We found it hard to believe that Denis was dying. He looked so happy and restful, and spoke with a voice that belied the anguish that was no doubt going on in his mind.

The Exclusive Brethren priests visited him during those last few weeks. When they were due to arrive, Denis asked me to stay in the background.

'It's best that you leave me alone with them,' he said. So I made myself scarce. I sat in the bedroom and cried until they had gone. I was afraid they had come to ask Denis's permission for the Exclusive Brethren to bury him. They do that sort of thing sometimes. I don't know what they said to him. I didn't ask him. Even though he had been out of the fellowship for more than twenty years, I would like to believe that they visited him as their friend. I'll never know, and it doesn't matter now.

Denis was getting more tired and preoccupied every day. I cooked his favourite foods and gently spoon-fed him in the desperate hope that it would keep him alive. He no longer wanted to talk. It was almost as if he was already in a different place. Building the room had been hard work for him, but the doctor said it had given him a reason to live a little longer, and it was something to take our minds off the inevitable. At last the room was completed and the carpet was laid. Denis looked around; he looked pleased, contented and happy.

'It's finished; you can use it now,' he said with a smile.

That weekend we had a party, a midwinter-Christmas party at the beginning of August, with crackers, balloons and Denis's favourite foods. He went to bed that Saturday night, and he stayed there. I wasn't with him when he died a week later. The doctors had assured me that he would be okay if I took a two-day break leaving the rest of the family to care for him. I will always regret that decision because he deteriorated very rapidly after I had left the house that Saturday morning. He had lived for eight weeks from the time the doctor had told him he was dying, longer than any of us had hoped for and long enough to do the things that he wanted to do.

Denis died at the very best time for him. In the spring, the time of year he liked best, on a day so special for him, and at just the right moment. It was six o'clock on Sunday morning, just as the Exclusive Brethren, all over New Zealand, were gathering together for the Breaking of Bread.

Goodbye, my friend.

Epilogue

The band was playing as the graduates in their black gowns and gold-lined hoods marched into the Founders Theatre, bare heads held high, trenchers in their left hands. I had felt rather indifferent to the whole capping procedure until I heard the band playing. It sent a tingling thrill through my body, giving me goose bumps on my arms. Some members of my family were seated in the audience, but I knew I would lose my step if I started gazing around for familiar faces. My friend Peter, who'd come to cheer me on, had found a seat near the procession route. He smiled as I passed, and I was glad he was there to support me. We were seated in alphabetical order, ready for the ceremonial walk up the steps and across the stage. But, first, the speeches.

I remembered some useless information from a high school prize-giving speech delivered by a headmaster more than forty years ago. 'All the atoms in the world, compressed, would fit into a matchbox and, being so heavy, would fall to the centre of the earth,' he had said. It's funny how we remember little things like that; it made me think of my school years. I wondered what university would have been like had I been allowed to go all those years ago. And if I had graduated, would I have been allowed to go to a capping ceremony? I brought my mind back to the present as the guest speaker stepped forward. 'Graduates, when you are capped and receive your degree certificate, you will become Waikato University Graduates for ever. *No one can take that away from you.*' He went on to say more, but I had heard the most important message of the day, a message that will stay in my mind for the rest of my life.

In the late 1970s, the Exclusive Brethren tried to take away the prestige of the university degrees earned by those who were fortunate enough to finish their studies before the embargo was placed on them in the early 1960s. I have heard that they were told by the MOG of the time to destroy their degrees. To the Exclusive Brethren, a university degree is worthless, a cause of pride, and therefore something to be ashamed of. I'm so glad I'm no longer in fellowship because no one is going to take my hard-earned degree away from me. No matter what else I do with my life, I will always be a university graduate.

Denis would have been so proud. I had done it all for him. It hadn't been easy after he died. I had lost the most important part of my life, the man who loved me unconditionally. We had been the best of friends for thirty-three years, and I missed him. Now that Denis had gone, I was grieving for Dad and Mum as well. All three had died within a few short years of each other. Denis and I had talked about how I would manage after he had gone. For six months I coped quite well, rather as if he was away on a long vacation. We had shared the leadership of a Church Home Cell group and I tried to keep this going. I was getting desperate. I was falling apart and nobody seemed to notice.

I was in a black hole and I wanted to hide. I appeared so calm and strong on the outside, but inside I was falling to pieces. We had a cellar under our house. Through a door in the hallway, and down some steep wooden steps, was a concrete-lined room originally designed as a large water tank. This is where I hid for three weeks, surfacing only to use the bathroom, to feed the dog and to make occasional cups of tea for family or friends, who mostly left me alone to get on with my grieving. It was dark and quiet in the cellar, and although I was not cold, I lay curled up in a corner for hours at a time. I thought about the unfairness of death and I screamed as long and hard as I wanted to, until I fell exhausted onto a mattress to sleep fitfully for an hour or two.

The journey out of the cellar began when a concerned neighbour persuaded me to see a doctor.

By August 1996, just twelve months after Denis died, I was ready to accept his challenge to go to university. I enrolled in a Bridging Course for Women at the end of that year, and completed my first seven papers at Waikato University in 1997. During my second year I applied for and was accepted as an exchange student for one semester at Edith Cowan University in Perth, Western Australia. When I returned, I set aside six months to write the original draft of this book before completing the rest of my degree at Massey University in Palmerston North.

I want to include here a letter I wrote in my journal a few years ago. From it you will learn a little more about my personal journey, and how, with the help of the memory of a loving and caring partner, I was able to face losing him, the most important part of my life.

> *Dear Denis,*
> *It is nearly four years since you started on that part of your journey where our paths parted. We had walked along together for thirty-three years. Thirty-three years of growing, and learning about ourselves as a couple, and about each other as individuals. The path was so rough and stony at the beginning, but eventually we fell into step, and were able to walk side by side. When you knew that it was time for us to go our separate ways, you took my hand and gently squeezed it, and began preparing me for the path ahead. You were so unselfish, saying that it was better that it happen now than in ten years' time. You knew that it would be so much harder for me if I were older. When we finally reached the fork in the road, you gave me some wise and practical words of advice and encouragement, and after waving a tearful goodbye, you headed towards the light.*

I know now that it was you who gave me the strength and confidence to go on without you. You had so much faith in me. You believed in me, you knew I could do it on my own. Your suggestion that I go to university was a good one. I've enjoyed the challenge. I could never have managed it while you were with me because you needed me to be there for you. I remember how pleased you always were to come home to a warm house and a nice meal. You used to boast to our friends that you had a 'Gourmet Cook' in your kitchen. I liked that.

You had sacrificed so much for me during the last twenty years of your life. I didn't fully understand this until I had written the book. You were right to say that I shouldn't write it in your lifetime. As you know, I did try, several times, but it just didn't work. And yet, I so much wish you were here now so that we could talk about those tough times when we thought we couldn't carry on, when being parents almost became too hard, and leaving our accustomed lifestyle with the Exclusive Brethren, even harder. I can't remember all the details now, but if you were here, you could remind me. You always said that two heads were better than one.

We were quite different from each other. At first I thought that our personalities would always clash, but our differences helped us to gain strength from one another. You were so black and white in your thinking, while my thoughts danced like a prism hanging in the window, reflecting every colour of the rainbow. You believed that something was either right or wrong, but I loved to find a compromise. Together we built a relationship based on love and respect. I'm glad we stayed together to enjoy that love. We so easily could have parted along the way, when side-paths and tangents beckoned and tempted us to go where the other couldn't follow. There were times when one of us had to wait for the other to catch up, and times when we had to backtrack to a mutual meeting place. But we made it in the end.

Now I have come to the real reason for writing this

letter to you, knowing that you are following every word as I write. I want to thank you for our life together, especially for allowing me to be my own person, knowing that that was contrary to our upbringing. You allowed me the freedom to make choices. You were flexible enough to allow me time and space to work on whatever creative project I was excited about at the time.

When I began recording our life together, I became very aware of the many sacrifices you had made for me. Although I am still very glad we were withdrawn from, I am sorry to have deprived you of so much and hope that my love and devotion to you compensated a little.

I want to say thank you for so many things, but it's all summed up in this; thank you Denis for loving me unconditionally. I will never forget you.

Goodbye, Den.

I began the first draft of this book in January 1999 while living in my garage in Taupo. I had taken a six-month break from university, just long enough to complete the first stage. I became a semi-recluse, seldom going out anywhere or communicating with friends. All my belongings — which now fill a five bedroom house — were stacked around the walls of the garage, giving me a close, warm feeling of being embraced by an accumulated past. It was only a few steps from my bed to the computer, and sometimes during the night, when so many thoughts raced through my mind, I would just have to get up and write all night then maybe not touch it for days. I found writing very therapeutic. As the memories came flooding back I was able to laugh, cry and occasionally get angry. Sometimes after writing a particularly difficult page I would just sit, very quiet and still, reliving painful experiences and letting go of the hurts.

I did a lot of forgiving of both myself and other people and gained a better understanding of the Exclusive Brethren and their belief system. I became much more mellow and compassionate, as I carefully thought about what I was writing, and about the many people involved. This healing process has continued through the editing phase.

I've thought quite a lot about the fear of God. I no longer believe all that stuff about God wanting to punish people. Because I had always associated God with male dominance, with power and control, I thought that God was 'out there' somewhere, waiting to pounce and punish. I no longer believe that because I know that 'The Kingdom of God is within'. Now I know that God is everywhere, that God is 'Love' and is on the inside of us shining out. Because God is Love, and is on the inside, I am free to choose to love people unconditionally, and without judging or wanting to change them. I need only be concerned with judging myself. It is not for me to say that the Exclusive Brethren or anyone else are sinners and should be punished for all the 'harmful and hurtful' things they do to people. All I want to do is love them anyway. As someone else put it, we are not punished *for* our sins, we are punished *by* them.

Yes, there *is* life after being withdrawn from — an abundant life that for most of us is full and rich with love and understanding, adventurous, worthwhile and of a quality of spirituality never dreamed of nor understood while in fellowship with the Exclusives. Once freed from the bonds of exclusive separatism one can begin to live the breadth of life as well as the length of it, making a worthwhile contribution to society.

I think heaven and hell are concepts designed to both encourage and threaten us into goodness. I personally believe that heaven is where God is, so I think of heaven in the present tense, here and now, rather than something we have to wait for. It is my understanding that a compassionate attitude brings me, and others closer to heaven. I think that Satan and hell are subjective, and are in direct contrast with God.

If I could sum up my life in a nutshell it would go something like this:

I was taught to be drab; inconspicuous,
To fade into the background; unnoticed,

> To be seen but not heard; submissive,
> With eyes and heart downcast; contrite.
> *Now I can laugh out loud and wear bright yellow!*

And my plans for the future?

> *For I know the plans I have for you, says the Lord, plans for good and not for evil, to give you a future and a hope.* Jeremiah 29:11 (*Living Bible*)

Appendix 1

Exclusive Brethren history

It is impossible to write a brief history of the Plymouth Exclusive Brethren with which all will agree. Those in fellowship would most likely avoid the task and yet be critical of anyone else who attempted to do so. Other breakaway groups will all have their own slant. What follows is strictly my own view, pieced together from various sources. It is not a topic that ever interested me when I was in fellowship, so I am dependent on foraged information. It should not be taken as a definitive history of the movement.

It all started back in 1800 when John Nelson Darby was born in Ireland to God-fearing upper-class parents. John was a bright lad, of genius intelligence. After completing his schooling he entered university to study law. After practising for a year, Darby decided not to pursue a career in law and turned instead to the Church of England, where he was trained, ordained as a clergyman and assigned to a church in Ireland. Darby was a conscientious and tireless worker for the church, spending much of his time as an itinerant evangelist and teacher. While still practising as a clergyman, Darby became friendly with other

Christians outside of his own church and was impressed with a small group of people who had started meeting together in Dublin in 1825. This small group, originally consisting of just a few men and women, met together in one of their homes and conducted their services without the aid of a clergyman. The reason the group formed and grew was a shared concern that clericalism was restricting the freedom of the Holy Spirit in the body (members) of the church. Darby's career as a clergyman was short-lived because in 1827 he joined this small but growing group of 'Brethren' and, in 1830, left the Church of England to devote his time to preaching, teaching, writing, composing hymns and to church planting. He became a valued and respected teacher in the Brethren movement, travelling throughout Europe and later to the United States, Australia and New Zealand.

Darby was a prolific writer. During his lifetime he wrote many tracts, articles for magazines and letters. These were later printed as his collected writings in 44 volumes (most were about 400 pages), all of which are still in print. His most important work — most copies would be found in private collections owned by Exclusive Brethren members and ex-members and maybe some of the other Brethren groups — would have to be the complete translation of the Bible into French, English and German, and the New Testament into Italian. His translation is thought by many Bible scholars to be one of the most accurate translations available. The Exclusive Brethren today use Darby's Bible and no other.

The Brethren movement grew rapidly during the twenty years from 1825 to 1845, attracting many well-born, highly educated people along with 'common' folk. Many of them were well versed in classical languages, and all were devout Christians. They met together in simple conditions and were bonded by a common desire to be led by the Holy Spirit rather than by ordained leadership.

John Nelson Darby is sometimes referred to as the father of modern-day fundamentalism and dispensationalism, dividing history into eight dispensations. Many of his early teachings, along with those of his compatriots, form the basics of most fundamentalist Christian churches. However, because of his later stand for separatism, Darby has had very little recognition, except among the Exclusive groups of the Brethren Church, which he is credited with founding after a disagreement and split with the original group. Darby spent a great deal of time with the Brethren in Plymouth, England, and it was there that the split took place. Some of the Brethren thought that the church (although they did not call themselves a church) should be autonomous with each separate meeting or group being responsible for their own decisions and policy-making, while still being under the umbrella of the whole Brethren movement. Others sided with Darby in the belief that the church was universal and what happened in one locality or part of the world directly affected those members in other parts. If you were 'in (or out) of fellowship' in one place, then you were also 'in (or out) of fellowship' with all others, no matter where in the world you were. Along with this went the expectation that all members were individual parts of the universal body and, as such, were to be treated, and judged, as separate individuals rather than as a group who were breaking bread together in any one place. It was also expected that if you were a member of the 'Exclusive Brethren' group you would not attend a service at any other Christian gathering. It was Darby who first taught that separation from evil was the bottom line, which, unfortunately, also eventually included separation from other Christians. The concept of separatism remains the focal point of the Exclusive Brethren teachings and, as a result, evangelism, or the proclamation of the teachings of Jesus Christ to the nations, has suffered to the point that it is, for them, now almost non-existent.

As a result of this split in the 1840s, two groups were formed. The so-called 'original' group — who believed in autonomy — became known by the others as 'Open Brethren', with an open door to any other Christian desiring to worship with them. The stricter, universal group, the 'Exclusive Brethren', led by Darby, gradually became more exclusive as 'outsiders' were discouraged from sharing their Breaking of Bread. The fact that the split occurred in Plymouth is what gives them the full name of either Plymouth Open Brethren or Plymouth Exclusive Brethren. The Open Brethren developed their own set of ordinances, including Believer's Baptism, while the Exclusive Brethren practised

Household Baptism, baptising infants by full immersion. Many of their other rituals remained similar, including the format of their meetings or services, although the Open Brethren had a more 'open door' policy toward non-members.

During the following years, both factions experienced several splits and divisions. In hindsight, some of these schisms — the doctrine of separation programmed the Exclusive Brethren group toward such things — could have been avoided, but history cannot be undone and, as a result, there are now several groups with both Open and/or Exclusive principles.

After the death of John Nelson Darby in 1882, and after yet another devastating split in 1890 over doctrinal differences, the Exclusive Brethren, again diminished in numbers, continued under the leadership of FER. *[FE Raven]*

The Exclusive Brethren are the remnants of those who follow the line down through JN Darby, FER, JT, JT Jnr, JHS, JSH, and his son BDH (the present Man of God in 2004). Although the Brethren movement started with the desire to have no one single ordained leader, singular universal leadership has always been the pattern, except for a six-year period between JT's death in 1953 and the rise to power of his son JT Jnr in 1959, when the leadership was in limbo and shared between 'Leading Brothers'. It is interesting to note that all the leaders died in service, and a (major) split or change accompanied each new leadership phase. I believe a reason for so many splits and divisions could be that, generally, the leader's teachings were not questioned. Another reason could be that there was always within the teachings a level of ambiguity that could only be resolved by the Man of God. When the MOG died, rivals and discontented potential leaders had room to assert their own views. The strictest of rivals for leadership was almost bound to prevail because God is perceived as being more severe than compassionate, and the Devil as out to weaken by way of compromise and the lowering of standards. Doctrines remained encapsulated in transcripts of meetings — they were never distilled into creeds.

Appendix 2

Is the Exclusive Brethren Church a cult?

It was around 1959–1960 that the Exclusive Brethren, under the leadership of JT Jnr, started to become more cult-like.

When we don't fully understand the way a particular group works, when we only know what the media present us with, or when we have been hurt in some way, it is tempting to categorise that group as a cult. Lack of understanding often leads us to believe that because members of some groups behave differently from what we think is 'normal', they must be 'abnormal'. There are thousands of recognised cults in the world today, many of them living reasonably 'normal' lives.

It is only when the occasional group goes off the rails and comes to our attention via the media that we say, 'why didn't someone stop them?' Or 'surely someone knew what was going on?'

For those people who have belonged to one of these groups, these questions are very relevant. We would all want to do our best to prevent another Jonestown tragedy or Waco siege, but at what point do we take away a group's right to worship or behave how they wish within the law?

Nevertheless, surely having families torn apart by extreme

separatism is not acceptable. It's not necessarily a group's *beliefs* that make it a cult, but the *behaviour* of its members towards other members, ex-members and to people outside the group. Most cults start with admirable ideals, with a sound belief system, but some develop into extreme authoritarian and totalitarian groups. I believe it is something to do with the power and domination of the leader.

Cults are not a new phenomenon; they can be traced right back through recorded history. Many groups still operating today date back beyond the 1950s; others flourished as part of the hippy counter-culture during the 1960s and 1970s. Those called New Religious Movements began during the 1980s and 1990s.

The American Family Foundation has a good definition of a cult: 'A group or movement exhibiting great or excessive devotion or dedication to some person, idea or thing, and employing unethical, manipulative or coercive techniques of persuasion and control (e.g. isolation from friends and family not in the group, debilitation, use of special methods to heighten suggestibility and subservience, powerful group pressures, information management, suspension of individuality or critical judgement, promotion of total dependency on the group and fear of leaving it), designed to advance the goals of the group's leaders, to the actual or possible detriment of members, their families, or the community.' (Quoted from *Captive Hearts, Captive Minds* by Tobias and Lalich.)

There are some obvious similarities to the Exclusives here. I hesitate to call the Exclusive Brethren a cult, but they have some definitely cult-like characteristics. Such groups provide the environment for a certain kind of leadership to flourish, and in turn the leader furnishes those conditions to maintain the group. Outside influences can undermine the authority of even the strongest leader, so Exclusive Brethren members (as with other similar groups) are kept in a constant state of 'busyness' to prevent their involvement with outside interests.

Living in a time warp

Exclusive Brethren live in a time warp and have a tendency to shun modern technology. There is a verse in the Bible that describes Satan as being the ruler and authority of the air, which means, for them, that anything using the airwaves is wrong. This includes radios, cellphones, radio-telephones, fax machines, computers, CD players, televisions and stereos, remote-controlled toys, and anything else using radio frequency remote controls. (Infra-red controlled garage-door openers are okay.) They don't use these things and they won't let their children touch them, either. However, some of their practices are contradictory. They need to use telephones to keep in touch with the MOG and with one another. However, telephones no longer operate by Morse code. Perhaps they haven't heard about satellites beaming telephone messages around the earth. I'm not sure how they talk themselves out of that one.

Submission and abuse

Total submission to a hierarchical system breeds abuse. In the case of the abused child in the security of home, the perpetrator is often a parent whom the child trusts and has been taught to obey. For the child, the seduction is gradual and usually persists for many years. Abuse in any age group includes sexual, verbal, physical, emotional, psychological and sociological abuse. The same pattern prevails in systems that abuse. It is not confined to but is common in hierarchical church communities. Those in power abuse their authority and their trust over the subservient — the women, the children and the less dominant men. It is so easy for the powerful to abuse their power while the abused and accused dare not challenge their authority. They are our 'Fathers', our leaders, our priests, our providers, our spiritual lifeline, our security, and through our unquestioning obedience our ticket to heaven. All this takes place in what is deemed to be a safe place —

a caring, loving community of God-fearing people. This subservience is part of the culture and becomes part of one's life. How dare we even question it? People who challenge those to whom they are expected to be subservient are dealt with summarily and with very few exceptions are thrown out, and so the system flourishes. From time to time the leader recognises and acknowledges superficial abuse patterns and there is a clean-up, but the basic pattern remains intact.

This insistence on submission allows abuse to continue and the perpetrators to hold their heads high within the Exclusive Brethren system. Abuse comes in many forms and an effective response to it — by those bold enough — is, of course, to stop being submissive. Victims identify submission as the one thing they have contributed to and can change — by ceasing to be subject. It is then convenient for the abuser to insist on submission as the essential prerequisite for recovery and allows the perpetrator to avoid facing their own involvement. True spiritual reflection would lead one to see that abuse of power and authority was the root of the problem. Insistence on submission is used by the men to avoid facing their own abusive behaviour and, apart from a few exceptions, the hierarchy does not squarely face this abuse issue because it is a male-dominated culture, led by the MOG who cannot be held accountable by his followers. This is not easy for the men to admit to when they are running the show, which is also why the women or children usually cop the blame. It is also why submission is perverted and its beauty turned to ashes.

Hope for the future?

Near the end of 2002 relatives and priests contacted many ex-members with what seemed like honest and genuine overtures of friendship and apologies for past hurts. There was great excitement in the outer camp, and communications with long lost family members were joyfully renewed. We naively welcomed the change, but unfortunately in some cases this change was only superficial. The sting in the tail had not been completely removed, and some of us were left feeling more hurt and rejected than before. We don't need shallow apologies; we want change, real change.

I hope in the future they might have a complete change of heart and genuinely and honestly begin repairing the damage. I guess I'm still looking for a miracle. I may be chasing rainbows, but I have been taught that with God all things are possible. But, until a genuine change comes about, not just on their terms but allowing equal justice on both sides, the problems will continue.

Exclusive Brethren teenagers are virtually cut off from society, and ill equipped to cope with life if they decide to leave. It's all part of the control tactics designed to keep them dependent on the Exclusive way of life. Perhaps the brighter, more adventurous ones who leave do so of their own accord, leaving behind the unquestioning and submissive ones. Maybe a few years down the track the Exclusive Brethren will have evolved into a completely different culture, quite different from the one I left in the 1970s.

I should explain about that word *evolution*, remembering how paranoid the Brethren are about their children being exposed to any teaching on 'evolution'. To them, evolution is a forbidden concept. It defies the creation story and suggests that people evolved from apes and that all life forms evolved from primitive single cells. I am using the word in a slightly different context. I have some ideas of my own about cultural evolution. I see the growth and development of certain groups as an evolution within themselves. If they consistently cull out the thinkers and questioners from their ranks, leaving only the submissive and compliant ones behind, then the cultural evolution of that group will become established. They are already becoming inbred — not only biologically but psychologically.

For example, present members born in 1960 — before extreme separatism — who married young and began their families immediately would now be grandparents. Stories and anecdotes from the preceding generations are considered morally suspect and would not be passed on. Any knowledge of withdrawn from family members would be expunged from their memories. In fact, any memories of a relatively 'normal' life prior to 1960 will gradually fade and die.

Appendix 3

An ongoing nightmare

I underestimated the extent of the trauma that my family suffered after leaving the Exclusive Brethren. Leaving such a close-knit group is extremely distressing for children, even more so than some of us have realised. Children between the ages of five and twelve years are growing into the 'rules' of family and society. If this process is disrupted then some children may need help to come to terms with their altered circumstances. I am including this 'memory', written by one of my sons. It may help parents who have been withdrawn from to understand, and to guide their children through this time of stress.

Paul's memories

It takes an effort of memory to remember the fears and problems of the past. It is not something to dwell on, but perhaps to remind myself, every now and then, of where I came from, and where I am going. I am more fully aware now about Dad's loss, and the suffering he felt losing his area of belonging — the Exclusive Brethren church. I will never forget the day Dad died and, in strength, took his stand with God and abandoned Man. He considered the word of God and His requirements for Dad were to stick by his family; an act of duty, not his own desire. His own desire or choice for himself would have been to remain where he was, with the Exclusive Brethren, and allow his family, or a part of it at least, to move on.

I was about eleven when we were withdrawn from. I don't know how the folks broached the subject to us children that day, but I do remember it was discussed. Where would we go? What would we do? What would our choice be? I have a vague feeling that Mum and Dad decided to take it to the children for their opinion. Perhaps they were resigned to splitting up: Dad with the Brethren; Mum out of it.

There has never been any doubt in my mind that I would have stayed with Dad, as he was going to stay with the Brethren, yet it was not what I really wanted. I will never forget how I knelt down with Dad by the sofa, the grey one with the wooden arm rests, and prayed aloud. I prayed for some time that the family would stay together. Dad broke down and cried while I prayed. I never discussed this with him ever again after that day. There was never any need to, I guess; all was clear to me and to Dad. Mum was angry with the Brethren; she had had enough. I suspect that although she threatened to leave, she would have stayed with her family if it had come to a separation. Perhaps Dad did not see that, or things may have turned out differently. As it was, we left the Exclusive Brethren as a family, and life began for all of us in one painful jolt.

Taught to see everyone as sinners, and dammed to hell, we all had many adjustments to make, and each of us had different problematical areas. For years, Mum and we kids felt threatened by Dad's desire to go back to the Brethren. Now I realise there was nothing to fear. Dad's desire was for the thing he knew and loved — the people, his folks, and his sisters who, I guess, he always got on better with than his brothers. All were left behind.

The family did not see the people and the depth of understanding and community love that Dad saw, but rather the system; the pointless restrictions, the lack of acceptance, and severely critical and judgemental attitudes, and had no desire for these. I guess neither party understood the other, but it does go to show how much Dad felt isolated after we left the Exclusive Brethren in 1974.

I can clearly remember not fitting in with the other boys at the Exclusive Brethren meetings (there were very few in my age group) and being ridiculed at school. I remember the pain of rejection, and developed a sensitivity that created a strong desire for acceptance from others. This, of course, only served to increase the rejection, so I do not have any fond memories of my childhood, either before we left the Exclusive Brethren or after.

After 1974, things got even worse for me. How does one make friends? How does one know what makes a friend? How does one be a friend to others? I did not, and still do not, know the answers to these questions. It is wonderful to observe my own children learn these lessons at an early age. Those first ten years, I believe, teach you many things about society, and how to be a part of society. We were taught to be apart from society, and although some found the answers to many mysteries, I did not. How does one show friendship to the opposite sex without inferring sexual or intimate reference? What are the codes, the signals, the words? How do I recognise and avoid, without offence? The answers to these questions, too, under normal circumstances, are learned in the first ten years of your life. I did not learn them; they are still a mystery.

This has been, and still is, a cause of great grief to me. For the past twenty-five years, it has perhaps been the number one problem I have failed to find a compromise for. I apparently, unknowingly, send clear signals to women, and, of course, cannot see or read the signals returned. I am usually left stunned by their reaction, wondering what I have done, and how I have offended. This is perhaps my final challenge, to behave in a predictable manner, in the unspoken, unwritten laws of society that I never did learn. I cannot entirely blame the Exclusive Brethren church, as many, if not most, of those people still learned some form of code for their own society. For some reason I did not.

Social events began for me at age twelve, when I acquired my first friend, only to lose him in a car accident three years later.

I have no fear of the Exclusive Brethren. In fact, I can objectively say that I would fit right in there now with them, better than any other church, and more readily than anyone else in the family. A clear reliance on God has given me a boldness without fear of such thoughts. I often think about returning there to preach the song of forgiveness and acceptance, while my faith in God remains stronger than any fear of man, or fear of rejection (which is always my greatest fear). I have no qualms about such thoughts.

It seems to me that the Exclusive Brethren church has fallen into the trap that JN Darby prophesied they would fall into: that their search for the truth would turn them from forgiveness to judgement, and thus they would condemn themselves before God. That prophecy was pointed out to me, many years ago, in a book of ministry written by JN Darby. I could hardly believe what I was reading, an exact description of what happened, written decades before by one of their own, who translated their Bible. If Jesus came to forgive, who are you, the Exclusive Brethren, to judge? This is the message for the Brethren, which would return them to reliance on God, and away from their reliance on their own understanding of how things should be.

So, as a teenager, I coped as best I could, learning too late that we all have a responsibility to society. It was amazing to discover that the Lord worked, to a huge extent, *outside* the Exclusive Brethren church, and was quite prepared to turn us over to the law for punishment! So, we are not exempt from His law, or society's law, after all!

It is sad to see the Exclusive Brethren afraid of excommunicated Brethren, considering them worse than the damned, as people who somehow will turn them from God's ways to wicked ways. A true belief and faith in God will not produce this fear of men. Only a belief and faith in the Exclusive Brethren, or any other church, and their teachings will produce this fear, a fear that results from worldly wisdom being taught instead of godly faith. I guess the first thing to recognise is that God is more powerful than Satan, and has already won the battle, so who fears evil when they rely on God? None should.

We used to see this fear in the streets. An Exclusive Brethren member would spot us walking toward them on the same side, and they would cross to the other side of the street. Not for the ordinary sinners would they do this, for in their eyes we were worse than mere worldly sinners, even though some of us were only children.

I feel no hate or dislike toward these people. I have tasted, and now enjoy, true faith in God, and feel so sad that they are missing out on the wonders of God's creation, which includes all the people on the earth.

There were many trials in our family during the 1970s and 1980s. I guess we were each too busy trying to cope with our own problems to pay much attention to the dilemmas of the other members of the family. Fortunately, in those days we were all poor, and there was nothing to come between us as a family. I often think this was a result of Dad's supreme commitment to his family, back in 1974, as we were never — after that day — threatened by the insecurity of not belonging in the family. It is clear to me that the Lord does look after His people, wherever they are, and this is, perhaps, another message for those leaving the Exclusive Brethren church: that the leaving is not a denial of God, or God's forsaking them. It is more likely to be that God is leading them out of it.

I will leave you with these sobering thoughts.